COLLECTOR'S
LIBRARY OF THE
CIVIL WAR

The brilliant son of an American President, brother-in-law of the Confederate President, a Southern general and the last commander east of the Mississippi River to surrender, Richard Taylor is nevertheless remembered best for his literate military memoirs, *Destruction and Reconstruction*. "Taylor wrote as he thought . . . with a firm hand on the hilt of his naked sword," observed a contemporary historian. "His book is himself in type—caustic, fiery, given unto satire, master of epigrams."

Thin, of average height, with hazel eyes and dark complexion, Dick Taylor looked delicate, but looks were deceiving. A friend recalled that "his absolute self-reliance amounted to total irreverence for any man's opinion." Possessed of strong prejudices, Taylor was as tactless with his enemies as he was deeply affectionate with his friends. He was well read, philosophical, and blessed with an unusual memory for facts and faces. These traits are reflected clearly in the pages of his book.

Taylor was born on January 27, 1826, near Louisville, Kentucky. While his father, Zachary, was achieving the military fame that would lead to the White House, his only son was acquiring a superb education in Europe and at both Harvard and Yale. After graduation, Taylor became one of the South's wealthiest sugar producers, first taking charge of a family estate in Louisiana, then using his inheritance to establish a 1,740-acre plantation worked by 75 slaves. He was active in state politics, and he avidly studied the works of the great military leaders of history. This was his sole preparation for the Civil War.

In spite of his inexperience, Taylor was appointed colonel of the 9th Louisiana Infantry Regiment in July of 1861, then brigadier general in October. His prowess as a soldier emerged in Stonewall Jackson's 1862 Valley Campaign (some of the best writing in *Destruction and Reconstruction* deals with this fighting). Although severely ill during the Seven Days' Battles near Richmond, he heroically commanded a brigade

TIME-LIFE BOOKS INC., ALEXANDRIA, VIRGINIA 22314

from an ambulance, struggling onto his horse at crucial moments. As major general in command of the District of Western Louisiana, Taylor won two decisive military victories in quick succession in 1864, at Sabine Cross Roads and Pleasant Hill. A personality clash with General E. Kirby Smith, his superior officer, led to administrative breakdowns, however, and Taylor requested that he be relieved from duty. His request was denied, and a few weeks later he was made a lieutenant-general and assigned the Department of Alabama, Mississippi and East Louisiana. On May 4, 1865, Taylor surrendered the last organized Confederate forces east of the Mississippi to Federal authorities.

Taylor refused to request a pardon at war's end because he believed his cause to have been correct and honorable. As a result, his citizenship was revoked and his land holdings confiscated, which ruined him financially. Making a living at several jobs, Taylor worked tirelessly to restore order in the South as well as citizenship to Jefferson Davis and other Confederate leaders. He died of dropsy on April 12, 1879, while visiting friends in New York, a few days after his memoirs appeared in book form.

Destruction and Reconstruction began in 1876 as a series of articles for the *North American Review.* The essays were highly praised for their lively style and incisive observations, and Taylor expanded his material into a book that quickly went through two editions in America and one in England. More than a century after the book's appearance, its pictures of Confederate political and military leaders, its dramatic scenes of war, and its flowing and sometimes poetic style give Taylor's reminiscences a credibility, freshness and personal touch that are timeless.

—THE EDITORS

Reprinted 1983 from the 1879 edition.
Cover design © 1981 Time-Life Books Inc.
Library of Congress CIP data following page 274.

This volume is bound in leather.

DESTRUCTION

AND

RECONSTRUCTION:

PERSONAL EXPERIENCES OF THE LATE WAR.

BY

RICHARD TAYLOR,
LIEUTENANT-GENERAL IN THE CONFEDERATE ARMY.

NEW YORK:
D. APPLETON AND COMPANY,
549 AND 551 BROADWAY.
1879.

PREFACE.

THESE reminiscences of Secession, War, and Reconstruction it has seemed to me a duty to record. An actor therein, accident of fortune afforded me exceptional advantages for an interior view.

The opinions expressed are sincerely entertained, but of their correctness such readers as I may find must judge. I have in most cases been a witness to the facts alleged, or have obtained them from the best sources. Where statements are made upon less authority, I have carefully endeavored to indicate it by the language employed.

R. TAYLOR.

December, 1877.

CONTENTS.

CHAPTER X.

CHAPTER XI.

CHAPTER XII.

CHAPTER XIII.

CHAPTER XIV.

CHAPTER XV.

CHAPTER XVI.

CHAPTER XVII.

DESTRUCTION AND RECONSTRUCTION.

CHAPTER I.

SECESSION.

THE history of the United States, as yet unwritten, will show the causes of the "Civil War" to have been in existence during the Colonial era, and to have cropped out into full view in the debates of the several State Assemblies on the adoption of the Federal Constitution, in which instrument Luther Martin, Patrick Henry, and others, insisted that they were implanted. African slavery at the time was universal, and its extinction in the North, as well as its extension in the South, was due to economic reasons alone.

The first serious difficulty of the Federal Government arose from the attempt to lay an excise on distilled spirits. The second arose from the hostility of New England traders to the policy of the Government in the war of 1812, by which their special interests were menaced; and there is now evidence to prove that, but for the unexpected peace, an attempt to disrupt the Union would then have been made.

The "Missouri Compromise" of 1820 was in reality a truce between antagonistic revenue systems, each seeking to gain the balance of power. For many years subsequently, slaves—as domestic servants—were taken to the Territories without exciting remark, and the "Nullification" movement in South Carolina was entirely directed against the tariff.

Anti-slavery was agitated from an early period, but failed to attract public attention for many years. At length, by unwearied industry, by ingeniously attaching itself to exciting questions of the day, with which it had no natural connection, it succeeded in making a lodgment in the public mind, which, like a subject exhausted by long effort, is exposed to the attack of some malignant fever, that in a normal condition of vigor would have been resisted. The common belief that slavery was the cause of civil war is incorrect, and Abolitionists are not justified in claiming the glory and spoils of the conflict and in pluming themselves as " choosers of the slain."

The vast immigration that poured into the country between the years 1840 and 1860 had a very important influence in directing the events of the latter year. The numbers were too great to be absorbed and assimilated by the native population. States in the West were controlled by German and Scandinavian voters, while the Irish took possession of the seaboard towns. Although the balance of party strength was not much affected by these naturalized voters, the modes of political thought were seriously disturbed, and a tendency was manifested to transfer exciting topics from the domain of argument to that of violence.

The aged and feeble President, Mr. Buchanan, unfitted for troublous times, was driven to and fro by ambitious leaders of his own party, as was the last weak Hapsburg who reigned in Spain by the rival factions of France and Austria.

Under these conditions the National Democratic Convention met at Charleston, South Carolina, in the spring of 1860, to declare the principles on which the ensuing presidential campaign was to be conducted, and select candidates for the offices of President and Vice-President. Appointed a delegate by the Democracy of my State, Louisiana, in company with others I reached Charleston two days in advance of the time. We were at once met by an invitation to join in council delegates from the Gulf States, to agree upon some common ground of action in the Convention, but declined for the reason that we were accredited to the National Convention, and had no authority to participate in other deliberations. This invitation and the terms in which it was conveyed argued badly for the harmony of the Convention itself, and for the preservation of the unity of the Democracy, then the only organization supported in all quarters of the country.

It may be interesting to recall the impression created at the time by the tone and temper of different delegations. New England adhered to the old tenets of the Jefferson school. Two leaders from Massachusetts, Messrs. Caleb Cushing and Benjamin F. Butler, of whom the former was chosen President of the Convention, warmly supported the candidacy of Mr. Jefferson Davis. New York, under the direction of Mr. Dean Richmond, gave its influence to Mr. Douglas. Of a combative temperament, Mr. Richmond was impressed with a belief that "secession" was but a bugbear to frighten the northern wing of the party. Thus he failed to appreciate the gravity of the situation, and impaired the value of unusual common sense and unselfish patriotism, qualities he possessed to an eminent degree. The anxieties of Pennsylvania as to candidates were accompanied by a philosophic indifference as to principles. The Northwest was ardent for Douglas, who divided with Guthrie Missouri, Kentucky, and Tennessee.

Maryland, Virginia, North Carolina, Georgia, and Louisiana held moderate opinions, and were ready to adopt any honorable means to preserve the unity of the party and country. The conduct of the South Carolina delegates was admirable. Representing the most advanced constituency in the Convention, they were singularly reticent, and abstained from adding fuel to the flames. They limited their rôle to that of dignified, courteous hosts, and played it as Carolina gentlemen are wont to do. From Alabama, Florida, Mississippi, Arkansas, and Texas came the fiery spirits, led by Mr. William L. Yancey of Alabama, an able rhetorician. This gentleman had persuaded his State Convention to pass a resolution, directing its delegates to withdraw from Charleston if the Democracy there assembled refused to adopt the extreme Southern view as to the rights of citizens in the territories. In this he was opposed by ex-Governor Winston, a man of conservative tendencies, and long the rival of Mr. Yancey in State politics. Both gentlemen were sent to Charleston, but the majority of their co-delegates sustained Mr. Yancey.

Several days after its organization the National Convention reached a point which made the withdrawal of Alabama imminent. Filled with anxious forebodings, I sought after nightfall the lodgings of Messrs. Slidell, Bayard, and Bright, United States senators, who had come to Charleston, not as delegates, but under the impulse of hostility to the principles and candidacy of Mr. Douglas. There, after pointing out the certain consequences of Alabama's impending action, I made an earnest appeal for peace and harmony, and with success. Mr. Yancey was sent for, came into our views after some discussion, and undertook to call his people together at that late hour, and secure their consent to disregard instructions. We waited until near dawn for Yancey's return, but his efforts failed of success. Governor Winston, originally opposed to instructions as unwise and dangerous, now insisted that they should be obeyed to the letter, and carried a majority of the Alabama delegates with him. Thus the last hope of preserving the unity of the National Democracy was destroyed, and by one who was its earnest advocate.

The withdrawal of Alabama, followed by other Southern States, the adjournment of a part of the Convention to Baltimore and of another part to Richmond, and the election of Lincoln by votes of Northern States, require no further mention.

In January, 1861, the General Assembly of Louisiana met. A member of the upper branch, and chairman of its Committee on Federal Relations, I reported, and assisted in passing, an act to call a Convention of the people of the State to consider of matters beyond the competency of the Assembly. The Convention met in March, and was presided over by ex-Governor and ex-United States Senator Alexander Mouton, a man of high character. I represented my own parish, St. Charles, and was appointed chairman of the Military and Defense Committee, on behalf of which two ordinances were reported and passed : one, to raise two regiments; the other, to authorize the Governor to expend a million of dollars in the purchase of arms and munitions. The officers of the two regiments were to be appointed by the Governor, and the men to be enlisted for five years, unless sooner discharged. More would have been desirable in the way of raising troops, but the temper of men's minds did not then justify the effort. The Governor declined to use his authority to purchase arms, assured as he was on all sides that there was no danger of war, and that the United States arsenal at Baton Rouge, completely in our power, would furnish more than we could need. It was vainly urged in reply that the stores of the arsenal were almost valueless, the arms being altered flint-lock muskets, and the accouterments out of date. The current was too strong to stem.

The Convention, by an immense majority of votes, adopted an ordinance declaring that Louisiana ceased to be a State within the Union. Indeed, similar action having already been taken by her neighbors, Louisiana of necessity followed. At the time and since, I marveled at the joyous and careless temper in which men, much my superiors in sagacity and experience, consummated these acts. There appeared the same general *gaîté de cœur* that M. Ollivier claimed for the Imperial Ministry when war was declared against Prussia. The attachment of northern and western people to the Union; their superiority in numbers, in wealth, and especially in mechanical resources; the command of the sea; the lust of rule and territory always felt by democracies, and nowhere to a greater degree than in the South—all these facts were laughed to scorn, or their mention was ascribed to timidity and treachery.

As soon as the Convention adjourned, finding myself out of harmony with prevailing opinion as to the certainty of war and necessity for preparation, I retired to my estate, determined to accept such responsibility only as came to me unsought.

The inauguration of President Lincoln; the confederation of South Carolina, Georgia, and the five Gulf States; the attitude of the border slave States, hoping to mediate; the assembling of Confederate forces at Pensacola, Charleston, and other points; the seizure of United States forts and arsenals; the attack on "Sumter"; war—these followed with bewildering rapidity, and the human agencies concerned seemed as unconscious as scene-shifters in some awful tragedy.

CHAPTER II.

I was drawn from my retreat by an invitation from General Bragg, a particular friend, to visit Pensacola, where he commanded the southern forces, composed of volunteers from the adjacent States. Full of enthusiasm for their cause, and of the best material, officers and men were, with few exceptions, without instruction, and the number of educated officers was, as in all the southern armies, too limited to satisfy the imperious demands of the staff, much less those of the drill-master. Besides, the vicious system of election of officers struck at the very root of that stern discipline without which raw men cannot be converted into soldiers.

The Confederate Government, then seated at Montgomery, weakly receded from its determination to accept no volunteers for short terms of service, and took regiments for twelve months. The same blindness smote the question of finance. Instead of laying taxes, which the general enthusiasm would have cheerfully endured, the Confederate authorities pledged their credit, and that too for an amount which might have implied a pact with Mr. Seward that, should war unhappily break out, its duration was to be strictly limited to sixty days. The effect of these errors was felt throughout the struggle.

General Bragg occupied Pensacola, the United States navy yard, and Fort Barrancas on the mainland; while Fort Pickens, on Santa Rosa island, was held by Federal troops, with several war vessels anchored outside the harbor. There was an understanding that no hostile movement would be made by either side without notice. Consequently, Bragg worked at his batteries bearing on Pickens, while Major Brown, the Federal commander, strengthened with sand bags and earth the weak landward curtain of his fort; and time was pleasantly passed by both parties in watching each other's occupation.

Some months before this period, when Florida enforced her assumed right to control all points within her limits, a small company of United States artillery, under Lieutenant Slemmer, was stationed at Barrancas, where it was helpless. After much manœuvring, the State forces of Florida induced Slemmer to retire from Barrancas to Pickens, then, *garrisoned* by one ordnance sergeant, and at the mercy of a corporal's guard in a rowboat. Fort Sumter, in Charleston harbor, was in a similar condition before Anderson retired to it with his company. The early seizure of these two fortresses would have spared the Confederates many serious embarrassments; but such small details were neglected at that time.

My visit to Pensacola was brought to a close by information from the Governor of Louisiana of my appointment to the colonelcy of the 9th Louisiana infantry, a regiment just formed at camp on the railway some miles north of New Orleans, and under orders for Richmond. Accepting the appointment, I hastened to the camp, inspected the command, ordered the Lieutenant Colonel—Randolph, a well-instructed officer for the time—to move by rail to Richmond as rapidly as transportation was furnished, and went on to New Orleans, as well to procure equipment, in which the regiment was deficient, as to give some hours to private affairs. It was known that there was a scarcity of small-arm ammunition in Virginia, owing to the rapid concentration of troops; and I was fortunate in obtaining from the Louisiana authorities a hundred thousand rounds, with which, together with some field equipment, I proceeded by express to Richmond, where I found my command, about a thousand strong, just arrived and preparing to go into camp. The town was filled with rumor of battle away north at Manassas, where Beauregard commanded the Confederate forces. A multitude of wild reports, all equally inflamed, reached my ears while looking after the transportation of my ammunition, of which I did not wish to lose sight. Reaching camp, I paraded the regiment, and stated the necessity for prompt action, and my purpose to make application to be sent to the front immediately. Officers and men were delighted with the prospect of active service, and largely supplied want of experience by zeal. Ammunition was served out, three days' rations were ordered for haversacks, and all camp equipage not absolutely essential was stored.

These details attended to, at 5 P. M. I visited the war office, presided over by General Pope Walker of Alabama. When the object of my visit was stated, the Secretary expressed much pleasure, as he was anxious to send troops forward, but had few in readiness to move, owing to the lack of ammunition, etc. As I had been in Richmond but a few hours, my desire to move and adequate state of preparation gained me some " redletter " marks at the war office. The Secretary thought that a train would be in readiness at 9 o'clock that night. Accordingly, the regiment was marched to the station, where we remained several weary hours. At length, long after midnight, our train made its appearance. As the usual time to Manassas was some six hours, we confidently expected to arrive in the early forenoon; but this expectation our engine brought to grief. It proved a machine of the most wheezy and helpless character, creeping snail-like on levels, and requiring the men to leave the carriages to help it up grades. As the morning wore on, the sound of guns, reëchoed from the Blue Ridge mountains on our left, became loud and constant. At every halt of the wretched engine the noise of battle grew more and more intense, as did our impatience. I hope the attention of the recording angel was engrossed that day in other directions. Later we met men, single or in squads, some with arms and some without, moving south, in which quarter they all appeared to have pressing engagements.

At dusk we gained Manassas Junction, near the field where, on that day, the battle of first " Manassas " had been fought and won. Bivouacking the men by the roadside, I sought through the darkness the headquarters of General Beau-

2

regard, to whom I was instructed to report. With much difficulty and delay the place was found, and a staff officer told me
that orders would be sent the following morning. By these I
was directed to select a suitable camp, thus indicating that no
immediate movement was contemplated.

The confusion that reigned about our camps for the next
few days was extreme. Regiments seemed to have lost their
colonels, colonels their regiments. Men of all arms and all
commands were mixed in the wildest way. A constant fusillade of small arms and singing of bullets were kept up, indica-
tive of a superfluity of disorder, if not of ammunition. One
of my men was severely wounded in camp by a " stray," and
derived no consolation from my suggestion that it was a delicate attention of our comrades to mitigate the disappointment
of missing the battle. The elation of our people at their success was natural. They had achieved all, and more than all,
that could have been expected of raw troops ; and some commands had emulated veterans by their steadiness under fire.
Settled to the routine of camp duty, I found many opportunities to go over the adjacent battle field with those who had
shared the action, then fresh in their memories. Once I had
the privilege of so doing in company with Generals Johnston
and Beauregard ; and I will now give my opinion of this, as I
purpose doing of such subsequent actions, and commanders
therein, as came within the range of my personal experience
during the war.

Although since the days of Nimrod war has been the constant occupation of men, the fingers of one hand suffice to
number the great commanders. The " unlearned " hardly think
of usurping Tyndall's place in the lecture room, or of taking
his cuneiform bricks from Rawlinson ; yet the world has been
much more prolific of learned scientists and philologers than of
able generals. Notwithstanding, the average American (and,
judging from the dictatorship of Maître Gambetta, the Frenchman) would not have hesitated to supersede Napoleon at Austerlitz or Nelson at Trafalgar. True, Cleon captured the Spar-
tan garrison, and Narses gained victories, and Bunyan wrote

the " Pilgrim's Progress ; " but pestilent demagogues and muti-
lated guardians of Eastern zenanas have not always been successful in war, nor the great and useful profession of tinkers
written allegory. As men without knowledge have at all times
usurped the right to criticise campaigns and commanders, they
will doubtless continue to do so despite the protests of professional soldiers, who discharge this duty in a reverent spirit,
knowing that the greatest is he who commits the fewest blunders.

General McDowell, the Federal commander at Manassas,
and a trained soldier of unusual acquirement, was so hounded
and worried by ignorant, impatient politicians and newspapers
as to be scarcely responsible for his acts. This may be said of
all the commanders in the beginning of the war, and notably of
Albert Sidney Johnston, whose early fall on the field of Shiloh was irreparable, and mayhap determined the fate of the
South. McDowell's plan of battle was excellent, and its execution by his mob no worse than might have been confidently
expected. The late Governor Andrew of Massachusetts observed that his men thought they were going to a town meeting, and this is exhaustive criticism. With soldiers at his disposal, McDowell would have succeeded in turning and over-
whelming Beauregard's left, driving him from his rail communications with Richmond, and preventing the junction of
Johnston from the valley. It appears that Beauregard was to
some extent surprised by the attack, contemplating movements
by his own centre and right. His exposed and weak left stub-
bornly resisted the shock of attacking masses, while he, with
coolness and personal daring most inspiriting to his men, brought
up assistance from centre and right ; and the ground was held
until Johnston, who had skillfully eluded Patterson, arrived
and began feeding our line, when the affair was soon decided.

There can be little question that with a strong brigade of
soldiers Johnston could have gone to Washington and Baltimore. Whether, with his means, he should have advanced, has
been too much and angrily discussed already. Napoleon held
that, no matter how great the confusion and exhaustion of a
victorious army might be, a defeated one must be a hundred-

fold worse, and action should be based on this. Assuredly, if there be justification in disregarding an axiom of Napoleon, the wild confusion of the Confederates after Manassas afforded it.

The first skirmishes and actions of the war proved that the Southron, untrained, was a better fighter than the Northerner —not because of more courage, but of the social and economic conditions by which he was surrounded. Devoted to agriculture in a sparsely populated country, the Southron was self-reliant, a practiced horseman, and skilled in the use of arms. The dense population of the North, the habit of association for commercial and manufacturing purposes, weakened individuality of character, and horsemanship and the use of arms were exceptional accomplishments. The rapid development of railways and manufactures in the West had assimilated the people of that region to their eastern neighbors, and the old race of frontier riflemen had wandered to the far interior of the continent. Instruction and discipline soon equalized differences, and battles were decided by generalship and numbers; and this was the experience of our kinsmen in their great civil war. The country squires who followed the banners of Newcastle and Rupert at first swept the eastern-counties yeomanry and the London train-bands from the field; but fiery and impetuous valor was at last overmatched by the disciplined purpose and stubborn constancy of Cromwell's Ironsides.

The value of the "initiative" in war cannot be overstated. It surpasses in power mere accession of numbers, as it requires neither transport nor commissariat. Holding it, a commander lays his plans deliberately, and executes them at his own appointed time and in his own way. The "defensive" is weak, lowering the morale of the army reduced to it, enforcing constant watchfulness lest threatened attacks become real, and keeping commander and troops in a state of anxious tension. These truisms would not deserve mention did not the public mind ignore the fact that their application is limited to trained soldiers, and often become impatient for the employment of proved ability to sustain sieges and hold lines in offensive movements. A collection of untrained men is neither more nor less than a

mob, in which individual courage goes for nothing. In movement each person finds his liberty of action merged in a crowd,
ignorant and incapable of direction. Every obstacle creates
confusion, speedily converted into panic by opposition. The
heroic defenders of Saragossa could not for a moment have
faced a battalion of French infantry in the open field. Osman's
solitary attempt to operate outside of Plevna met with no success; and the recent defeat of Moukhtar may be ascribed to
incaution in taking position too far from his line of defense,
where, when attacked, manœuvres of which his people were incapable became necessary.

CHAPTER III.

AFTER the action at Manassas, the summer and winter of 1861 wore away without movements of special note in our quarter, excepting the defeat of the Federals at Ball's Bluff, on the Potomac, by a detached brigade of Confederates, commanded by General Evans of South Carolina, a West-Pointer enjoying the sobriquet of *Shanks* from the thinness of his legs.

In the organization of our army, my regiment was brigaded with the 6th, 7th, and 8th regiments of the Louisiana infantry, and placed under General William H. T. Walker of Georgia. Graduated from West Point in the summer of 1837, this officer joined the 6th United States infantry operating against the Seminoles in Florida. On Christmas day following was fought the battle of Okeechobee, the severest fight of that Indian war. The savages were posted on a thickly jungled island in the lake, through the waters of which, breast-high, the troops advanced several hundred yards to the attack. The loss on our side was heavy, but the Indians were so completely routed as to break their spirit. Colonel Zachary Taylor commanded, and there won his yellow sash and grade. Walker was desperately wounded, and the medical people gave him up; but he laughed at their predictions and recovered. In the war with Mexico, assaulting Molino del Rey, he received several wounds, all pronounced fatal, and science thought itself avenged. Again he got well, as he said, to spite the doctors. Always a martyr to asthma, he rarely enjoyed sleep but in a sitting posture; yet he was as cheerful and full of restless activity as the celebrated Earl of Peterborough. Peace with Mexico established, Walker became commandant of cadets at West Point. His ability as an instructor, and his lofty, martial bearing, deeply impressed his new brigade and prepared it for stern work. Subsequently Walker died on the field near Atlanta, defending the soil of his native State—a death of all others he would have chosen. I have dwelt somewhat on his character, because it was one of the strangest I have met. No enterprise was too rash to awaken his ardor, if it necessitated daring courage and self-devotion. Truly, he might have come forth from the pages of old Froissart. It is with unaffected feeling that I recall his memory and hang before it my humble wreath of immortelles.

In camp our army experienced much suffering and loss of strength. Drawn almost exclusively from rural districts, where families lived isolated, the men were scourged with mumps, whooping-cough, and measles, diseases readily overcome by childhood in urban populations. Measles proved as virulent as smallpox or cholera. Sudden changes of temperature drove the eruption from the surface to the internal organs, and fevers, lung and typhoid, and dysenteries followed. My regiment was fearfully smitten, and I passed days in hospital, nursing the sick and trying to comfort the last moments of many poor lads, dying so far from home and friends. Time and frequent changes of camp brought improvement, but my own health gave way. A persistent low fever sapped my strength and impaired the use of my limbs. General Johnston kindly ordered me off to the Fauquier springs, sulphur waters, some twenty miles to the south. There I was joined and carefully nursed by a devoted sister, and after some weeks slowly regained health.

On the eve of returning to the army, I learned of my promotion to brigadier, to relieve General Walker, transferred to a brigade of Georgians. This promotion seriously embarrassed me. Of the four colonels whose regiments constituted the brigade, I was the junior in commission, and the other three had been present and "won their spurs" at the recent battle, so far the only important one of the war. Besides, my known friendship for President Davis, with whom I was connected by his first marriage with my elder sister, would justify the opinion that my promotion was due to favoritism. Arrived at head-quarters, I obtained leave to go to Richmond, where, after an affectionate reception, the President listened to the story of my feelings, the reasons on which they were based, and the request that the promotion should be revoked. He replied that he would take a day for reflection before deciding the matter. The following day I was told that the answer to my appeal would be forwarded to the army, to which I immediately returned. The President had employed the delay in writing a letter to the senior officers of the brigade, in which he began by stating that promotions to the grade of general officer were by law intrusted to him, and were made for considerations of public good, of which he alone was judge. He then, out of abundant kindness for me, went on to soothe the feelings of these officers with a tenderness and delicacy of touch worthy a woman's hand, and so effectually as to secure me their hearty support. No wonder that all who enjoy the friendship of Jefferson Davis love him as Jonathan did David.

Several weeks without notable incident were devoted to instruction, especially in marching, the only military quality for which Southern troops had no aptitude. Owing to the good traditions left by my predecessor, Walker, and the zeal of officers and men, the brigade made great progress.

With the army at this time was a battalion of three companies from Louisiana, commanded by Major Wheat. These detached companies had been thrown together previous to the fight at Manassas, where Wheat was severely wounded. The strongest of the three, and giving character to all, was called the "Tigers." Recruited on the levee and in the alleys of New Orleans, the men might have come out of "Alsatia," where they would have been worthy subjects of that illustrious potentate, "Duke Hildebrod." The captain, who had succeeded to the immediate command of these worthies on the advancement of Wheat, enjoying the luxury of many aliases, called himself White, perhaps out of respect for the purity of the patriotic garb lately assumed. So villainous was the reputation of this battalion that every commander desired to be rid of it; and

General Johnston assigned it to me, despite my efforts to decline
the honor of such society. He promised, however, to sustain
me in any measures to enforce discipline, and but a few hours
elapsed before the fulfillment of the promise was exacted. For
some disorder after tattoo, several "Tigers" were arrested and
placed in charge of the brigade guard. Their comrades attempted to force the guard and release them. The attempt
failed, and two ringleaders were captured and put in irons for
the night. On the ensuing morning an order for a general
court-martial was obtained from army headquarters, and the
court met at 10 A. M. The prisoners were found guilty, and
sentenced to be shot at sunset. I ordered the "firing party" to
be detailed from their own company; but Wheat and his officers
begged to be spared this hard duty, fearing that the "Tigers"
would refuse to fire on their comrades. I insisted for the sake
of the example, and pointed out the serious consequences of
disobedience by their men. The brigade, under arms, was
marched out; and as the news had spread, many thousands from
other commands flocked to witness the scene. The firing party,
ten "Tigers," was drawn up fifteen paces from the prisoners,
the brigade provost gave the command to fire, and the unhappy
men fell dead without a struggle. This account is given because
it was the first military execution in the Army of Northern
Virginia; and punishment, so closely following offense, produced a marked effect. But Major "Bob" Wheat deserves an
extended notice.

In the early summer of 1846, after the victories of Palo
Alto and Resaca de la Palma, the United States Army under
General Zachary Taylor lay near the town of Matamoros. Visiting the hospital of a recently joined volunteer corps from the
States, I remarked a bright-eyed youth of some nineteen years,
wan with disease, but cheery withal. The interest he inspired
led to his removal to army headquarters, where he soon recovered health and became a pet. This was Bob Wheat, son of an
Episcopal clergyman, who had left school to come to the war.
He next went to Cuba with Lopez, was wounded and captured,
but escaped the garrote to follow Walker to Nicaragua. Ex-

hausting the capacities of South American patriots to *pronounce*, he quitted their society in disgust, and joined Garibaldi in Italy, whence his keen scent of combat summoned him home in convenient time to receive a bullet at Manassas. The most complete Dugald Dalgetty possible, he had "all the defects of the good qualities" of that doughty warrior.

Some months after the time of which I am writing, a body of Federal horse was captured in the valley of Virginia. The colonel commanding, who had been dismounted in the fray, approached me. A stalwart man, with huge mustaches, cavalry boots adorned with spurs worthy of a *caballero*, slouched hat, and plume, he strode along with the nonchalant air of one who had wooed Dame Fortune too long to be cast down by her frowns. Suddenly Major Wheat, near by, sprang from his horse with a cry of "Percy! old boy!" "Why, Bob!" was echoed back, and a warm embrace was exchanged. Colonel Percy Wyndham, an Englishman in the Federal service, had last parted from Wheat in Italy, or some other country where the pleasant business of killing was going on, and now fraternized with his friend in the manner described.

Poor Wheat! A month later, and he slept his last sleep on the bloody field of Cold Harbor. He lies there in a soldier's grave. Gallant spirit! let us hope that his readiness to die for his cause has made "the scarlet of his sins like unto wool."

As the autumn of the year 1861 passed away, the question of army organization pressed for solution, while divergent opinions were held by the Government at Richmond and General Johnston. The latter sent me to President Davis to explain his views and urge their adoption. My mission met with no success; but in discharging it, I was made aware of the estrangement growing up between these eminent persons, which subsequently became "the spring of woes unnumbered." An earnest effort made by me to remove the cloud, then "no greater than a man's hand," failed; though the elevation of character of the two men, which made them listen patiently to my appeals, justified hope. Time but served to widen the breach. Without the knowledge and despite the wishes of General Johnston, the descendants of the ancient dwellers in the cave of Adullam gathered themselves behind his shield, and shot their arrows at President Davis and his advisers, weakening the influence of the head of the cause for which all were struggling.

Immediately after the birth of the Confederacy, a resolution was adopted by the " Provisional Congress " declaring that military and naval officers, resigning the service of the United States Government to enter that of the Confederate, would preserve their relative rank. Later on, the President was authorized to make five appointments to the grade of general. These appointments were announced after the battle of Manassas, and in the following order of seniority: Samuel Cooper, Albert Sidney Johnston, Robert E. Lee, Joseph E. Johnston, and G. T. Beauregard.

Near the close of President Buchanan's administration, in 1860, died General Jesup, Quartermaster-General of the United States army; and Joseph E. Johnston, then lieutenant-colonel of cavalry, was appointed to the vacancy. Now the Quartermaster-General had the rank, pay, and emoluments of a brigadier-general; but the rank was staff, and by law this officer could not exercise command over troops unless by special assignment. When, in the spring of 1861, the officers in question entered the service of the Confederacy, Cooper had been Adjutant-General of the United States Army, with the rank of colonel; Albert Sidney Johnston, colonel and brigadier-general by brevet, and on duty as such ; Lee, lieutenant-colonel of cavalry, senior to Joseph E. Johnston in the line before the latter's appointment above mentioned ; Beauregard, major of engineers. In arranging the order of seniority of generals, President Davis held to the superiority of line to staff rank, while Joseph E. Johnston took the opposite view, and sincerely believed that injustice was done him.

After the grave and wondrous scenes through which we have passed, all this seems like "a tempest in a tea-pot;" but it had much influence and deserves attention.

General Beauregard, who about this time was transferred to the army in the West, commanded by Albert Sidney Johnston, was also known to have grievances. Whatever their source, it could not have been *rank;* but it is due to this General—a gentleman of taste—to say that no utterances came from him. Indiscreet persons at Richmond, claiming the privilege and discharging the duty of friendship, gave tongue to loud and frequent plaints, and increased the confusion of the hour.

As the year 1862 opened, and the time for active movements drew near, weighty cares attended the commander of the Army of Northern Virginia. The folly of accepting regiments for the short period of twelve months, to which allusion has been made, was now apparent. Having taken service in the spring of 1861, the time of many of the troops would expire just as the Federal host in their front might be expected to advance. A large majority of the men were willing to reënlist, provided that they could first go home to arrange private affairs; and fortunately, the fearful condition of the country permitted the granting of furloughs on a large scale. Except on a few pikes, movements were impossible, and an army could no more have marched across country than across Chesapeake bay. Closet warriors in cozy studies, with smooth macadamized roadways before their doors, sneer at the idea of military movements being arrested by mud. I apprehend that these gentlemen have never served in a bad country during the rainy season, and are ignorant of the fact that, in his Russian campaign, the elements proved too strong for the genius of Napoleon.

General Johnston met the difficulties of his position with great coolness, tact, and judgment; but his burden was by no means lightened by the interference of certain politicians at Richmond. These were perhaps inflamed by the success that had attended the tactical efforts of their Washington peers. At all events, they now threw themselves upon military questions with much ardor. Their leader was Alexander H. Stephens of Georgia, Vice-President of the Confederacy, who is entitled to a place by himself.

Like the celebrated John Randolph of Roanoke, Mr. Stephens has an acute intellect attached to a frail and meagre body. As was said by the witty Canon of St. Paul's of Francis Jeffrey, his mind is in a state of indecent exposure. A trained and skill-ful politician, he was for many years before the war returned to the United States House of Representatives from the district in which he resides, and his "device" seems always to have been, " Fiat justitia, ruat cœlum." When, in December, 1849, the Congress assembled, there was a Whig administration, and the same party had a small majority in the lower House, of which Mr. Stephens, an ardent Whig, was a member; but he could not see his way to support his party's candidate for Speaker, and this inability to find a road, plain mayhap to weaker organs, secured the control of the House to his political adversaries. During the exciting period preceding " secession" Mr. Stephens held and avowed moderate opinions; but, swept along by the resistless torrent surrounding him, he discovered and proclaimed that "slavery was the corner-stone of the con-federacy." In the strong vernacular of the West, this was "rather piling the agony" on the humanitarians, whose sym-pathies were not much quickened toward us thereby. As the struggle progressed, Mr. Stephens, with all the impartiality of an equity judge, marked many of the virtues of the Government north of the Potomac, and all the vices of that on his own side of the river. Regarding the military questions in hand he en-tertained and publicly expressed original opinions, which I will attempt to convey as accurately as possible. The war was for principles and rights, and it was in defense of these, as well as of their property, that the people had taken up arms. They could always be relied on when a battle was imminent; but, when no fighting was to be done, they had best be at home attending to their families and interests. As their intelligence was equal to their patriotism, they were as capable of judging of the necessity of their presence with the colors as the com-manders of armies, who were but professional soldiers fighting for rank and pay, and most of them without property in the South. It may be observed that such opinions are more com-fortably cherished by political gentlemen, two hundred miles away, than by commanders immediately in front of the enemy.

In July, 1865, two months after the close of the great war,

I visited Washington in the hope of effecting some change in the condition of Jefferson Davis, then ill and a prisoner at Fortress Monroe; and this visit was protracted to November before ·its object was accomplished. In the latter part of October of the same year Mr. Stephens came to Washington, where he was the object of much attention on the part of people controlling the Congress and the country. Desiring his coöperation in behalf of Mr. Davis, I sought and found him sitting near a fire (for he is of a chilly nature), smoking his pipe. He heard me in severe politeness, and, without unnecessary expenditure of enthusiasm, promised his assistance. Since the war Mr. Stephens has again found a seat in the Congress, where, unlike the rebel brigadiers, his presence is not a rock of offense to the loyal mind.*

---

* The foregoing sketch of Mr. Stephens appeared substantially in the "North American Review," but the date of the interview in Washington was not stated. Thereupon Mr. Stephens, in print, seized on July, and declared that, as he was a prisoner in Fort Warren during that month, the interview was a "Munchausenism." He also disputes the correctness of the opinions concerning military matters ascribed to him, although scores of his associates at Richmond will attest it. Again, he assumes the non-existence of twelve-months' regiments because some took service for the war, etc.

Like other ills, feeble health has its compensations, especially for those who unite restless vanity and ambition to a feminine desire for sympathy. It has been much the habit of Mr. Stephens to date controversial epistles from "a sick chamber," as do ladies in a delicate situation. A diplomatist of the last century, the Chevalier D'Eon, by usurping the privileges of the opposite sex, inspired grave doubts concerning his own.

CHAPTER IV.

PURSUING "the even tenor of his way," Johnston rapidly increased the efficiency of his army. Furloughed men returned in large numbers before their leaves had terminated, many bringing new recruits with them. Divisions were formed, and officers selected to command them. Some islands of dry land appeared amid the sea of mud, when the movement of the Federal forces in our front changed the theatre of war and opened the important campaign of 1862.

When overtaken by unexpected calamity African tribes destroy the fetich previously worshiped, and with much noise seek some new idol in which they can incarnate their vanities and hopes. Stunned by the rout at Manassas, the North pulled down an old veteran, Scott, and his lieutenant, McDowell, and set up McClellan, who caught the public eye at the moment by reason of some minor successes in Western Virginia, where the Confederate General, Robert Garnett, was killed. It is but fair to admit that the South had not emulated the wisdom of Solomon nor the modesty of Godolphin. The capture of Fort Sumter, with its garrison of less than a hundred men, was hardly Gibraltar; yet it would put the grandiloquent hidalgoes of Spain on their mettle to make more clatter over the downfall of the cross of St. George from that historic rock. McClellan was the young Napoleon, the very god of war in his latest avatar. While this was absurd, and in the end injurious to McClellan, it was of service to his Government; for it strengthened his loins to the task before him—a task demanding the highest order of ability and the influence of a demigod. A great war was to be carried on, and a great army, the most complex of machines, was necessary.

The cardinal principles on which the art of war is based are few and unchangeable, resembling in this the code of morality; but their application varies as the theatre of the war, the genius and temper of the people engaged, and the kind of arms employed. The United States had never possessed a great army. The entire force engaged in the war against Mexico would scarcely have made a respectable *corps d'armée*, and to study the organization of great armies and campaigns a recurrence to the Napoleonic era was necessary. The Governments of Europe for a half century had been improving armaments, and changing the tactical unit of formation and manœuvre to correspond to such improvement. The Italian campaign of Louis Napoleon established some advance in field artillery, but the supreme importance of breech-loaders was not admitted until Sadowa, in 1866. All this must be considered in determining the value of McClellan's work. Taking the raw material intrusted to him, he converted it into a great military machine, complete in all its parts, fitted for its intended purpose. Moreover, he resisted the natural impatience of his Government and people, and the follies of politicians and newspapers, and for months refused to put his machine at work before all its delicate adjustments were perfected. Thus, much in its own despite, the North obtained armies and the foundation of success. The correctness of the system adopted by McClellan proved equal to all emergencies, and remained unchanged until the close of the war. Disappointed in his hands, and suffering painful defeats in those of his immediate successors, the "Army of the Potomac" always recovered, showed itself a vital organism, and finally triumphed. McClellan organized victory for his section, and those who deem the preservation of the "Union" the first of earthly duties should not cease to do him reverence.

I have here written of McClellan, not as a leader, but an organizer of armies; and as such he deserves to rank with the Von Moltkes, Scharnhorsts, and Louvois of history.

Constant struggle against the fatal interference of politicians with his military plans and duties separated McClellan from the civil department of his Government, and led him to adopt a policy of his own. The military road to Richmond, and the only one as events proved, was by the peninsula and the James river, and it was his duty so to advise. He insisted, and had his way; but not for long. A little of that selfishness which serves lower intelligences as an instinct of self-preservation would have shown him that his most dangerous enemies were not in his front. The Administration at Washington had to deal with a people blind with rage, an ignorant and meddlesome Congress, and a wolfish horde of place-hunters. A sudden dash of the Confederates on the capital might change the attitude of foreign powers. These political considerations weighed heavily at the seat of government, but were of small moment to the military commander. In a conflict between civil policy and military strategy, the latter must yield. The jealousy manifested by the Venetian and Dutch republics toward their commanders has often been criticised; but it should be remembered that they kept the military in strict subjection to the civil power; and when they were overthrown, it was by foreign invasion, not by military usurpation. Their annals afford no example of the declaration by their generals that the special purpose of republican armies is to preserve civil order and enforce civil law.

After the battle of Chickamauga, in 1863, General Grant was promoted to the command of the armies of the United States, and called to Washington. In a conference between him, President Lincoln, and Secretary Stanton, the approaching campaign in Virginia was discussed. Grant said that the advance on Richmond should be made by the James river. It was replied that the Government required the interposition of an army between Lee and Washington, and could not consent at that late day to the adoption of a plan which would be taken by the public as a confession of previous error. Grant observed that he was indifferent as to routes; but if the Government preferred its own, so often tried, to the one he suggested, it must be prepared for the additional loss of a hundred thousand men. The men were promised, Grant accepted the governmental plan of campaign,

3

and was supported to the end.   The above came to me well authenticated, and I have no doubt of its correctness.*

---

* Some of the early pages of this work were published in the number of the "North American Review" for January, 1878, including the above account of a conference at Washington between President Lincoln, Secretary Stanton, and General Grant.   In the "New York Herald" of May 27, 1878, appears an interview with General Grant, in which the latter says, "The whole story is a fabrication, and whoever vouched for it to General Taylor vouched for a fiction."   General Halleck, who was at the time in question Chief of Staff at the war office, related the story of this conference to me in New Orleans, where he was on a visit from Louisville, Ky., then his headquarters.   Several years later General Joseph E. Johnston gave me the same account, which he had from another officer of the United States Army, also at the time in the war office.   A letter from General Johnston, confirming the accuracy of my relation, has been published.   Since, I have received a letter, dated New York, June 6, 1878, wherein the writer states that in Washington, in 1868 or 1869, he had an account of this conference, as I give it, from General John A. Logan of Illinois.   When calling for reënforcements, after his losses in the Wilderness, General Grant reminded Stanton of his opposition to the land route in their conference, but added that "he would now fight it out on this line if it takes all summer."   The writer of this communication is quite unknown to me, but manifests his sincerity by suggesting that I should write to General Logan, who, he doubts not, will confirm his statement.   I have not so written, because I have no acquaintance with General Logan, and no desire to press the matter further. From many sources comes evidence that *a conference* was held, which General Grant seems to deny.   Moreover, I cannot forget that in one notable instance a question of fact was raised against General Grant, with much burden of evidence ; and while declaiming any wish or intent of entering on another, one may hold in all charity that General Grant's memory may be as treacherous about *facts* as mine proved about a *date*, when, in a letter to the "Herald," I stupidly gave two years after General· Halleck's death as the time of his conversation with me.   These considerations have determined me to let the account of the conference stand as originally written.

During his operations on the peninsula and near Richmond, McClellan complained much of want of support; but the constancy with which President Lincoln adhered to him was, under the circumstances, surprising. He had drifted away from the dominant Washington sentiment, and alienated the sympathies of his Government. His fall was inevitable; the affection of the army but hastened it; even victory could not save him. He adopted the habit of saying, "My army," "My soldiers." Such phraseology may be employed by a Frederick or Napoleon, sovereigns as well as generals; but officers command the armies of their governments. General McClellan is an upright, patriotic man, incapable of wrong-doing, and has a high standard of morality, to which he lives more closely than most men do to a lower one; but it is to be remembered that the examples of the good are temptations and opportunities to the unscrupulous. The habit of thought underlying such language, or soon engendered by its use, has made Mexico and the South American republics the wonder and scorn of civilization.

The foregoing account of McClellan's downfall is deemed pertinent because he was the central figure in the Northern field, and laid the foundation of Northern success. Above all, he and a gallant band of officers supporting him impressed a generous, chivalric spirit on the war, which soon faded away; and the future historian, in recounting some later operations, will doubt if he is dealing with campaigns of generals or expeditions of brigands.

The intention of McClellan to transfer his base from Washington to some point farther south was known to Johnston, but there was doubt whether Fredericksburg or the Peninsula would be selected. To meet either contingency, Johnston in the spring of 1862 moved his army from Manassas to the vicinity of Orange Court House, where he was within easy reach of both Fredericksburg and Richmond. The movement was executed with the quiet precision characteristic of Johnston, unrivaled as a master of logistics.

I was ordered to withdraw the infantry pickets from the lower Bull Run after nightfall, and move on a road through the county of Prince William, east of the line of railway from Manassas to Orange. This road was tough and heavy, and crossed by frequent streams, affluents of the neighboring Potomac. These furnished occupation and instruction to a small body of pioneers, recently organized, while the difficulties of the road drew heavily on the marching capacity—or rather incapacity— of the men. Straggling was then, and continued throughout to be, the vice of Southern armies. The climate of the South was not favorable to pedestrian exercise, and, centaur-like, its inhabitants, from infancy to old age, passed their lives on horseback, seldom walking the most insignificant distance. When brought into the field, the men were as ignorant of the art of marching as babes, and required for their instruction the same patient, unwearied attention. On this and subsequent marches frequent halts were made, to enable stragglers to close up; and I set the example to mounted officers of riding to the rear of the column, to encourage the weary by relieving them of their arms, and occasionally giving a footsore fellow a cast on my horse. The men appreciated this care and attention, followed advice as to the fitting of their shoes, cold bathing of feet, and healing of abrasions, and soon held it a disgrace to fall out of ranks. Before a month had passed the brigade learned how to march, and, in the Valley with Jackson, covered long distances without leaving a straggler behind. Indeed, in several instances it emulated the achievement of Crauford's "Light Brigade," whose wonderful march to join Wellington at Talavera remains the stoutest feat of modern soldiership.

Arrived at the Rappahannock, I found the railway bridge floored for the passage of troops and trains. The army, with the exception of Ewell's division, composed of Elzey's, Trimball's, and my brigades, had passed the Rapidan, and was lying around Orange Court House, where General Johnston had his headquarters. Some horse, under Stuart, remained north of the Rappahannock, toward Manassas.

For the first time Ewell had his division together and under his immediate command; and as we remained for many days between the rivers, I had abundant opportunities for studying

the original character of " Dick Ewell." We had known each
other for many years, but now our friendship and intercourse
became close and constant. Graduated from West Point in
1840, Ewell joined the 1st regiment of United States dragoons,
and, saving the Mexican war, in which he served with such distinction as a young cavalryman could gain, his whole military
life had been passed on the plains, where, as he often asserted,
he had learned all about commanding fifty United States dragoons, and forgotten everything else. In this he did himself
injustice, as his career proves ; but he was of a singular modesty.
Bright, prominent eyes, a bomb-shaped, bald head, and a nose
like that of Francis of Valois, gave him a striking resemblance
to a woodcock ; and this was increased by a bird-like habit of
putting his head on one side to utter his quaint speeches. He
fancied that he had some mysterious internal malady, and would
eat nothing but frumenty, a preparation of wheat; and his
plaintive way of talking of his disease, as if he were some one
else, was droll in the extreme. His nervousness prevented him
from taking regular sleep, and he passed nights curled around a
camp-stool, in positions to dislocate an ordinary person's joints
and drive the " caoutchouc man " to despair. On such occasions, after long silence, he would suddenly direct his eyes and
nose toward me with " General Taylor ! What do you suppose
President Davis made me a major-general for ? "—beginning
with a sharp accent and ending with a gentle lisp. Superbly
mounted, he was the boldest of horsemen, invariably leaving
the roads to take timber and water. No follower of the
" Pytchley " or " Quorn " could have lived with him across
country. With a fine tactical eye on the battle field, he was
never content with his own plan until he had secured the approval of another's judgment, and chafed under the restraint of
command, preparing to fight with the skirmish line. On two
occasions in the Valley, during the temporary absence of Jackson from the front, Ewell summoned me to his side, and immediately rushed forward among the skirmishers, where some
sharp work was going on. Having refreshed himself, he returned with the hope that " old Jackson would not catch him

at it." He always spoke of Jackson, several years his junior, as " old," and told me in confidence that he admired his genius, but was certain of his lunacy, and that he never saw one of Jackson's couriers approach without expecting an order to assault the north pole.

Later, after he had heard Jackson seriously declare that he never ate pepper because it produced a weakness in his left leg, he was confirmed in this opinion. With all his oddities, perhaps in some measure because of them, Ewell was adored by officers and men.

Orders from headquarters directed all surplus provisions, in the country between the Rappahannock and Rapidan, to be sent south of the latter stream. Executing these orders strictly, as we daily expected to rejoin the army, the division began to be straitened for supplies. The commissary of my brigade, Major Davis, was the very pearl of commissaries. Indefatigable in discharge of duty, he had as fine a nose for bullocks and bacon as Major Monsoon for sherry. The commissaries of the other brigades were less efficient, and for some days drew rations from Davis; but it soon became my duty to take care of my own command, and General Ewell's attention was called to the subject. The General thought that it was impossible so rich a country could be exhausted, and sallied forth on a cattle hunt himself. Late in the day he returned with a bull, jaded as was he of.Ballyraggan after he had been goaded to the summit of that classic pass, and venerable enough to have fertilized the milky mothers of the herds of our early Presidents, whose former estates lie in this vicinity. With a triumphant air Ewell showed me his plunder. I observed that the bull was a most respectable animal, but would hardly afford much subsistence to eight thousand men. "Ah! I was thinking of my fifty dragoons," replied the General. The joke spread, and doubtless furnished sauce for the happy few to whose lot the bull fell.

Meantime, the cavalry force in our front had been withdrawn, and the Federal pickets made their appearance on the north bank of the Rappahannock, occasionally exchanging a shot with ours across the stream. This served to enliven us for a day or two, and kept Ewell busy, as he always feared lest some one would get under fire before him.   At length a fire of artillery and small arms was opened from the north end of the bridge, near the south end of which my brigade was camped.   Ordering the command to move out, I galloped down to the river, where I found Ewell assisting with his own hands to place some guns in position.   The affair was over in a few minutes.   The enemy had quietly run up two pieces of artillery, supported by dismounted horsemen, and opened fire on my camp; but the promptness with which the men had moved prevented loss, saving one or two brush huts, and a few mess pans.

The bridge had previously been prepared for burning, Ewell's orders being to destroy all railway bridges behind him, to prevent the use of the rails by the Federals.   During the little *alerte* mentioned, I saw smoke rising from the bridge, which was soon a mass of flame.   Now, this was the only bridge for some miles up or down; and though the river was fordable at many points, the fords were deep and impassable after rains.   Its premature destruction not only prevented us from scouting and foraging on the north bank, but gave notice to the enemy of our purpose to abandon the country.   Annoyed, and doubtless expressing the feeling in my countenance, as I watched the flames, Ewell, after a long silence, said, " You don't like it."   Whereupon I related the following from Bugeaud's "Maxims" :   At the close of the Napoleonic wars, Bugeaud, a young colonel, commanded a French regiment on the Swiss frontier.   A stream spanned by a bridge, but fordable above and below, separated him from an Austrian force of four times his strength.   He first determined to destroy the bridge, but reflected that if left it might tempt the enemy, whenever he moved, to neglect the fords.   Accordingly, he masked his regiment as near his end of the bridge as the topography of the ground permitted, and waited.   The Austrians moved by the bridge, and Bugeaud, seizing the moment, fell upon them in the act of crossing and destroyed the entire force.   Moral : 'Tis easier to watch and defend one bridge than many miles of fordable water.   " Why did you keep the story until the bridge was burnt ? " exclaimed Ewell.   Subsequently, alleging that he had small opportunity for study after leaving West Point, he drew from me whatever some reading and a good memory could supply; but his shrewd remarks changed many erroneous opinions I had formed, and our " talks " were of more value to me than to him.

As our next move, hourly expected, would take us beyond the reach of railways, I here reduced the brigade to light marching order. My own kit, consisting of a change of under-wear and a tent " fly," could be carried on my horse. A fly can be put up in a moment, and by stopping the weather end with boughs a comfortable hut is made. The men carried each his blanket, an extra shirt and drawers, two pairs of socks (woolen), and a pair of extra shoes. These, with his arm and ammunition, were a sufficient load for strong marching. Tents, especially in a wooded country, are not only a nuisance, involving much trans-portation, the bane of armies, but are detrimental to health. In cool weather they are certain to be tightly closed, and the number of men occupying them breeds a foul atmosphere. The rapidity with which men learn to shelter themselves, and their ingenuity in accomplishing it under unfavorable conditions, are surprising. My people grumbled no little at being " stripped," but soon admitted that they were better for it, and came to des-pise useless *impedimenta*.

I early adopted two customs, and adhered to them throughout the war. The first was to examine at every halt the adjacent roads and paths, their direction and condition; distances of nearest towns and cross-roads; the country, its capacity to fur-nish supplies, as well as general topography, etc., all of which was embodied in a rude sketch, with notes to impress it on mem-ory. The second was to imagine while on the march an enemy before me to be attacked, or to be received in my position, and make the necessary dispositions for either contingency. My imaginary manœuvres were sad blunders, but I corrected them by experience drawn from actual battles, and can safely affirm that such slight success as I had in command was due to these customs. Assuredly, a knowledge of details will not make a great general; but there can be no greatness in war without such knowledge, for genius is but a capacity to grasp and apply details.

These observations are not for the "heaven-born," who from their closets scan with eagle glance fields of battle, whose mighty pens slay their thousands and their tens of thousands, and in whose "Serbonian" inkstands "armies whole" disappear; but it is hoped that they may prove useful to the young adopting the profession of arms, who may feel assured that the details of the art of war afford "scope and verge" for the employment of all their faculties. Conscientious study will not perhaps make them great, but it will make them respectable; and when the responsibility of command comes, they will not disgrace their flag, injure their cause, nor murder their men.

CHAPTER V.

THE VALLEY CAMPAIGN.

AT length the expected order to march came, and we moved south to Gordonsville. In one of his letters to Madame du Deffand, Horace Walpole writes of the English spring as "coming in with its accustomed severity," and such was our experience of a Virginian spring; or rather, it may be said that winter returned with renewed energy, and we had for several days snow, sleet, rain, and all possible abominations in the way of weather. Arrived at Gordonsville, whence the army had departed for the Peninsula, we met orders to join Jackson in the Valley, and marched thither by Swift Run "Gap"—the local name for mountain passes. Swift Run, an affluent of the Rapidan, has its source in this gap. The orders mentioned were the last received from General Joseph E. Johnston, from whom subsequent events separated me until the close of the war; and occasion is thus furnished for the expression of opinion of his character and services.

In the full vigor of mature manhood, erect, alert, quick, and decisive of speech, General Johnston was the beau ideal of a soldier. Without the least proneness to blandishments, he gained and held the affection and confidence of his men. Brave and impetuous in action, he had been often wounded, and no officer of the general staff of the old United States army had seen so much actual service with troops. During the Mexican war he was permitted to take command of a voltigeur regiment, and rendered brilliant service. In 1854 he resigned from the engineers to accept the lieutenant-colonelcy of a cavalry regiment. When the civil war became certain, a Virginian by birth, he left the position of Quartermaster-General of the United States, and offered his sword to the Confederacy. To the East, as his great namesake Albert Sidney to the West, he was "the rose and fair expectancy" of our cause; and his timely march from Patterson's front in the Valley to assist Beauregard át Manassas confirmed public opinion of his capacity. Yet he cannot be said to have proved a fortunate commander. Leaving out of view Bentonville and the closing scenes in North Carolina, which were rather the spasmodic efforts of despair than regular military movements, General Johnston's " offensive" must be limited to Seven Pines or Fair Oaks. Here his plan was well considered and singularly favored of fortune. Some two corps of McClellan's army were posted on the southwest or Richmond side of the Chickahominy, and a sudden rise of that stream swept away bridges and overflowed the adjacent lowlands, cutting off these corps from their supports. They ought to have been crushed, but Johnston fell, severely wounded; upon which confusion ensued, and no results of importance were attained: Official reports fail, most unwisely, to fix the responsibility of the failure, and I do not desire to add to the gossip prevailing then and since.

From his own account of the war we can gather that Johnston regrets he did not fight on the Oostenaula, after Polk had joined him. It appears that in a council two of his three corps commanders, Polk, Hardee, and Hood, were opposed to fighting there; but to call a council at all was a weakness not to be expected of a general of Johnston's ability and self-reliant nature.

I have written of him as a master of logistics, and his skill in handling troops was great. As a retreat, the precision and coolness of his movements during the Georgia campaign would have enhanced the reputation of Moreau; but it never seems to have occurred to him to assume the offensive during the many turning movements of his flanks, movements involving time and distance. Dispassionate reflection would have brought him to the conclusion that Lee was even more overweighted in Virginia than he in Georgia; that his Government had given him every available man, only leaving small garrisons at Wilmington, Charleston, Savannah, and Mobile; that Forrest's command in Mississippi, operating on Sherman's communications, was virtually doing his work, while it was idle to expect assistance from the trans-Mississippi region. Certainly, no more egregious blunder was possible than that of relieving him from command in front of Atlanta. If he intended to fight there, he was entitled to execute his plan. Had he abandoned Atlanta without a struggle, his removal would have met the approval of the army and public, an approval which, under the circumstances of its action, the Richmond Government failed to receive.

I am persuaded that General Johnston's mind was so jaundiced by the unfortunate disagreement with President Davis, to which allusion has been made in an earlier part of these reminiscences, as to seriously cloud his judgment and impair his usefulness. He sincerely believed himself the Esau of the Government, grudgingly fed on bitter herbs, while a favored Jacob enjoyed the flesh-pots. Having known him intimately for many years, having served under his command and studied his methods, I feel confident that his great abilities under happier conditions would have distinctly modified, if not changed, the current of events. Destiny willed that Davis and Johnston should be brought into collision, and the breach, once made, was never repaired. Each misjudged the other to the end.

Ewell's division reached the western base of Swift Run Gap on a lovely spring evening, April 30, 1862, and in crossing the Blue Ridge seemed to have left winter and its rigors behind. Jackson, whom we moved to join, had suddenly that morning marched toward McDowell, some eighty miles west, where, after uniting with a force under General Edward Johnson, he defeated the Federal general Milroy. Some days later he as suddenly returned. Meanwhile we were ordered to remain in camp on the Shenandoah near Conrad's store, at which place a bridge spanned the stream.

The great Valley of Virginia was before us in all its beauty. Fields of wheat spread far and wide, interspersed with woodlands, bright in their robes of tender green. Wherever appropriate sites existed, quaint old mills, with turning wheels, were busily grinding the previous year's harvest; and grove and eminence showed comfortable homesteads. The soft vernal influence shed a languid grace over the scene. The theatre of war in this region was from Staunton to the Potomac, one hundred and twenty miles, with an average width of some twenty-five miles; and the Blue Ridge and Alleghanies bounded it east and west. Drained by the Shenandoah with its numerous affluents, the surface was nowhere flat, but a succession of graceful swells, occasionally rising into abrupt hills. Resting on limestone, the soil was productive, especially of wheat, and the underlying rock furnished abundant metal for the construction of roads. Railway communication was limited to the Virginia Central, which entered the Valley by a tunnel east of Staunton and passed westward through that town; to the Manassas Gap, which traversed the Blue Ridge at the pass of that name and ended at Strasburg; and to the Winchester and Harper's Ferry, thirty miles long. The first extended to Richmond by Charlottesville and Gordonsville, crossing at the former place the line from Washington and Alexandria to Lynchburg; the second connected Strasburg and Front Royal, in the Valley, with the same line at Manassas Junction; and the last united with the Baltimore and Ohio at Harper's Ferry. Frequent passes or gaps in the mountains, through which wagon roads had been constructed, afforded easy access from east and west; and pikes were excellent, though unmetaled roads became heavy after rains.

But the glory of the Valley is Massanutten. Rising abruptly from the plain near Harrisonburg, twenty-five miles north of Staunton, this lovely mountain extends fifty miles, and as suddenly ends near Strasburg. Parallel with the Blue Ridge, and of equal height, its sharp peaks have a bolder and more picturesque aspect, while the abruptness of its slopes gives the appearance of greater altitude. Midway of Massanutten, a gap with good road affords communication between Newmarket and Luray. The eastern or Luray valley, much narrower than the one west of Massanutten, is drained by the east branch of the Shenandoah, which is joined at Front Royal, near the northern end of the mountain, by its western affluent, whence the united waters flow north, at the base of the Blue Ridge, to meet the Potomac at Harper's Ferry.

The inhabitants of this favored region were worthy of their inheritance. The north and south were peopled by scions of old colonial families, and the proud names of the " Old Dominion" abounded. In the central counties of Rockingham and Shenandoah were many descendants of German settlers. These were thrifty, substantial farmers, and, like their kinsmen of Pennsylvania, expressed their opulence in huge barns and fat cattle. The devotion of all to the Southern cause was wonderful. Jackson, a Valley man by reason of his residence at Lexington, south of Staunton, was their hero and idol. The women sent husbands, sons, lovers, to battle as cheerfully as to marriage feasts. No oppression, no destitution could abate their zeal. Upon a march I was accosted by two elderly sisters, who told me they had secreted a large quantity of bacon in a well on their estate, hard by. Federals had been in possession of the country, and, fearing the indiscretion of their slaves, they had done the work at night with their own hands, and now desired to *give* the meat to their people. Wives and daughters of millers, whose husbands and brothers were in arms, worked the mills night and day to furnish flour to their soldiers. To the last, women would go distances to carry the modicum of food between themselves and starvation to a suffering Confederate. Should the sons of Virginia ever commit dishonorable acts, grim indeed will be their reception on the further shores of Styx. They can expect no recognition from the mothers who bore them.

Ere the war closed, the Valley was ravaged with a cruelty surpassing that inflicted on the Palatinate two hundred years ago. That foul deed smirched the fame of Louvois and Turenne, and public opinion, in what has been deemed a ruder age, forced an apology from the " Grand Monarque." Yet we have seen the official report of a Federal general wherein are recounted the many barns, mills, and other buildings destroyed, concluding with the assertion that "a crow flying over the Valley must take rations with him." In the opinion of the admirers of the officer making this report, the achievement on which it is based ranks with Marengo. Moreover, this same officer, General Sheridan, many years after the close of the war, denounced several hundred thousands of his fellow citizens as "banditti," and solicited permission of his Government to deal with them as such. May we not well ask whether religion, education, science and art combined have lessened the brutality of man since the days of Wallenstein and Tilly?

While in camp near Conrad's store, the 7th Louisiana, Colonel Hays, a crack regiment, on picket down stream, had a spirited affair, in which the enemy was driven with the loss of a score of prisoners. Shortly after, for convenience of supplies, I was directed to cross the river and camp some miles to the southwest. The command was in superb condition, and a four-gun battery from Bedford county, Virginia, Captain Bowyer, had recently been added to it. The four regiments, 6th, 7th, 8th, and 9th Louisiana, would average above eight hundred bayonets. Of Wheat's battalion of "Tigers" and the 7th I have written. The 6th, Colonel Seymour, recruited in New Orleans, was composed of Irishmen, stout, hardy fellows, turbulent in camp and requiring a strong hand, but responding to kindness and justice, and ready to follow their officers to the death. The 9th, Colonel Stafford, was from North Louisiana. Planters or sons of planters, many of them men of fortune, soldiering was a hard task to which they only became reconciled by reflecting that it was "niddering" in gentlemen to assume voluntarily the discharge of duties and then shirk. The 8th, Colonel Kelly, was from the Attakapas—"Acadians," the race of which Longfellow sings in "Evangeline." A home-loving, simple people, few spoke English, fewer still had ever before moved ten miles from their natal *cabanas;* and the war to them was "a liberal education," as was the society of the lady of quality to honest Dick Steele. They had all the light gayety of the Gaul, and, after the manner of their ancestors, were born cooks. A capital regimental band accompanied them, and whenever weather and ground permitted, even after long marches, they would waltz and "polk" in couples with as much zest as if their arms encircled the supple waists of the Célestines and Mélazies of their native Téche. The Valley soldiers were largely of the Presbyterian faith, and of a solemn, pious demeanor, and looked askant at the caperings of my Creoles, holding them to be "devices and snares."

The brigade adjutant, Captain (afterward Colonel) Eustace Surget, who remained with me until the war closed, was from Mississippi, where he had large estates. Without the slightest military training, by study and zeal, he soon made himself an accomplished staff officer. Of singular coolness in battle, he never blundered, and, though much exposed, pulled through without a scratch. My aide, Lieutenant Hamilton, grandson of General Hamilton of South Carolina, was a cadet in his second year at West Point when war was declared, upon which he returned to his State—a gay, cheery lad, with all the pluck of his race.

At nightfall of the second day in this camp, an order came from General Jackson to join him at Newmarket, twenty odd miles north; and it was stated that my division commander, Ewell, had been apprised of the order. Our position was near a pike leading south of west to Harrisonburg, whence, to gain Newmarket, the great Valley pike ran due north. All roads near our camp had been examined and sketched, and among them was a road running northwest over the southern foot-hills of Massanutten, and joining the Valley pike some distance to the north of Harrisonburg. It was called the Keazletown road, from a little German village on the flank of Massanutten; and as it was the hypothenuse of the triangle, and reported good except at two points, I decided to take it. That night a pioneer party was sent forward to light fires and repair the road for artillery and trains. Early dawn saw us in motion, with lovely weather, a fairish road, and men in high health and spirits.

Later in the day a mounted officer was dispatched to report our approach and select a camp, which proved to be beyond Jackson's forces, then lying in the fields on both sides of the pike. Over three thousand strong, neat in fresh clothing of gray with white gaiters, bands playing at the head of their regiments, not a straggler, but every man in his place, stepping jauntily as on parade, though it had marched twenty miles and more, in open column with arms at "right shoulder shift," and rays of the declining sun flaming on polished bayonets, the brigade moved down the broad, smooth pike, and wheeled on to its camping ground. Jackson's men, by thousands, had gathered on either side of the road to see us pass. Indeed, it was a martial sight, and no man with a spark of sacred fire in his heart but would have striven hard to prove worthy of such a command.

After attending to necessary camp details, I sought Jackson, whom I had never met. And here it may be remarked that he then by no means held the place in public estimation which he subsequently attained. His Manassas reputation was much impaired by operations in the Valley, to which he had been sent after that action. The winter march on Romney had resulted in little except to freeze and discontent his troops; which discontent was shared and expressed by the authorities at Richmond, and Jackson resigned. The influence of Colonel Alek Boteler, seconded by that of the Governor of Virginia, induced him to withdraw the resignation. At Kernstown, three miles south of Winchester, he was roughly handled by the Federal General Shields, and only saved from serious disaster by the failure of that officer to push his advantage, though Shields was usually energetic.

The mounted officer who had been sent on in advance pointed out a figure perched on the topmost rail of a fence overlooking the road and field, and said it was Jackson. Approaching, I saluted and declared my name and rank, then waited for a response. Before this came I had time to see a pair of cavalry boots covering feet of gigantic size, a mangy cap with visor drawn low, a heavy, dark beard, and weary eyes—eyes I afterward saw filled with intense but never brilliant light. A low, gentle voice inquired the road and distance marched that day. "Keazletown road, six and twenty miles." "You seem to have

4

no stragglers." "Never allow straggling." "You must teach my people; they straggle badly." A bow in reply. Just then my creoles started their band and a waltz. After a contemplative suck at a lemon, "Thoughtless fellows for serious work" came forth. I expressed a hope that the work would not be less well done because of the gayety. A return to the lemon gave me the opportunity to retire. Where Jackson got his lemons "no fellow could find out," but he was rarely without one. To have lived twelve miles from that fruit would have disturbed him as much as it did the witty Dean.

Quite late that night General Jackson came to my camp fire, where he stayed some hours. He said we would move at dawn, asked a few questions about the marching of my men, which seemed to have impressed him, and then remained silent. If silence be golden, he was a "bonanza." He sucked lemons, ate hard-tack, and drank water, and praying and fighting appeared to be his idea of the "whole duty of man."

In the gray of the morning, as I was forming my column on the pike, Jackson appeared and gave the route—north— which, from the situation of its camp, put my brigade in advance of the army. After moving a short distance in this direction, the head of the column was turned to the east and took the road over Massanutten gap to Luray. Scarce a word was spoken on the march, as Jackson rode with me. From time to time a courier would gallop up, report, and return toward Luray. An ungraceful horseman, mounted on a sorry chestnut with a shambling gait, his huge feet with outturned toes thrust into his stirrups, and such parts of his countenance as the low visor of his shocking cap failed to conceal wearing a wooden look, our new commander was not prepossessing. That night we crossed the east branch of the Shenandoah by a bridge, and camped on the stream, near Luray. Here, after three long marches, we were but a short distance below Conrad's store, a point we had left several days before. I began to think that Jackson was an unconscious poet, and, as an ardent lover of nature, desired to give strangers an opportunity to admire the beauties of his Valley. It seemed hard lines to be wandering like sentimental travelers about the country, instead of gaining "kudos" on the Peninsula.

Off the next morning, my command still in advance, and Jackson riding with me. The road led north between the east bank of the river and the western base of the Blue Ridge. Rain had fallen and softened it, so as to delay the wagon trains in rear. Past midday we reached a wood extending from the mountain to the river, when a mounted officer from the rear called Jackson's attention, who rode back with him. A moment later, there rushed out of the wood to meet us a young, rather well-looking woman, afterward widely known as Belle Boyd. Breathless with speed and agitation, some time elapsed before she found her voice. Then, with much volubility, she said we were near Front Royal, beyond the wood; that the town was filled with Federals, whose camp was on the west side of the river, where they had guns in position to cover the wagon bridge, but none bearing on the railway bridge below the former; that they believed Jackson to be west of Massanutten, near Harrisonburg; that General Banks, the Federal commander, was at Winchester, twenty miles northwest of Front Royal, where he was slowly concentrating his widely scattered forces to meet Jackson's advance, which was expected some days later. All this she told with the precision of a staff officer making a report, and it was true to the letter. Jackson was possessed of these facts before he left Newmarket, and based his movements upon them; but, as he never told anything, it was news to me, and gave me an idea of the strategic value of Massanutten—pointed out, indeed, by Washington before the Revolution. There also dawned on me quite another view of our leader than the one from which I had been regarding him for two days past.

Convinced of the correctness of the woman's statements, I hurried forward at "a double," hoping to surprise the enemy's idlers in the town, or swarm over the wagon bridge with them and secure it. Doubtless this was rash, but I felt immensely "cocky" about my brigade, and believed that it would prove equal to any demand. Before we had cleared the wood Jackson came galloping from the rear, followed by a company of horse.

He ordered me to deploy my leading regiment as skirmishers on both sides of the road and continue the advance, then passed on. We speedily came in sight of Front Royal, but the enemy had taken the alarm, and his men were scurrying over the bridge to their camp, where troops could be seen forming. The situation of the village is surpassingly beautiful. It lies near the east bank of the Shenandoah, which just below unites all its waters, and looks directly on the northern peaks of Massanutten. The Blue Ridge, with Manassas Gap, through which passes the railway, overhangs it on the east; distant Alleghany bounds the horizon to the west; and down the Shenandoah, the eye ranges over a fertile, well-farmed country. Two bridges spanned the river—a wagon bridge above, a railway bridge some yards lower. A good pike led to Winchester, twenty miles, and another followed the river north, whence many cross-roads united with the Valley pike near Winchester. The river, swollen by rain, was deep and turbulent, with a strong current. The Federals were posted on the west bank, here somewhat higher than the opposite, and a short distance above the junction of waters, with batteries bearing more especially on the upper bridge.

Under instructions, my brigade was drawn up in line, a little retired from the river, but overlooking it—the Federals and their guns in full view. So far, not a shot had been fired. I rode down to the river's brink to get a better look at the enemy through a field-glass, when my horse, heated by the march, stepped into the water to drink. Instantly a brisk fire was opened on me, bullets striking all around and raising a little shower-bath. Like many a foolish fellow, I found it easier to get into than out of a difficulty. I had not yet led my command into action, and, remembering that one must "strut" one's little part to the best advantage, sat my horse with all the composure I could muster. A provident camel, on the eve of a desert journey, would not have laid in a greater supply of water than did my thoughtless beast. At last he raised his head, looked placidly around, turned, and walked up the bank.

This little incident was not without value, for my men welcomed me with a cheer; upon which, as if in response, the ene-

my's guns opened, and, having the range, inflicted some loss on
my line. We had no guns up to reply, and, in advance as has
been mentioned, had outmarched the troops behind us. Motionless as a statue, Jackson sat his horse some few yards away, and
seemed lost in thought. Perhaps the circumstances mentioned
some pages back had obscured his star; but if so, a few short
hours swept away the cloud, and it blazed, Sirius-like, over
the land. I approached him with the suggestion that the railway bridge might be passed by stepping on the cross-ties, as the
enemy's guns bore less directly on it than on the upper bridge.
He nodded approval. The 8th regiment was on the right of
my line, near at hand; and dismounting, Colonel Kelly led it
across under a sharp musketry fire. Several men fell to disappear in the dark water beneath; but the movement continued
with great rapidity, considering the difficulty of walking on ties,
and Kelly with his leading files gained the opposite shore.
Thereupon the enemy fired combustibles previously placed near
the center of the wagon bridge. The loss of this structure
would have seriously delayed us, as the railway bridge was not
floored, and I looked at Jackson, who, near by, was watching
Kelly's progress. Again he nodded, and my command rushed
at the bridge. Concealed by the cloud of smoke, the suddenness of the movement saved us from much loss; but it was
rather a near thing. My horse and clothing were scorched, and
many men burned their hands severely while throwing brands
into the river. We were soon over, and the enemy in full flight
to Winchester, with loss of camp, guns, and prisoners. Just as
I emerged from flames and smoke, Jackson was by my side.
How he got there was a mystery, as the bridge was thronged
with my men going at full speed; but smoke and fire had de-
cidedly freshened up his costume.

In the angle formed by the two branches of the river was
another camp held by a Federal regiment from Maryland. This
was captured by a gallant little regiment of Marylanders, Colonel Bradley Johnson, on our side. I had no connection with
this spirited affair, saving that these Marylanders had acted
with my command during the day, though not attached to it.

We followed the enemy on the Winchester road, but to little purpose, as we had few horsemen over the river. Carried away by his ardor, my commissary, Major Davis, gathered a score of mounted orderlies and couriers, and pursued until a volley from the enemy's rear guard laid him low on the road, shot through the head. During my service west of the Mississippi River, I sent for the colonel of a mounted regiment from western Texas, a land of herdsmen, and asked him if he could furnish men to hunt and drive in cattle. "Why! bless you, sir, I have men who can find cattle where there *aint any*," was his reply. Whatever were poor Davis's abilities as to non-existent supplies, he could find all the country afforded, and had a wonderful way of cajoling old women out of potatoes, cabbages, onions, and other garden stuff, giving variety to camp rations, and of no small importance in preserving the health of troops. We buried him in a field near the place of his fall. He was much beloved by the command, and many gathered quietly around the grave. As there was no chaplain at hand, I repeated such portions of the service for the dead as a long neglect of pious things enabled me to recall.

Late in the night Jackson came out of the darkness and seated himself by my camp fire. He mentioned that I would move with him in the morning, then relapsed into silence. I fancied he looked at me kindly, and interpreted it into an approval of the conduct of the brigade. The events of the day, anticipations of the morrow, the death of Davis, drove away sleep, and I watched Jackson. For hours he sat silent and motionless, with eyes fixed on the fire. I took up the idea that he was inwardly praying, and he remained throughout the night.

Off in the morning, Jackson leading the way, my brigade, a small body of horse, and a section of the Rockbridge (Virginia) artillery forming the column. Major Wheat, with his battalion of "Tigers," was directed to keep close to the guns. Sturdy marchers, they trotted along with the horse and artillery at Jackson's heels, and after several hours were some distance in advance of the brigade, with which I remained.

A volley in front, followed by wild cheers, stirred us up to a "double," and we speedily came upon a moving spectacle. Jackson had struck the Valley. pike at Middletown, twelve miles south of Winchester, along which a large body of Federal horse, with many wagons, was hastening north. He had attacked at once with his handful of men, overwhelmed resistance, and cap-tured prisoners and wagons. The gentle Tigers were looting right merrily, diving in and out of wagons with the activity of rabbits in a warren ; but this occupation was abandoned on my approach, and in a moment they were in line, looking as solemn and virtuous as deacons at a funeral. Prisoners and spoil were promptly secured. The horse was from New England, a section in which horsemanship was an unknown art, and some of the riders were strapped to their steeds. Ordered to dismount, they explained their condition, and were given time to unbuckle. Many breastplates and other protective devices were seen here, and later at Winchester. We did not know whether the Fed-erals had organized cuirassiers, or were recurring to the customs of Gustavus Adolphus. I saw a poor fellow lying dead on the pike, pierced through breastplate and body by a rifle ball. Iron-clad men are of small account before modern weapons.

A part of the Federal column had passed north before Jack-son reached the pike, and this, with his mounted men, he pur-sued. Something more than a mile to the south a road left the pike and led directly west, where the Federal General Fremont, of whom we shall hear more, commanded "the Mountain De-partment." Attacked in front, as described, a body of Federals, horse, artillery, and infantry, with some wagons, took this road, and, after moving a short distance, drew up on a crest, with un-limbered guns. Their number was unknown, and for a moment they looked threatening. The brigade was rapidly formed and marched straight upon them, when their guns opened. A shell knocked over several men of the 7th regiment, and a second, as I rode forward to an eminence to get a view, struck the ground under my horse and exploded. The saddle cloth on both sides was torn away, and I and Adjutant Surget, who was just behind me, were nearly smothered with earth ; but neither man nor horse received a scratch. The enemy soon limbered up and fled west.   By some well-directed shots, as they crossed a hill, our guns sent wagons flying in the air, with which "P. P. C." we left them and marched north.

At dusk we overtook Jackson, pushing the enemy with his little mounted force, himself in advance of all.   I rode with him, and we kept on through the darkness.   There was not resistance enough to deploy infantry.   A flash, a report, and a whistling bullet from some covert met us, but there were few casualties.   I quite remember thinking at the time that Jackson was invulnerable, and that persons near him shared that quality. An officer, riding hard, overtook us, who proved to be the chief quartermaster of the army.   He reported the wagon trains far behind, impeded by a bad road in Luray Valley.   "The ammunition wagons?" sternly.   "All right, sir.   They were in advance, and I doubled teams on them and brought them through." "Ah!" in a tone of relief.

To give countenance to this quartermaster, if such can be given of a dark night, I remarked jocosely: "Never mind the wagons.   There are quantities of stores in Winchester, and the General has invited me to breakfast there to-morrow."

Jackson, who had no more capacity for jests than a Scotchman, took this seriously, and reached out to touch me on the arm.   In fact, he was of Scotch-Irish descent, and his unconsciousness of jokes was *de race*.   Without physical wants himself, he forgot that others were differently constituted, and paid little heed to commissariat; but woe to the man who failed to bring up ammunition!   In advance, his trains were left far behind.   In retreat, he would fight for a wheelbarrow.

Some time after midnight, by roads more direct from Front Royal, other troops came on the pike, and I halted my jaded people by the roadside, where they built fires and took a turn at their haversacks.

Moving with the first light of morning, we came to Kernstown, three miles from Winchester, and the place of Jackson's fight with Shields.   Here heavy and sustained firing, artillery and small arms, was heard.   A staff officer approached at full speed to summon me to Jackson's presence and move up my command. A gallop of a mile or more brought me to him. Winchester was in sight, a mile to the north. To the east Ewell with a large part of the army was fighting briskly and driving the enemy on to the town. On the west a high ridge, overlooking the country to the south and southeast, was occupied by a heavy mass of Federals with guns in position. Jackson was on the pike, and near him were several regiments lying down for shelter, as the fire from the ridge was heavy and searching. A Virginian battery, Rockbridge artillery, was fighting at a great disadvantage, and already much cut up. Poetic authority asserts that " Old Virginny never tires," and the conduct of this battery justified the assertion of the muses. With scarce a leg or wheel for man and horse, gun or caisson, to stand on, it continued to hammer away at the crushing fire above.

Jackson, impassive as ever, pointed to the ridge and said, " You must carry it." I replied that my command would be up by the time I could inspect the ground, and rode to the left for that purpose. A small stream, Abraham's creek, flowed from the west through the little vale at the southern base of the ridge, the ascent of which was steep, though nowhere abrupt. At one point a broad, shallow, trough-like depression broke the surface, which was further interrupted by some low copse, outcropping stone, and two fences. On the summit the Federal lines were posted behind a stone wall, along a road coming west from the pike. Worn somewhat into the soil, this road served as a countersink and strengthened the position. Further west, there was a break in the ridge, which was occupied by a body of horse, the extreme right of the enemy's line.

There was scarce time to mark these features before the head of my column appeared, when it was filed to the left, close to the base of the ridge, for protection from the plunging fire. Meanwhile, the Rockbridge battery held on manfully and engaged the enemy's attention. Riding on the flank of my column, between it and the hostile line, I saw Jackson beside me. This was not the place for the commander of the army, and I ventured to tell him so ; but he paid no attention to the remark.

We reached the shallow depression spoken of, where the enemy could depress his guns, and his fire became close and fatal. Many men fell, and the whistling of shot and shell occasioned much ducking of heads in the column. This annoyed me no little, as it was but child's play to the work immediately in hand. Always an admirer of delightful "Uncle Toby," I had contracted the most villainous habit of his beloved army in Flanders, and, forgetting Jackson's presence, ripped out, "What the h— are you dodging for? If there is any more of it, you will be halted under this fire for an hour." The sharp tones of a familiar voice produced the desired effect, and the men looked as if they had swallowed ramrods; but I shall never forget the reproachful surprise expressed in Jackson's face. He placed his hand on my shoulder, said in a gentle voice, "I am afraid you are a wicked fellow," turned, and rode back to the pike.

The proper ground gained, the column faced to the front and began the ascent. At the moment the sun rose over the Blue Ridge, without cloud or mist to obscure his rays. It was a lovely Sabbath morning, the 25th of May, 1862. The clear, pure atmosphere brought the Blue Ridge and Alleghany and Massanutten almost overhead. Even the cloud of murderous smoke from the guns above made beautiful spirals in the air, and the broad fields of luxuriant wheat glistened with dew. It is remarkable how, in the midst of the most absorbing cares, one's attention may be fixed by some insignificant object, as mine was by the flight past the line of a bluebird, one of the brightest-plumaged of our feathered tribes, bearing a worm in his beak, breakfast for his callow brood. Birdie had been on the war path, and was carrying home spoil.

As we mounted we came in full view of both armies, whose efforts in other quarters had been slackened to await the result of our movement. I felt an anxiety amounting to pain for the brigade to acquit itself handsomely; and this feeling was shared by every man in it. About half way up, the enemy's horse from his right charged; and to meet it, I directed Lieutenant-Colonel Nicholls, whose regiment, the 8th, was on the left, to withhold slightly his two flank companies. By one volley, which emptied some saddles, Nicholls drove off the horse, but was soon after severely wounded. Progress was not stayed by this incident. Closing the many gaps made by the fierce fire, steadied the rather by it, and preserving an alignment that would have been creditable on parade, the brigade, with cadenced step and eyes on the foe, swept grandly over copse and ledge and fence, to crown the heights from which the enemy had melted away. Loud cheers went up from our army, prolonged to the east, where warm-hearted Ewell cheered himself hoarse, and led forward his men with renewed energy. In truth, it was a gallant feat of arms, worthy of the pen of him who immortalized the charge of the "Buffs" at Albuera.

Breaking into column, we pursued closely. Jackson came up and grasped my hand, worth a thousand words from another, and we were soon in the streets of Winchester, a quaint old town of some five thousand inhabitants. There was a little fighting in the streets, but the people were all abroad—certainly all the women and babies. They were frantic with delight, only regretting that so many "Yankees" had escaped, and seriously impeded our movements. A buxom, comely dame of some five and thirty summers, with bright eyes and tight ankles, and conscious of these advantages, was especially demonstrative, exclaiming, "Oh! you are too late—too late!" Whereupon, a tall creole from the Téche sprang from the ranks of the 8th regiment, just passing, clasped her in his arms, and imprinted a sounding kiss on her ripe lips, with "Madame! je n'arrive jamais trop tard." A loud laugh followed, and the dame, with a rosy face but merry twinkle in her eye, escaped.

Past the town, we could see the Federals flying north on the Harper's Ferry and Martinsburg roads. Cavalry, of which there was a considerable force with the army, might have reaped a rich harvest, but none came forward. Raised in the adjoining region, our troopers were gossiping with their friends, or worse. Perhaps they thought that the war was over. Jackson joined me, and, in response to my question, "Where is the cavalry?" glowered and was silent. After several miles, finding that we were doing no good—as indeed infantry, preserving its organization, cannot hope to overtake a flying enemy — I turned into the fields and camped.

Here I will " say my say " about Confederate cavalry; and though there were exceptions to the following remarks, they were too few to qualify their general correctness. The difficulty of converting raw men into soldiers is enhanced manifold when they are mounted. Both man and horse require training, and facilities for rambling, with temptation so to do, are increased. There was but little time, and it may be said less disposition, to establish camps of instruction. Living on horseback, fearless and dashing, the men of the South afforded the best possible material for cavalry. They had every quality but discipline, and resembled Prince Charming, whose manifold gifts, bestowed by her sisters, were rendered useless by the malignant fairy. Scores of them wandered about the country like locusts, and were only less destructive to their own people than the enemy. The universal devotion of Southern women to their cause led them to give indiscriminately to all wearing the gray. Cavalry officers naturally desired to have as large commands as possible, and were too much indulged in this desire. Brigades and regiments were permitted to do work appropriate to squadrons and companies, and the cattle were unnecessarily broken down. Assuredly, our cavalry rendered much excellent service, especially when dismounted and fighting as infantry. Such able officers as Stuart, Hampton, and the younger Lees in the east, Forrest, Green, and Wheeler in the west, developed much talent for war; but their achievements, however distinguished, fell far below the standard that would have been reached had not the want of discipline impaired their efforts and those of their men.

After the camp was established, I rode back to Winchester to look after my wounded and see my sister, the same who had nursed me the previous autumn. By a second marriage she was Mrs. Dandridge, and resided in the town. Her husband, Mr. Dandridge, was on duty at Richmond. Depot of all Federal forces in the Valley, Winchester was filled with stores. Prisoners, guns, and wagons, in large numbers, had fallen into our hands. Of especial value were ordnance and medical stores.

The following day my command was moved ten miles north on the pike leading by Charlestown to Harper's Ferry, and after a day some miles east toward the Shenandoah. This was in consequence of the operations of the Federal General Shields, who, in command of a considerable force to the east of the Blue Ridge, passed Manassas Gap and drove from Front Royal a regiment of Georgians, left there by Jackson. Meanwhile, a part of the army was pushed forward to Martinsburg and beyond, while another part threatened and shelled Harper's Ferry. Jackson himself was engaged in forwarding captured stores to Staunton.

On Saturday, May 31, I received orders to move through Winchester, clear the town of stragglers, and continue to Strasburg. Few or no stragglers were found in Winchester, whence the sick and wounded, except extreme cases, had been taken. I stopped for a moment, at a house near the field of the 25th, to see Colonel Nicholls. He had suffered amputation of the arm that morning, and the surgeons forbade his removal; so that, much to my regret and more to his own, he was left. We reached camp at Strasburg after dark, a march of thirty odd miles, weather very warm. Winder, with his brigade, came in later, after a longer march from the direction of Harper's Ferry. Jackson sat some time at my camp fire that night, and was more communicative than I remember him before or after. He said Fremont, with a large force, was three miles west of our present camp, and must be defeated in the morning. Shields was moving up Luray Valley, and might cross Massanutten to Newmarket, or continue south until he turned the mountain to fall on our trains near Harrisonburg. The importance of preserving the immense trains, filled with captured stores, was great, and would engage much of his personal attention; while he relied on the army, under Ewell's direction, to deal promptly with Fremont. This he told in a low, gentle voice, and with many interruptions to afford time, as I thought and believe, for inward prayer. The men said that his anxiety about the wagons was because of the lemons among the stores.

Dawn of the following day (Sunday) was ushered in by the

sound of Fremont's guns.   Our lines had been early drawn out
to meet him, and skirmishers pushed up to the front to attack.
Much cannonading, with some rattle of small arms, ensued.   The
country was densely wooded, and little save the smoke from the
enemy's guns could be seen.   My brigade was in reserve a short
distance to the rear and out of the line of fire ; and here a ludi-
crous incident occurred.   Many slaves from Louisiana had accompanied their masters to the war, and were a great nuisance
on a march, foraging far and wide for " prog " for their owners'
messes.   To abate this, they had been put under discipline and
made to march in rear of the regiments to which they pertained.
They were now, some scores, assembled under a large tree,
laughing, chattering, and cooking breakfast.   On a sudden, a
shell burst in the tree-top, rattling down leaves and branches
in fine style, and the rapid decampment of the servitors was
most amusing.   But I must pause to give an account of my own
servant, Tom Strother, who deserves honorable and affectionate
mention at my hands, and serves to illustrate a phase of Southern life now passed away.

As under feudal institutions the arms of heiresses were quartered with those of the families into which they married, in the
South their slaves adopted the surname of the mistress; and one
curious in genealogy could trace the descent and alliances of an
old family by finding out the names used by different slaves on
the estate.   Those of the same name were a little clannish, preserving traditions of the family from which their fathers had
come, and magnifying its importance.   In childhood I often
listened with credulous ears to wondrous tales of the magnifi-
cence of my forefathers in Virginia and Maryland, who, these
imaginative Africans insisted, dwelt in palaces, surrounded by
brave, handsome sons, lovely, virtuous daughters, and countless
devoted servants.   The characters of many Southern children
were doubtless influenced by such tales, impressive from the
good faith of the narrators.   My paternal grandmother was
Miss Sarah Strother of Virginia, and from her estate came these
Strother negroes.   Tom, three years my senior, was my foster
brother and early playmate.   His uncle, Charles Porter Strother

(to give him his full name), had been body servant to my grand-father, Colonel Richard Taylor, whom he attended in his last illness. He then filled the same office to my father, following him through his Indian and Mexican campaigns, and dying at Washington a year before his master. Tom served in Florida and Mexico as "aide-de-camp" to his uncle, after which he married and became father of a large family. On this account I hesitated to bring him to Virginia, but he would come, and was a model servant. Tall, powerful, black as ebony, he was a mirror of truth and honesty. Always cheerful, I never heard him laugh or knew of his speaking unless spoken to. He could light a fire in a minute under the most unfavorable conditions and with the most unpromising material, made the best coffee to be tasted outside of a creole kitchen, was a "dab" at camp stews and roasts, groomed my horses (one of which he rode near me), washed my linen, and was never behind time. Occasionally, when camped near a house, he would obtain starch and flat-irons, and get up my extra shirt in a way to excite the envy of a professional clear-starcher; but such red-letter days were few.

I used to fancy that there was a mute sympathy between General Jackson and Tom, as they sat silent by a camp fire, the latter respectfully withdrawn; and an incident here at Strasburg cemented this friendship. When my command was called into action, I left Tom on a hill where all was quiet. Thereafter, from a change in the enemy's dispositions, the place became rather hot, and Jackson, passing by, advised Tom to move; but he replied, if the General pleased, his master told him to stay there and would know where to find him, and he did not believe shells would trouble him. Two or three nights later, Jackson was at my fire when Tom came to give me some coffee; whereupon Jackson rose and gravely shook him by the hand, and then told me the above.

After the war was closed, Tom returned with me to New Orleans, found his wife and children all right, and is now prosperous. My readers have had so much fighting lately, and are about to have so much more, as to render unnecessary an apology for introducing Tom's history.

To return. Cannonading continued without much effect, and Ewell summoned me to his presence, directing the brigade to remain in position till further orders. Jackson, busy with his trains, was not at the moment on the field, which he visited several times during the day, though I did not happen to see him. To reach Ewell, it was necessary to pass under some heavy shelling, and I found myself open to the reproach visited previously on my men. Whether from fatigue, loss of sleep, or what, there I was, nervous as a lady, ducking like a mandarin. It was disgusting, and, hoping that no one saw me, I resolved to take it out of myself the first opportunity. There is a story of Turenne, the greatest soldier of the Bourbons, which, if not true, is *ben trovato*. Of a nervous temperament, his legs on the eve of an action trembled to such an extent as to make it difficult to mount his horse. Looking at them contemptuously, he said: "If you could foresee the danger into which I am going to take you, you would tremble more." It was with a similar feeling, not only for my legs, but for my entire carcass, that I reached Ewell, and told him I was no more good than a frightened deer. He laughed, and replied: "Nonsense! 'tis Tom's strong coffee. Better give it up. Remain here in charge while I go out to the skirmishers. I can't make out what these people are about, for my skirmish line has stopped them. They won't advance, but stay out there in the wood, making a great fuss with their guns; and I do not wish to commit myself to much advance while Jackson is absent." With this, he put spurs to his horse and was off, and soon a brisk fusillade was heard, which seemed gradually to recede. During Ewell's absence, surrounded by his staff, I contrived to sit my horse quietly. Returning, he said: "I am completely puzzled. I have just driven everything back to the main body, which is large. Dense wood everywhere. Jackson told me not to commit myself too far. At this rate my attentions are not likely to become serious enough to commit any one. I wish Jackson was here himself." I suggested that my brigade might be moved to the extreme right, near the Capon road, by which Fremont had marched, and attempt to strike that road, as this would enable us to find out something. He replied: "Do so; that may stir them up, and I am sick of this fiddling about." Had Ewell been in command, he would have "pitched in" long before; but he was controlled by instructions not to be drawn too far from the pike.

We found the right of our line held by a Mississippi regiment, the colonel of which told me that he had advanced just before and driven the enemy. Several of his men were wounded, and he was bleeding profusely from a hit in his leg, which he was engaged in binding with a handkerchief, remarking that "it did not pester him much." Learning our purpose, he was eager to go in with us, and was not at all pleased to hear that I declined to change General Ewell's dispositions. A plucky fellow, this colonel, whose name, if ever known, I cannot recall. The brigade moved forward until the enemy was reached, when, wheeling to the left, it walked down his line. The expression is used advisedly, for it was nothing but a "walk-over." Sheep would have made as much resistance as we met. Men decamped without firing, or threw down their arms and surrendered, and it was so easy that I began to think of traps. At length we got under fire from our own skirmishers, and suffered some casualties, the only ones received in the movement.

Our whole skirmish line was advancing briskly as the Federals retired. I sought Ewell, and reported. We had a fine game before us, and the temptation to play it was great; but Jackson's orders were imperative and wise. He had his stores to save, Shields to guard against, Lee's grand strategy to promote; and all this he accomplished, alarming Washington, fastening McDowell's strong corps at Fredericksburg and preventing its junction with McClellan, on whose right flank he subsequently threw himself at Cold Harbor. He could not waste time chasing Fremont, but we, who looked from a lower standpoint, grumbled and shared the men's opinion about the *lemon wagons*.

The prisoners taken in our promenade were Germans, speaking no English; and we had a similar experience a few days later. In the Federal Army was a German corps, the 11th,

5

commanded by General O. O. Howard, and called by both sides "the Flying Dutchmen." Since the time of Arminius the Germans have been a brave people; to-day, in military renown, they lead the van of the nations; but they require a cause and leaders. In our Revolutionary struggle the Hessians were unfortunate at Bennington, Saratoga, and Trenton. We have millions of German citizens, and excellent citizens they are. Let us hope that the foregoing facts may be commended to them, so their ways may be ways of peace in their adopted land.

Although the movement along the enemy's line was successful, as described, it was rash and foolish. Fremont had troops which, had they been in the place of these Germans, would have made us pass one of Rabelais's unpleasant quarters of an hour. Alarm and disgust at my own nervousness occasioned it, proving weak nerves to be the source of rash acts.

Fremont made no further sign, and as the day declined the army was recalled to the pike and marched south. Jackson, in person, gave me instructions to draw up my brigade facing west, on some hills above the pike, and distant from it several hundred yards, where I was to remain. He said that the road was crowded, and he wanted time to clear it, that Fremont was safe for the night, and our cavalry toward Winchester reported Banks returned to that place from the Potomac, but not likely to move south before the following day; then rode off, and so rapidly as to give me no time to inquire how long I was to remain, or if the cavalry would advise me in the event that Banks changed his purpose. This was near sunset, and by the time the command was in position darkness fell upon us. No fires were allowed, and, stacking arms, the men rested, munching cold rations from their haversacks. It was their first opportunity for a bite since early morning.

I threw myself on the ground, and tried in vain to sleep. No sound could be heard save the clattering of hoofs on the pike, which as the night wore on became constant. Hour after hour passed, when, thinking I heard firing to the north, I mounted and looked for the pike. The darkness was so intense that it could not have been found but for the white limestone.

Some mounted men were passing, whom I halted to question. They said their command had gone on to rejoin the army, and, they supposed, had missed me in the dark; but there was a squadron behind, near the enemy's advance, which, a large cavalry force, had moved from Winchester at an early period of the day and driven our people south. This was pleasant; for Winder's brigade had marched several hours since, and a wide interval existed between us.

More firing, near and distinct, was heard, and the command was ordered down to the pike, which it reached after much stumbling and swearing, and some confusion. Fortunately, the battery, Captain Bowyer, had been sent forward at dusk to get forage, and an orderly was dispatched to put it on the march. The 6th (Irish) regiment was in rear, and I took two companies for a rear guard. The column had scarce got into motion before a party of horse rushed through the guard, knocking down several men, one of whom was severely bruised. There was a little pistol-shooting and sabre-hacking, and for some minutes things were rather mixed. The enemy's cavalry had charged ours, and driven it on the infantry. One Federal was captured and his horse given to the bruised man, who congratulated the rider on his promotion to a respectable service. I dismounted, gave my horse to Tom to lead, and marched with the guard. From time to time the enemy would charge, but we could hear him coming and be ready. The guard would halt, about face, front rank with fixed bayonets kneel, rear rank fire, when, by the light of the flash, we could see emptied saddles. Our pursuers' fire was wild, passing over head; so we had few casualties, and these slight; but they were bold and enterprising, and well led, often charging close up to the bayonets. I remarked this, whereupon the Irishmen answered, "Devil thank 'em for that same." There was no danger on the flanks. The white of the pike alone guided us. Owls could not have found their way across the fields. The face of the country has been described as a succession of rolling swells, and later the enemy got up guns, but always fired from the summits, so that his shells passed far above us, exploding in the fields. Had the guns been trained low, with canister, it might have proved uncomfortable, for the pike ran straight to the south. "It was a fine night intirely for divarsion," said the Irishmen, with which sentiment I did not agree; but they were as steady as clocks and chirpy as crickets, indulging in many a jest whenever the attentions of our friends in the rear were slackened. They had heard of Shields's proximity, and knew him to be an Irishman by birth, and that he had Irish regiments with him. During an interlude I was asked if it was not probable that we would encounter Shields, and answering affirmatively, heard: "Them Germans is poor creatures, but Shields's boys will be after fighting." Expressing a belief that my "boys" could match Shields's any day, I received loud assurance from half a hundred Tipperary throats: "You may bet your life on that, sor." Thus we beguiled the weary hours. During the night I desired to relieve the guard, but was diverted from my purpose by scornful howls of "We are the boys to see it out." As Argyle's to the tartan, my heart has warmed to an Irishman since that night.

Daylight came, and I tried to brace myself for hotter work, when a body of troops was reported in position to the south of my column. This proved to be Charles Winder with his (formerly Jackson's own) brigade. An accomplished soldier and true brother-in-arms, he had heard the enemy's guns during the night, and, knowing me to be in rear, halted and formed line to await me. His men were fed and rested, and he insisted on taking my place in the rear. Passing through Winder's line, we moved slowly, with frequent halts, so as to remain near, the enemy pressing hard during the morning. The day was uncommonly hot, the sun like fire, and water scarce along the road; and our men suffered greatly.

Just after midday my brisk young aide, Hamilton, whom I had left with Winder to bring early intelligence, came to report that officer in trouble and want of assistance. My men were so jaded as to make me unwilling to retrace ground if it could be avoided; so they were ordered to form line on the crest of the slope at hand, and I went to Winder, a mile to the rear. His brigade, renowned as the "Stonewall," was deployed on both sides of the pike, on which he had four guns. Large masses of cavalry, with guns and some sharp-shooters, were pressing him closely, while far to the north clouds of dust marked the approach of troops. His line was on one of the many swells crossing the pike at right angles, and a gentle slope led to the next crest south, beyond which my brigade was forming. The problem was to retire without giving the enemy, eager and persistent, an opportunity to charge. The situation looked so blue that I offered to move back my command ; but Winder thought he could pull through, and splendidly did he accomplish it. Regiment by regiment, gun by gun, the brigade was withdrawn, always checking the enemy, though boldly led. Winder, cool as a professor playing the new German game, directed every movement in person, and the men were worthy of him and of their first commander, Jackson. It was very close work in the vale before he reached the next crest, and heavy volleys were necessary to stay our plucky foes ; but, once there, my command showed so strong as to impress the enemy, who halted to reconnoiter, and the two brigades were united without further trouble.

The position was good, my battery was at hand, and our men were so fatigued that we debated whether it was not more comfortable to fight than retreat. We could hold the ground for hours against cavalry, and night would probably come before infantry got up, while retreat was certain to bring the cavalry on us. At this juncture up came General Turner Ashby, followed by a considerable force of horse, with guns. This officer had been engaged in destroying bridges in Luray Valley, to prevent Shields from crossing that branch of the Shenandoah, and now came, much to our satisfaction, to take charge of the rear. He proceeded to pay his respects to our friends, and soon took them off our hands. We remained an hour to rest the men and give Ashby time to make his dispositions, then moved on.

Before sunset heavy clouds gathered, and the intense heat was broken by a regular downpour, in the midst of which we crossed the bridge over the west branch of the Shenandoah—a large stream—at Mount Jackson, and camped. There was not a dry thread about my person, and my boots would have furnished a respectable bath. Notwithstanding the flood, Tom soon had a fire, and was off to hunt forage for man and beast. Here we were less than ten miles from Newmarket, between which and this point the army was camped. Jackson was easy about Massanutten Gap. Shields must march south of the mountain to reach him, while the river, just crossed, was now impassable except by bridge.

We remained thirty-six hours in this camp, from the evening of the 2d until the morning of the 4th of June—a welcome rest to all. Two days of light marching carried us thence to Harrisonburg, thirty miles. Here Jackson quitted the pike leading to Staunton, and took the road to Port Republic. This village, twelve miles southeast of Harrisonburg, lies at the base of the Blue Ridge, on the east bank of the Shenandoah. Several streams unite here to form the east (locally called south) branch of that river; and here too was the only bridge from Front Royal south, all others having been destroyed by Ashby to prevent Shields from crossing. This commander was pushing a part of his force south, from Front Royal and Luray, on the east bank.

The army passed the night of June 5 in camp three miles from Harrisonburg toward Port Republic. Ewell's division, which I had rejoined for the first time since we met Jackson, was in rear; and the rear brigade was General George Stewart's, composed of one Maryland and two Virginia regiments. My command was immediately in advance of Stewart's. Ashby had burnt the bridge at Mount Jackson to delay Fremont, and was camped with his horse in advance of Harrisonburg. The road to Port Republic was heavy from recent rains, causing much delay to trains, so that we did not move on the morning of the 6th. Early in the day Fremont, reënforced from Banks, got up; and his cavalry, vigorously led, pushed Ashby through Harrisonburg, where a sharp action occurred, resulting in the capture of many Federals—among others, Colonel Percy Wyndham, commanding brigade, whose meeting with Major Wheat has been described. Later, while Ewell was conversing with me, a message from Ashby took him to the rear. Federal cavalry, supported by infantry, was advancing on Ashby. Stewart's brigade was lying in a wood, under cover of which Ewell placed it in position. A severe struggle ensued; the enemy was driven, and many prisoners were taken. I had ridden back with Ewell, and so witnessed the affair, uncommonly spirited, and creditable to both sides. Colonel Kane of Philadelphia was among the prisoners and painfully wounded. Having known his father, Judge Kane, as well as his brother, the Arctic explorer, I solicited and obtained from Jackson his parole.

Colonel Nicholls, left wounded near Winchester, had married a short time previous to the war, and his young wife now appeared, seeking to join her husband. Jackson referred her request to Ewell, who passed it to me. Of this I was informed by Captain Nicholls, 8th regiment, brother to the colonel, killed a few days after at Cold Harbor. Much cavalry skirmishing was still going on around Harrisonburg, dangerous for a lady to pass through; and besides, she had come from Port Republic, seen our situation, and might be indiscreet. These considerations were stated to Captain Nicholls, but his sister-in-law insisted on seeing me. A small, fairy-like creature, plucky as a "Dandie Dinmont" terrier, and with a heart as big as Massanutten, she was seated in a nondescript trap, drawn by two mules, driven by a negro. One look from the great, tearful eyes made of me an abject coward, and I basely shuffled the refusal to let her pass on to Jackson. The Parthian glance of contempt that reached me through her tears showed that the lady understood and despised my paltering. Nicholls was speedily exchanged, became a general officer, lost a foot at Chancellorsville, and, after leading his people up out of captivity, is now the conservative Governor of Louisiana.

The skirmishing spoken of in the above connection developed into severe work, in which General Ashby was killed. Alluding to his death in an official report, Jackson says, "As a partisan officer I never knew his superior." Like Claverhouse, "with a face that painters loved to limn and ladies look upon," he was the most daring and accomplished rider in a region of horsemen. His courage was so brilliant as to elicit applause from friend and foe, but he was without capacity or disposition to enforce discipline on his men. I witnessed his deep chagrin at the conduct of our troopers after the enemy had been driven from Winchester in May. With proper organization and discipline, his bold riders under his lead might have accomplished all that the lamented Nolan claimed as possible for light cavalry. Popular imagination, especially the female, is much in error as to these matters. Graceful young cavaliers, with flowing locks, leaping cannon to saber countless foes, make a captivating picture. In the language of Bosquet, "'Tis beautiful, but 'tis not war"; and grave mishaps have been occasioned by this misconception. Valor is as necessary now as ever in war, but disciplined, subordinated valor, admitting the courage and energies of all to be welded and directed to a common end. It is much to be desired that the ladies would consent to correct their opinions; for, after all, their approval stimulates our best fighting.

On the 7th of June we marched to a place within four miles of Port Republic, called Cross Keys, where several roads met. Near at hand was the meeting-house of a sect of German Quakers, Tunkers or Dunkards, as they are indifferently named. Here Jackson determined to await and fight Fremont, who followed him hard; but as a part of Shields's force was now unpleasantly near, he pushed on to Port Republic with Winder's and other infantry, and a battery, which camped on the hither bank of the river. Jackson himself, with his staff and a mounted escort, crossed the bridge and passed the night in the village.

Ewell, in immediate charge at Cross Keys, was ready early in the morning of the 8th, when Fremont attacked. The ground was undulating, with much wood, and no extended view could be had. In my front the attack, if such it could be called, was feeble in the extreme—an affair of skirmishers, in which the enemy yielded to the slightest pressure. A staff officer of Jackson's, in hot haste, came with orders from his chief to march my brigade double-quick to Port Republic. Elzey's brigade, in second line to the rear, was asked to take my place and relieve my skirmishers; then, advising the staff officer to notify Ewell, whom he had not seen, we started on the run, for such a message from Jackson meant business. Two of the intervening miles were quickly passed, when another officer appeared with orders to halt. In half an hour, during which the sound of battle at Cross Keys thickened, Jackson came. As before stated, he had passed the night in the village, with his staff and escort. Up as usual at dawn, he started alone to recross the bridge, leaving his people to follow. The bridge was a few yards below the last house in the village, and some mist overhung the river. Under cover of this a small body of horse, with one gun, from Shields's forces, had reached the east end of the bridge and trained the gun on it. Jackson was within an ace of capture. As he spurred across, the gun was fired on him, but without effect, and the sound brought up staff and escort, when the horse retired north. This incident occasioned the order to me. After relating it (all save his own danger), Jackson passed on to Ewell. Thither I followed, to remain in reserve until the general forward movement in the afternoon, by which Fremont was driven back with loss of prisoners. We did not persist far, as Shields's force was near upon us. From Ewell I learned that there had been some pretty fighting in the morning, though less than might have been expected from Fremont's numbers. I know not if the presence of this commander had a benumbing influence on his troops, but certainly his advanced cavalry and infantry had proved bold and enterprising.

In the evening we moved to the river and camped. Winder's and other brigades crossed the bridge, and during the night Ewell, with most of the army, drew near, leaving Trimble's brigade and the horse at Cross Keys. No one apprehended another advance by Fremont. The following morning, Sunday, June 9, my command passed the bridge, moved several hundred yards down the road, and halted. Our trains had gone east over the Blue Ridge. The sun appeared above the mountain while the men were quietly breakfasting. Suddenly, from below, was heard the din of battle, loud and sustained, artillery and small arms. The men sprang into ranks, formed column, and marched, and I galloped forward a short mile to see the following scene:

From the mountain, clothed to its base with undergrowth and timber, a level—clear, open, and smooth—extended to the river. This plain was some thousand yards in width. Half a mile north, a gorge, through which flowed a small stream, cut the mountain at a right angle. The northern shoulder of this gorge projected farther into the plain than the southern, and on an elevated plateau of the shoulder were placed six guns, sweeping every inch of the plain to the south. Federal lines, their right touching the river, were advancing steadily, with banners flying and arms gleaming in the sun. A gallant show, they came on. Winder's and another brigade, with a battery, opposed them. This small force was suffering cruelly, and its skirmishers were driven in on their thin supporting line. As my Irishmen predicted, "Shields's boys were after fighting." Below, Ewell was hurrying his men over the bridge, but it looked as if we should be doubled up on him ere he could cross and develop much strength. Jackson was on the road, a little in advance of his line, where the fire was hottest, with reins on his horse's neck, seemingly in prayer. Attracted by my approach, he said, in his usual voice, "Delightful excitement." I replied that it was pleasant to learn he was enjoying himself, but thought he might have an indigestion of such fun if the six-gun battery was not silenced. He summoned a young officer from his staff, and pointed up the mountain. The head of my approaching column was turned short up the slope, and speedily came to a path running parallel with the river. We took this path, the guide leading the way. From him I learned that the plateau occupied by the battery had been used for a charcoal kiln, and the path we were following, made by the burners in hauling wood, came upon the gorge opposite the battery. Moving briskly, we reached the hither side a few yards from the guns. Infantry was posted near, and riflemen were in the undergrowth on the slope above. Our approach, masked by timber, was unexpected. The battery was firing rapidly, enabled from elevation to fire over the advancing lines. The head of my column began to deploy under cover for attack, when the sounds of battle to our rear appeared to recede, and a loud Federal cheer was heard, proving Jackson to be hard pressed. It was rather an anxious moment, demanding instant action. Leaving a staff officer to direct my rear regiment—the 7th, Colonel Hays—to form in the wood as a reserve, I ordered the attack, though the deployment was not completed, and our rapid march by a narrow path had occasioned some disorder. With a rush and shout the gorge was passed and we were in the battery. Surprise had aided us, but the enemy's infantry rallied in a moment and drove us out. We returned, to be driven a second time. The riflemen on the slope worried us no little, and two companies of the 9th regiment were sent up the gorge to gain ground above and dislodge them, which was accomplished. The fighting in and around the battery was hand to hand, and many fell from bayonet wounds. Even the artillerymen used their rammers in a way not laid down in the Manual, and died at their guns. As Conan said to the devil, " 'Twas claw for claw." I called for Hays, but he, the promptest of men, and his splendid regiment, could not be found. Something unexpected had occurred, but there was no time for speculation. With a desperate rally, in which I believe the drummer-boys shared, we carried the battery for the third time, and held it. Infantry and riflemen had been driven off, and we began to feel a little comfortable, when the enemy, arrested in his advance by our attack, appeared. He had countermarched, and, with left near the river, came into full view of our situation. Wheeling to the right, with colors advanced, like a solid wall he marched straight upon us. There seemed nothing left but to set our backs to the mountain and die hard. At the instant, crashing through the underwood, came Ewell, outriding staff and escort. He produced the effect of a reënforcement, and was welcomed with cheers. The line before us halted and threw forward skirmishers. A moment later, a shell came shrieking along it, loud Confederate cheers reached our delighted ears, and Jackson, freed from his toils, rushed up like a whirlwind, the enemy in rapid retreat. We turned the captured guns on them as they passed, Ewell serving as a gunner. Though rapid, the retreat never became a rout. Fortune had refused her smiles, but Shields's brave "boys" preserved their organization and were formidable to the last; and had Shields himself, with his whole command, been on the field, we should have had tough work indeed.

Jackson came up, with intense light in his eyes, grasped my hand, and said the brigade should have the captured battery. I thought the men would go mad with cheering, especially the Irishmen. A huge fellow, with one eye closed and half his whiskers burned by powder, was riding cock-horse on a gun, and, catching my attention, yelled out, "We told you to bet on your boys." Their success against brother Patlanders seemed doubly welcome. Strange people, these Irish! Fighting every one's battles, and cheerfully taking the hot end of the poker, they are only found wanting when engaged in what they believe to be their national cause. Excepting the defense of Limerick under brilliant Sarsfield, I recall no domestic struggle in which they have shown their worth.

While Jackson pursued the enemy without much effect, as his cavalry, left in front of Fremont, could not get over till late, we attended to the wounded and performed the last offices to the dead, our own and the Federal. I have never seen so many dead and wounded in the same limited space. A large farm-house on the plain, opposite the mouth of the gorge, was converted into a hospital. Ere long my lost 7th regiment, sadly cut up, rejoined. This regiment was in rear of the column when we left Jackson to gain the path in the woods, and before it filed out of the road his thin line was so pressed that Jackson ordered Hays to stop the enemy's rush. This was done, for the 7th would have stopped a herd of elephants, but at a fearful cost. Colonel Hays was severely wounded, among many others, and the number of killed was large. Upon my promotion to Major-General, Hays succeeded to the command of the brigade, served through the war, returned to the practice of the law, and died in New Orleans. He was brother to Colonel Jack Hays, formerly of Texas, now of California, and shared much of the fighting ability of that renowned partisan.

The young officer who guided us through the wood deserves mention, as he was one of the first to reach the battery, where he was killed. Lieutenant English, near Harper's Ferry, Virginia, proved to be his name and place of birth.

Many hours passed in discharge of sad duties to the wounded and dead, during which Fremont appeared on the opposite bank of the river and opened his guns; but, observing doubtless our occupation, he ceased his fire, and after a short time withdrew. It may be added here that Jackson had caused such alarm at Washington as to start Milroy, Banks, Fremont, and Shields toward that capital, and the great valley was cleared of the enemy.

We passed the night high up the mountain, where we moved to reach our supply wagons. A cold rain was falling, and before we found them every one was tired and famished. I rather took it out of the train-master for pushing so far up, although I had lunched comfortably from the haversack of a dead Federal. It is not pleasant to think of now, but war *is* a little hardening.

On the 12th of June the army moved down to the river, above Port Republic, where the valley was wide, with many trees, and no enemy to worry or make us afraid. Here closed Jackson's wonderful Valley campaign of 1862.*

The Louisiana brigade marched from its camp near Conrad's

---

* A part of the foregoing text was published in the number of the "North American Review" for March, 1878, under the title of "Stonewall Jackson and the Valley Campaign." In a kind and friendly letter, dated New York, March 21, General Shields corrects some misapprehensions into which I had fallen, more especially concerning his *personal* connection with the events described. I had been unable to procure a copy of General Shields's report, which, he informs me in the same letter, was suppressed by Secretary Stanton.

store, to join Jackson at Newmarket, on the 21st of May. In twenty days it marched over two hundred miles, fought in five actions, of which three were severe, and several skirmishes, and, though it had suffered heavy loss in officers and men, was yet strong, hard as nails, and full of confidence. I have felt it a duty to set forth the achievements of the brigade, than which no man ever led braver into action, in their proper light, because such reputation as I gained in this campaign is to be ascribed to its excellence.

For the first time since several weeks, friend Ewell and I had a chance to renew our talks; but events soon parted us again. Subsequently he was wounded in the knee at the second battle of Manassas, and suffered amputation of the leg in consequence. His absence of mind nearly proved fatal. Forgetting his condition, he suddenly started to walk, came down on the stump, imperfectly healed, and produced violent hæmorrhage.

About the close of the war he married Mrs. Brown, a widow, and daughter of Judge Campbell, a distinguished citizen of Tennessee, who had represented the United States at the court of St. Petersburg, where this lady was born. She was a kinswoman of Ewell, and said to have been his early love. He brought her to New Orleans in 1866, where I hastened to see him. He took me by the hand and presented me to "my wife, Mrs. Brown." How well I remember our chat! How he talked of his plans and hopes and happiness, and of his great lot of books, which he was afraid he would never be able to read through. The while "my wife, Mrs. Brown," sat by, handsome as a picture, smiling on her General, as well she might, so noble a gentleman. A few short years, and both he and his wife passed away within an hour of each other; but his last years were made happy by her companionship, and comfortable by the wealth she had brought him. Dear Dick Ewell! Virginia never bred a truer gentleman, a braver soldier, nor an odder, more lovable fellow.

On the second day in this camp General Winder came to me and said that he had asked leave to go to Richmond, been refused, and resigned. He commanded Jackson's old brigade, and was aggrieved by some unjust interference. Holding Winder in high esteem, I hoped to save him to the army, and went to Jackson, to whose magnanimity I appealed, and to arouse this dwelt on the rich harvest of glory he had reaped in his brilliant campaign. Observing him closely, I caught a glimpse of the man's inner nature. It was but a glimpse. The curtain closed, and he was absorbed in prayer. Yet in that moment I saw an ambition boundless as Cromwell's, and as merciless. This latter quality was exhibited in his treatment of General Richard Garnett, cousin to Robert Garnett, before mentioned, and his codisciple at West Point. I have never met officer or soldier, present at Kernstown, who failed to condemn the harsh treatment of Garnett after that action. Richard Garnett was subsequently restored to command at my instance near Jackson, and fell on the field of Gettysburg.

No reply was made to my effort for Winder, and I rose to take my leave, when Jackson said he would ride with me. We passed silently along the way to my camp, where he left me. That night a few lines came from Winder, to inform me that Jackson had called on him, and his resignation was withdrawn.

Charles Winder was born in Maryland, graduated at West Point in 1850, embarked soon thereafter for California in charge of a detachment of recruits, was wrecked on the coast, and saved his men by his coolness and energy. He left the United States army to join the Confederacy, and was killed at Cedar Run some weeks after this period. Had he lived, he would have reached and adorned high position.

And now a great weariness and depression fell upon me. I was threatened with a return of the illness experienced the previous autumn. For many weeks I had received no intelligence from my family. New Orleans had fallen, and my wife and children resided there or on an estate near the city. I hoped to learn of them at Richmond; change might benefit health, and matters were quiet in the Valley. Accordingly, a short leave was asked for and granted; and although I returned within three days to join my command on the march to Cold Harbor, we were absorbed in the larger army operating against McClellan, and I saw but little of Jackson.

I have written that he was ambitious; and his ambition was vast, all-absorbing. Like the unhappy wretch from whose shoulders sprang the foul serpent, he loathed it, perhaps feared it; but he could not escape it—it was himself—nor rend it—it was his own flesh. He fought it with prayer, constant and earnest— Apollyon and Christian in ceaseless combat. What limit to set to his ability I know not, for he was ever superior to occasion. Under ordinary circumstances it was difficult to estimate him because of his peculiarities—peculiarities that would have made a lesser man absurd, but that served to enhance his martial fame, as those of Samuel Johnson did his literary eminence. He once observed, in reply to an allusion to his severe marching, that it was better to lose one man in marching than five in fighting; and, acting on this, he invariably surprised the enemy— Milroy at McDowell, Banks and Fremont in the Valley, McClellan's right at Cold Harbor, Pope at second Manassas.

Fortunate in his death, he fell at the summit of glory, before the sun of the Confederacy had set, ere defeat, and suffering, and selfishness could turn their fangs upon him. As one man, the South wept for him; foreign nations shared the grief; even Federals praised him. With Wolfe and Nelson and Havelock, he took his place in the hearts of English-speaking peoples.

In the first years of this century, a great battle was fought on the plains of the Danube. A determined charge on the Austrian center gained the victory for France. The courage and example of a private soldier, who there fell, contributed much to the success of the charge. Ever after, at the parades of his battalion, the name of Latour d'Auvergne was first called, when the oldest sergeant stepped to the front and answered, "Died on the field of honor." In Valhalla, beyond the grave, where spirits of warriors assemble, when on the roll of heroes the name of Jackson is reached, it will be for the majestic shade of Lee to pronounce the highest eulogy known to our race— "Died on the field of duty."

I reached Richmond, by Charlottesville and Lynchburg, the

day after leaving camp, and went to the war office, where I found letters from my family. My wife and children had left New Orleans on a steamer just as Farragut's fleet arrived, and were on the Atchafalaya River with friends, all well. While reading my letters, an acquaintance in high position in the office greeted me, but went on to say, if I knew what was afoot, my stay in Richmond would be short. Taking the hint, and feeling improved in health in consequence of relief from anxiety about my family, I returned to the station at once, and took rail to Charlottesville. Arrived there, I met the Valley army in march to the southeast, and joined my command.

That night we camped between Charlottesville and Gordonsville, in Orange County, the birthplace of my father. A distant kinsman, whom I had never met, came to invite me to his house in the neighborhood. Learning that I always slept in camp, he seemed so much distressed as to get my consent to breakfast with him, if he would engage to have breakfast at the barbarous hour of sunrise. His house was a little distant from the road; so, the following morning, he sent a mounted groom to show the way. My aide, young Hamilton, accompanied me, and Tom of course followed. It was a fine old mansion, surrounded by well-kept grounds. This immediate region had not yet been touched by war. Flowering plants and rose trees, in full bloom, attested the glorious wealth of June. On the broad portico, to welcome us, stood the host, with his fresh, charming wife, and, a little retired, a white-headed butler. Greetings over with host and lady, this delightful creature, with ebon face beaming hospitality, advanced, holding a salver, on which rested a huge silver goblet filled with Virginia's nectar, mint julep. Quantities of cracked ice rattled refreshingly in the goblet; sprigs of fragant mint peered above its broad rim; a mass of white sugar, too sweetly indolent to melt, rested on the mint; and, like rose buds on a snow bank, luscious strawberries crowned the sugar. Ah! that julep! Mars ne'er received such tipple from the hands of Ganymede. Breakfast was announced, and what a breakfast! A beautiful service, snowy table cloth, damask napkins, long unknown; above all, a lovely woman in

6

crisp gown, with more and handsomer roses on her cheek than
in her garden. 'Twas an idyl in the midst of the stern reali-
ties of war! The table groaned beneath its viands. Sable servitors brought in, hot and hot from the kitchen, cakes of wondrous forms, inventions of the tropical imagination of Africa,
inflamed by Virginian hospitality. I was rather a moderate
trencherman, but the performance of Hamilton was Gargan-
tuan, alarming. Duty dragged us from this Eden; yet in hurried adieus I did not forget to claim of the fair hostess the
privilege of a cousin. I watched Hamilton narrowly for a time.
The youth wore a sodden, apoplectic look, quite out of his
usual brisk form. A gallop of some miles put him right, but
for many days he dilated on the breakfast with the gusto of one
of Hannibal's veterans on the delights of Capua.

CHAPTER VI.

"THE SEVEN DAYS AROUND RICHMOND."

LEAVING Gordonsville, we proceeded in a southeasterly direction, passing Louisa Court House and Frederickshall, and camped at Ashland on the Fredericksburg Railway, twelve miles north of Richmond, on the evening of the 25th of June. To deceive the enemy, General Lee had sent to the Valley a considerable force under Generals Whiting, Hood, and Lawton. The movement was openly made and speedily known at Washington, where it produced the desired impression, that Jackson would invade Maryland from the Valley. These troops reached Staunton by rail on the 17th, and, without leaving the train, turned back to Gordonsville, where they united with Jackson. The line from Gordonsville to Frederickshall, south of which point it had been interrupted, was used to facilitate our movement, but this was slow and uncertain. The advance frequently halted or changed direction. We were pushing between McDowell and McClellan's right, over ground recently occupied by the enemy. Bridges had been destroyed, and, to conceal the movement, no guides were trusted—an over-caution occasioning delay.

During the day and night of the 25th I suffered from severe pains in the head and loins, and on the morning of the 26th found it impossible to mount my horse; so the brigade marched under the senior colonel, Seymour, 6th regiment. A small ambulance was left with me, and my staff was directed to accompany Seymour and send back word if an engagement was imminent. Several messages came during the day, the last after nightfall, reporting the command to be camped near Pole Green

Church, beyond the Chickahominy; so far, no fighting. Lying on the floor of a vacant house at Ashland, I had scarce consciousness to comprehend these messages. Pains in head and back continued, with loss of power to move my limbs.

Toward daylight of the 27th sleep came from exhaustion, and lasted some hours. From this I was aroused by sounds of artillery, loud and constant, brought by the easterly wind. Tom raised me into a sitting posture, and administered a cup of strong coffee. The sound of battle continued until it became unendurable, and I was put into the ambulance by Tom and the driver, the former following with the horses. We took the route by which the troops had marched, the din of conflict increasing with every mile, the rattle of small arms mingling with the thud of guns. After weary hours of rough road, every jolt on which threatened to destroy my remaining vitality, we approached Cold Harbor and met numbers of wounded. Among these was General Elzey, with a dreadful wound in the head and face. His aide was taking him to the rear in an ambulance, and, recognizing Tom, stopped a moment to tell of the fight. Ewell's division, to which Elzey and I belonged, had just been engaged with heavy loss. This was too much for any illness, and I managed somehow to struggle on to my horse and get into the action.

It was a wild scene. Battle was raging furiously. Shot, shell, and ball exploded and whistled. Hundreds of wounded were being carried off, while the ground was strewn with dead. Dense thickets of small pines covered much of the field, further obscured by clouds of smoke. The first troops encountered were D. H. Hill's, and, making way through these, I came upon Winder's, moving across the front from right to left. Then succeeded Elzey's of Ewell's division, and, across the road leading to Gaines's Mill, my own. Mangled and bleeding, as were all of Ewell's, it was holding the ground it had won close to the enemy's line, but unable to advance. The sun was setting as I joined, and at the moment cheers came up from our left, raised by Winder's command, which had turned and was sweeping the Federal right, while Lawton's Georgians, fresh and eager,

attacked in our front. The enemy gave way, and, under cover
of the night, retired over the Chickahominy. Firing continued
for two hours, though darkness concealed everything.

The loss in my command was distressing. Wheat, of whom
I have written, was gone, and Seymour, and many others. I
had a wretched feeling of guilt, especially about Seymour, who
led the brigade and died in my place. Colonel Seymour was
born in Georgia, but had long resided in New Orleans, where
he edited the leading commercial paper—a man of culture, respected of all. In early life he had served in Indian and Mexican wars, and his high spirit brought him to this, though past
middle age. Brave old Seymour! I can see him now, mounting the hill at Winchester, on foot, with sword and cap in hand,
his thin gray locks streaming, turning to his sturdy Irishmen
with "Steady, men! dress to the right!" Georgia has been
fertile of worthies, but will produce none more deserving than
Colonel Seymour.

The following morning, while looking to the burial of the
dead and care of the wounded, I had an opportunity of examin-
ing the field of battle. The campaign around Richmond is too
well known to justify me in entering into details, and I shall
confine myself to events within my own experience, only en-
larging on such general features as are necessary to explain
criticism.

The Chickahominy, a sluggish stream and subject to floods,
flows through a low, marshy bottom, draining the country between the Pamunky or York and James Rivers, into which last
it discharges many miles below Richmond. The upper portion
of its course from the crossing of the Central Railroad, six miles
north of Richmond, to Long Bridge, some three times that distance to the southeast, is parallel with both the above-mentioned
rivers. The bridges with which we were concerned at and after
Cold Harbor were the Federal military bridges, Grapevine,
York River Railroad, Bottom's, and Long, the lowermost; after
which the stream, affected by tide, spread over a marshy country. The upper or Grapevine Bridge was on the road leading
due south from Cold Harbor, and, passing Savage's Station on

York River Railroad, united with the Williamsburg road, which ran east from Richmond to Bottom's Bridge. A branch from this Williamsburg road continued on the south bank of the Chickahominy to Long Bridge, where it joined the Charles City, Darbytown, and Newmarket roads coming south-southeast from Richmond. Many other roads, with no names or confusing ones, crossed this region, which was densely wooded and intersected by sluggish streams, draining the marshes into both the Chickahominy and James. We came upon two of these country roads leading in quite different directions, but bearing the same name, Grapevine; and it will astound advocates of phonics to learn that the name of *Darby* (whence Darbytown) was thus pronounced, while it was spelt and written *Enroughty*. A German philologist might have discovered, unaided, the connection between the sound and the letters ; but it would hardly have occurred to mortals of less erudition.

At the beginning of operations in this Richmond campaign, Lee had seventy-five thousand men, McClellan one hundred thousand. Round numbers are here given, but they are taken from official sources. A high opinion has been expressed of the strategy of Lee, by which Jackson's forces from the Valley were suddenly thrust between McDowell and McClellan's right, and it deserves all praise ; but the tactics on the field were vastly inferior to the strategy. Indeed, it may be confidently asserted that from Cold Harbor to Malvern Hill, inclusive, there was nothing but a series of blunders, one after another, and all huge. The Confederate commanders knew no more about the topography of the country than they did about Central Africa. Here was a limited district, the whole of it within a day's march of the city of Richmond, capital of Virginia and the Confederacy, almost the first spot on the continent occupied by the British race, the Chickahominy itself classic by legends of Captain John Smith and Pocahontas; and yet we were profoundly ignorant of the country, were without maps, sketches, or proper guides, and nearly as helpless as if we had been suddenly transferred to the banks of the Lualaba. The day before the battle of Malvern Hill, President Davis could not find a guide with intelligence enough to show him the way from one of our columns to another; and this fact I have from him. People find a small cable in the middle of the ocean, a thousand fathoms below the surface. For two days we lost McClellan's great army in a few miles of woodland, and never had any definite knowledge of its movements. Let it be remembered, too, that McClellan had opened the peninsular campaign weeks before, indicating this very region to be the necessary theatre of conflict; that the Confederate commander (up to the time of his wound at Fair Oaks), General Johnston, had been a topographical engineer in the United States army; while his successor, General Lee—another engineer—had been on duty at the war office in Richmond and in constant intercourse with President Davis, who was educated at West Point and served seven years; and then think of our ignorance in a military sense of the ground over which we were called to fight. Every one must agree that it was amazing. Even now, I can scarcely realize it. McClellan was as superior to us in knowledge of our own land as were the Germans to the French in their late war, and owed the success of his retreat to it, although credit must be given to his ability. We had much praying at various headquarters, and large reliance on special providences; but none were vouchsafed, by pillar of cloud or fire, to supplement our ignorance; so we blundered on like people trying to read without knowledge of their letters.

To return to the field of Cold Harbor, the morning (Saturday) after the battle. McClellan had chosen an excellent position, covering his military bridges over the Chickahominy. His left, resting on the river, and his center were covered by a small stream, one of its affluents, boggy and of difficult passage. His right was on high ground, near Cold Harbor, in a dense thicket of pine-scrub, with artillery massed. This position, three miles in extent, and enfiladed in front by heavy guns on the south bank of the Chickahominy, was held by three lines of infantry, one above the other on the rising ground, which was crowned with numerous batteries, concealed by timber. McClellan reported thirty-six thousand men present, including Sykes's and

Porter's regulars; but reënforcements brought over during the action probably increased this number to fifty thousand. Lee had forty thousand on the field.

Longstreet attacked on our right, near the river, A. P. Hill on his left. Jackson approached Cold Harbor from the north, his divisions in column on one road as follows: Ewell's, Whiting's, Lawton's (Georgians), and Winder's. At Cold Harbor Jackson united with the division of D. H. Hill, in advance of him, and directed it to *find* and attack the enemy's right. His own divisions, in the order above named, were to come up on D. H. Hill's right and connect it with A. P. Hill's left. Artillery was only employed by the Confederates late in the day, and on their extreme left.

D. H. Hill and Ewell were speedily engaged, and suffered heavily, as did A. P. Hill and Longstreet, all attacking in front. Ignorance of the ground, densely wooded, and want of guides occasioned confusion and delay in the divisions to Ewell's rear. Lawton came to Ewell's support, Whiting to A. P. Hill's; while of the three brigades of the last division, the second went to Longstreet's right, the third to A. P. Hill's center, and the first was taken by Winder, with a fine soldierly instinct, from right to left, across the battle, to reënforce D. H. Hill and turn the Federal position. This movement was decisive, and if executed earlier would have saved loss of men and time. So much for fighting on unknown ground.

During the day of Saturday, McClellan remained on the south bank of the Chickahominy with guns in position guarding his bridges; and the only movement made by Lee was to send Stuart's cavalry east to the river terminus of the York Railway, and Ewell's division to the bridge of that line over the Chickahominy and to Bottom's, a short distance below. Late in the evening General Lee informed me that I would remain the following day to guard Bottom's and the railway bridges, while Stuart's cavalry watched the river below to Long Bridge and beyond. From all indications, he thought that McClellan would withdraw during the night, and expected to cross the river in the morning to unite with Magruder and

Huger in pursuit. Holmes's division was to be brought from the south side of the James to bar the enemy's road; and he expressed some confidence that his dispositions would inflict serious loss on McClellan's army, if he could receive prompt and accurate information of that General's movements. Meantime, I would remain until the following (Sunday) evening, unless sooner convinced of the enemy's designs, when I would cross Grapevine Bridge and follow Jackson. It is to be presumed that General Lee disclosed so much of his plans to his subordinates as he deemed necessary to insure their intelligent execution.

The morning light showed that the Federals had destroyed a part of the railway bridge near the center of the stream. We were opposite to Savage's Station (on the line toward Richmond), from which distinct sounds reached us, but dense forest limited vision to the margin of the river. Smoke rising above the trees, and explosions, indicated the destruction of stores. In the afternoon, a great noise of battle came—artillery, small arms, shouts. This, as we afterward learned, was Magruder's engagement at Savage's Station, but this din of combat was silenced to our ears by the following incident: A train was heard approaching from Savage's. Gathering speed, it came rushing on, and quickly emerged from the forest, two engines drawing a long string of carriages. Reaching the bridge, the engines exploded with terrific noise, followed in succession by explosions of the carriages, laden with ammunition. Shells burst in all directions, the river was lashed into foam, trees were torn for acres around, and several of my men were wounded. The enemy had taken this means of destroying surplus ammunition.

After this queer action had ceased, as sunset was approaching, and all quiet at Bottom's Bridge, we moved up stream and crossed Grapevine Bridge, repaired by Jackson earlier in the day. Darkness fell as we bivouacked on the low ground south of the river. A heavy rain came down, converting the ground into a lake, in the midst of which a half-drowned courier, with a dispatch, was brought to me. With difficulty, underneath an ambulance, a light was struck to read the dispatch, which proved to be from Magruder, asking for reënforcements in front of Savage's Station, where he was then engaged. Several hours had elapsed since the courier left Magruder, and he could tell nothing beyond the fact of the engagement, the noise of which we had heard. It must be borne in mind that, during the operations north of the Chickahominy, the divisions of Magruder and Huger had remained in position between McClellan's left and Richmond.

In the night the enemy disappeared from Savage's, near which we passed the following (Monday) morning, in march to rejoin Jackson. We encountered troops of Magruder's, Huger's, and other divisions, seeking to find their proper routes. Countless questions about roads were asked in vain. At length, we discovered that Jackson had followed the one nearest the Chickahominy, and about noon overtook the rear of his column, halted in the road. Artillery could be heard in front, and a staff officer was sent to find out the meaning of it.

Enfeebled by pain, I used an ambulance to husband my little strength for emergencies; and I think it was here that General Wade Hampton, accompanied by Senator Wigfall, came up to me. Hampton had been promoted to brigadier for gallantry at Manassas, where he was wounded, but not yet assigned to a command. Wigfall had left the army to take a seat in the Confederate Congress as Senator from Texas, and from him I learned that he was in hopes some brigadier would be killed to make a place for Hampton, to whom, as volunteer aide, he proposed to attach himself and see the fun. Finding me extended in an ambulance, he doubtless thought he had met his opportunity, and felt aggrieved that I was not *in extremis*. Hampton took command of a brigade in Jackson's old division the next day, and perhaps his friend Wigfall enjoyed himself at Malvern Hill.

The staff officer returned from the front and reported the situation. D. H. Hill's division was at White Oak Swamp Creek, a slough, and one of "despond" to us, draining to the Chickahominy. The enemy held the high ground beyond, and artillery fire was continuous, but no infantry was engaged. There was no change until nightfall, when we bivouacked where we were. Our loss, *one* artilleryman mortally wounded, proved that no serious effort to pass the slough was made; yet a prize was in reach worth the loss of thousands. While we were idly shelling the wood, behind which lay Franklin's corps—the right of McClellan's army—scarce a rifle shot to the southwest, but concealed by intervening forest, Longstreet and A. P. Hill were fighting the bloody engagement of Frazier's Farm with Heintzelman and McCall, the Federal center and left. Again, fractions against masses; for of the two divisions expected to support them, Magruder's and Huger's, the latter did not get up, and the former was taken off by a misleading message from Holmes, who, from the south bank of the James, had reached the Newmarket road a day later than was intended. Longstreet and Hill fought into the night, held a large part of the field, and captured many prisoners (including General McCall) and guns, but their own loss was severe. After the action, Franklin quietly passed within a few yards of them, joined Heintzelman, and with him gained Malvern Hill, which McClellan had fortified during the day, employing for the purpose the commands of Keyes and Porter.

On the succeeding morning (July 1), Jackson followed the enemy's track from White Oak Swamp Creek toward Malvern Hill, passing the field of Frazier's Farm, and Magruder's division, which had arrived in the night and relieved the exhausted commands of Longstreet and Hill.

Malvern Hill was a desperate position to attack in front, though, like Cold Harbor, it could be turned on the right. Here McClellan was posted with his whole force. His right was covered by Turkey Creek, an affluent of the James; his left was near that river and protected by gunboats, which, though hidden by timber, threw shells across his entire front. Distance and uncertainty of aim saved us from much loss by these projectiles, but their shriek and elongated form astonished our landward men, who called them lamp posts. By its height, Malvern Hill dominated the ground to the north, the James River, and the Newmarket road on which we approached, and was crowned with a numerous and heavy artillery. On our side, from inferior elevation, artillery labored under a great disadvantage, and was brought into action in detail to be overpowered.

The left attack was assigned to Jackson, the right to Magruder, supported by Huger and Holmes—Longstreet and A. P. Hill in reserve. Jackson's dispositions were as follows: On the extreme left, the division of Whiting, then artillery supported by a brigade under Wade Hampton, my brigade, and on my right the division of D. H. Hill. In reserve were the remainder of Ewell's division and the brigades of Winder, Lawton, and Cunningham. It was perhaps 3 o'clock of the afternoon before these dispositions were completed.

As it was General Lee's intention to open from his right, Magruder was waited for, who, following Jackson on the road, was necessarily later in getting into position. Orders were for Hill to attack with the bayonet as soon as he heard the cheers of Magruder's charge. To be ready, Hill advanced over open ground to some timber within four hundred yards of the enemy's line, but suffered in doing so. Artillery sent to his support was crippled and driven off. It was 5 o'clock or after when a loud shout and some firing were heard on the right, and, supposing this to be Magruder's attack, Hill led his men to the charge. He carried the first line of the enemy, who, unoccupied elsewhere, reënforced at once, and Hill was beaten off with severe loss. The brigades of Trimble, Lawton, Winder, and Cunningham were sent to his assistance, but could accomplish nothing beyond holding the ground. About sunset, after Hill's attack had failed, Magruder got into position and led on his men with similar fortune. Like Hill, he and his troops displayed superb courage and suffered enormously; but it was not to be; such partial attacks were without the first element of success. My brigade was not moved from its position, but experienced some loss by artillery.

After the action, Stuart arrived from the north side of the Chickahominy, where he had been since Cold Harbor. Had he been brought over the Long Bridge two days earlier, McClellan's huge trains on the Charles City road would have fallen an easy prey to his cavalry, and he could have blocked the roads through the forest.

McClellan's guns continued firing long after nightfall, but the ensuing morning found him and his army at Harrison's Landing, in an impregnable position. Here ended the campaign around Richmond.

The strategy displayed on the Confederate side was magnificent, and gave opportunity for resplendent success; but this opportunity was lost by tactical mistakes, occasioned by want of knowledge of the theatre of action, and it is to be feared that Time, when he renders his verdict, will declare the gallant dead who fell at Gaines's Mill, Cold Harbor, Frazier's Farm, and Malvern Hill, to have been sacrificed on the altar of the bloodiest of all Molochs—Ignorance.

The crisis of my illness now came in a paralysis of the lower limbs, and I was taken to Richmond, where I learned of my promotion to major-general, on the recommendation of Jackson, for services in the Valley, and assignment to a distant field.

Having expressed an opinion of McClellan as an organizer of armies, I will now treat of his conduct as a commander in this and his subsequent campaign. His first operations on the peninsula were marked by a slowness and hesitancy to be expected of an engineer, with small experience in handling troops. His opponent, General Magruder, was a man of singular versatility. Of a boiling, headlong courage, he was too excitable for high command. Widely known for social attractions, he had a histrionic vein, and indeed was fond of private theatricals. Few managers could have surpassed him in imposing on an audience a score of supernumeraries for a grand army. Accordingly, with scarce a tenth the force, he made McClellan reconnoiter and deploy with all the caution of old Melas, till Johnston came up. It is true that McClellan steadily improved, and gained confidence in himself and his army; yet he seemed to regard the latter as a parent does a child, and, like the first Frederick William's gigantic grenadiers, too precious for gunpowder.

His position in front of Richmond, necessitated by the establishment of his base on York River, was vicious, because his army was separated by the Chickahominy, a stream subject to heavy floods, which swept away bridges and made the adjacent lowlands impassable. Attacked at Fair Oaks while the river was in flood, he displayed energy, but owed the escape of his two exposed corps to Johnston's wound and the subsequent blunders of the Confederates. To operate against Richmond on the north bank of the James, his proper plan was to clear that river and rest his left upon it, or to make the Potomac and Rappahannock his base, as the line of rail from Aquia and Fredericksburg was but little longer than the York River line. This, keeping him more directly between the Confederate army and Washington, would have given him McDowell's corps, the withdrawal of which from his direction he earnestly objected to. The true line of attack was on the south of the James, where Grant was subsequently forced by the ability of Lee; but it should be observed that after he took the field, McClellan had not the liberty of action accorded to Grant. That Lee caught his right " in the air " at Hanover and Cold Harbor, McClellan ascribes to his Government's interference with and withdrawal of McDowell's corps. Reserving this, he fought well at Gaines's Mill, Cold Harbor, and Frazier's Farm. Always protecting his selected line of retreat, bringing off his movable stores, and preserving the organization of his army, he restored its spirit and *morale* by turning at Malvern Hill to inflict a bloody repulse on his enemy. In his official report he speaks of his movement from the Chickahominy to Harrison's Landing on the James as a change of base, previously determined. This his detractors sneer at as an afterthought, thereby unwittingly enhancing his merit. Regarded as a change of base, carefully considered and provided for, it was most creditable ; but if suddenly and unexpectedly forced upon him, he exhibited a courage, vigor, and presence of mind worthy of the greatest commanders.

Safe at Harrison's Landing, in communication with the fleet, the army was transferred from McClellan to the command of General Pope ; and the influence of McClellan on his troops can not be correctly estimated without some allusion to this officer, under whose command the Federal Army of the Potomac suffered such mortifying defeat. Of an effrontery while danger was remote equaled by helplessness when it was present, and mendacity after it had passed, the annals of despotism scarce afford an example of the elevation of such a favorite. It has been said that his talent for the relation of obscene stories engaged the attention and confidence of President Lincoln. However this may be, great was the consternation at Washington produced by his incapacity. The bitterness of official rancor was sweetened, and in honeyed phrase McClellan was implored to save the capital. He displayed an unselfish patriotism by accepting the task without conditions for himself, but it may be doubted if he was right in leaving devoted friends under the scalping-knife, speedily applied, as might have been foreseen.

With vigor he restored order and spirit to the army, and led it, through the passes of South Mountain, to face Lee, who was stretched from Chambersburg to Harper's Ferry. Having unaccountably permitted his cavalry to separate from him, and deprived himself of adequate means of information, Lee was to some extent taken unawares. His thin lines at Antietam, slowly fed with men jaded by heavy marching, were sorely pressed. There was a moment, as Hooker's advance was stayed by the wound of its leader, when McClellan, with *storgé* of battle, might have led on his reserves and swept the field. Hard would it have been for the Confederates, with the river in rear; but this seemed beyond McClellan or outside of his nature. Antietam was a drawn battle, and Lee recrossed into Virginia at his leisure.

While it may be confidently believed that McClellan would have continued to improve by experience in the field, it is doubtful if he possessed that divine spark which impels a commander, at the accepted moment, to throw every man on the enemy and grasp complete victory. But his Government gave him no further opportunity. He disappeared from the war, to be succeeded by mediocrity, too well recognized to disturb the susceptibility of a War Secretary who, like Louvois, was able, but jealous of merit and lustful of power.

Although in the last months of the war, after he had assumed command of the armies of the Confederacy, I had some correspondence with General Lee, I never met him again, and indeed was widely separated from him, and it now behooves me to set forth an opinion of his place in Southern history. Of all the men I have seen, he was best entitled to the epithet of distinguished; and so marked was his appearance in this particular, that he would not have passed unnoticed through the streets of any capital. Reserved almost to coldness, his calm dignity repelled familiarity: not that he seemed without sympathies, but that he had so conquered his own weaknesses as to prevent the confession of others before him. At the outbreak of the war his reputation was exclusively that of an engineer, in which branch of the military service of the United States he had, with a short exception, passed his career. He was early sent to Western Virginia on a forlorn hope against Rosecrans, where he had no success; for success was impossible. Yet his lofty character was respected of all and compelled public confidence. Indeed, his character seemed perfect, his bath in Stygian waters complete; not a vulnerable spot remained: *totus teres atque rotundus.* His soldiers reverenced him and had unbounded confidence in him, for he shared all their privations, and they saw him ever unshaken of fortune. Tender and protecting love he did not inspire: such love is given to weakness, not to strength. Not only was he destitute of a vulgar greed for fame, he would not extend a hand to welcome it when it came unbidden. He was without ambition, and, like Washington, into whose family connection he had married, kept duty as his guide.

The strategy by which he openly, to attract attention, reënforced Jackson in the Valley, to thrust him between McDowell and McClellan at Cold Harbor, deserves to rank with Marlborough's cross march in Germany and Napoleon's rapid concentration around Ulm; though his tactical manœuvres on the field were inferior to the strategy. His wonderful defensive campaign in 1864 stands with that of Napoleon in 1813; and the comparison only fails by an absence of sharp returns to the offensive. The historian of the Federal Army of the Potomac states (and, as far as I have seen, uncontradicted) that Grant's army, at second Cold Harbor, refused to obey the order to attack, so distressed was it by constant butchery. In such a condition of *morale* an advance upon it might have changed history. In truth, the genius of Lee for offensive war had suffered by a too long service as an engineer. Like Erskine in the House of Commons, it was not his forte. In both the Antietam and Gettysburg campaigns he allowed his cavalry to separate from him, and was left without intelligence of the enemy's movements until he was upon him. In both, too, his army was widely scattered, and had to be brought into action by piecemeal. There was an abundance of supplies in the country immediately around Harper's Ferry, and had he remained concentrated there, the surrender of Miles would have been advanced, and McClellan met under favorable conditions. His own report of Gettysburg confesses his mistakes; for he was of too lofty a nature to seek scapegoats, and all the rambling accounts of that action I have seen published add but little to his report. These criticisms are written with unaffected diffidence; but it is only by studying the campaigns of great commanders that the art of war can be illustrated.

Nevertheless, from the moment Lee succeeded to the command of the army in Virginia, he was *facile princeps* in the war, towering above all on both sides, as the pyramid of Ghizeh above the desert. Steadfast to the end, he upheld the waning fortunes of the Confederacy as did Hector those of Troy. Last scene of all, at his surrender, his greatness and dignity made of his adversary but a humble accessory; and if departed intelligences 'be permitted to take ken of the affairs of this world, the soul of Light Horse Harry rejoices that his own eulogy of Washington, "First in war, first in peace, first in the hearts of his countrymen," is now, by the united voice of the South, applied to his noble son.

7

Foregoing criticisms have indicated the tendency of engineer service to unfit men for command. It was once said of a certain colonel that he was an admirable officer when absent from soldiers. No amount of theoretical training can supply the knowledge gained by direct and immediate association with troops. The ablest and most promising graduates from West Point are annually assigned to the engineer and ordnance corps. After some years they become scientists, perhaps pedants, but not soldiers. Whatever may be the ultimate destination of such young men, they should be placed on duty for at least one year with each arm of the service, and all officers of the general staff below the highest grades should be returned to the line for limited periods. In no other way can a healthy connection between line and staff be preserved. The United States will doubtless continue to maintain an army, however small, as a model, if for no other purpose, for volunteers, the reliance of the country in the event of a serious war. It ought to have the best possible article for the money, and, to secure this, should establish a camp of instruction, composed of all arms, where officers could study the actual movements of troops.

CHAPTER VII.

A MONTH of rest at Richmond restored my health, which subsequently remained good; but in leaving Virginia I was separated from my brigade, endeared by so many memories. It remained with Lee's army, and gained distinction in many battles. As the last preserved of Benjamin on the rock of Rimmon, scarce a handful survived the war; but its story would comprise much of that of the Army of Northern Virginia, and I hope some survivor, who endured till the end, will relate it. A braver command never formed line of battle.

And now I turned my steps toward the West, where, beyond the "father of waters," two years of hard work and much fighting awaited me. The most direct route to the Southwest was by Chattanooga, where General Bragg was concentrating the Army of Tennessee. This officer had requested the War Department to assign me to duty with his army as chief of staff, and it was suggested to me to call on him *en route*. He had reached Chattanooga in advance of his troops, then moving from Tupelo in northern Mississippi. In the two days passed at Chattanooga, General Bragg communicated to me his plan of campaign into Kentucky, which was excellent, giving promise of large results if vigorously executed; and I think its failure may be ascribed to the infirmities of the commander.

Born in North Carolina, graduated from West Point in 1837, Bragg served long and creditably in the United States artillery. In the war with Mexico he gained much celebrity, especially at Buena Vista, to the success of which action, under the immediate eye of General Zachary Taylor, he largely contributed.

Resigning the service, he married a lady of Louisiana and purchased an estate on the Bayou Lafourche, where he resided at the outbreak of civil war. Promoted to the rank of general after the death of Albert Sidney Johnston, he succeeded Beauregard, retired by ill health, in command of the Army of Tennessee. Possessing experience in and talent for war, he was the most laborious of commanders, devoting every moment to the discharge of his duties. As a disciplinarian he far surpassed any of the senior Confederate generals; but his method and manner were harsh, and he could have won the affections of his troops only by leading them to victory. He furnished a striking illustration of the necessity of a healthy body for a sound intellect. Many years of dyspepsia had made his temper sour and petulant; and he was intolerant to a degree of neglect of duty, or what he esteemed to be such, by his officers. A striking instance of this occurred during my visit. At dinner, surrounded by his numerous staff, I inquired for one of his division commanders, a man widely known and respected, and received this answer: " General —— is an old woman, utterly worthless." Such a declaration, privately made, would have been serious; but publicly, and certain to be repeated, it was astonishing.

As soon as we had withdrawn to his private room, I asked by whom he intended to relieve General ——. " Oh! by no one. I have but one or two fitted for high command, and have in vain asked the War Department for capable people." To my suggestion that he could hardly expect hearty coöperation from officers of whom he permitted himself to speak contemptuously, he replied: " I speak the truth. The Government is to blame for placing such men in high position." From that hour I had misgivings as to General Bragg's success, and felt no regret at the refusal of the authorities to assign me to duty with him. It may be said of his subordinate commanders that they supported him wonderfully, in despite of his temper, though that ultimately produced dissatisfaction and wrangling. Feeble health, too, unfitted him to sustain long-continued pressure of responsibility, and he failed in the execution of his own plan.

The movement into Kentucky was made by two lines. General Kirby Smith led a subordinate force from Knoxville, East Tennessee, through Cumberland Gap, and, defeating the Federals in a spirited action at Richmond, Kentucky, reached Lexington, in the center of the State, and threatened Cincinnati. Bragg moved on a line west of the Cumberland range toward Louisville, on the Ohio River; and this movement forced the Federal commander, Buell, to march north to the same point by a parallel road, farther west. Buell left garrisons at Nashville and other important places, and sought to preserve his communications with Louisville, his base. Weakened by detachments, as well as by the necessity of a retrograde movement, Bragg should have brought him to action before he reached Louisville. Defeated, the Federals would have been driven north of the Ohio to reorganize, and Bragg could have wintered his army in the fertile and powerful State of Kentucky, isolating the garrisons in his rear; or, if this was impossible, which does not appear, he should have concentrated against Buell when the latter, heavily reënforced, marched south from Louisville to regain Nashville. But he fought a severe action at Perryville with a fraction of his army, and retired to Central Tennessee. The ensuing winter, at Murfreesboro, he contested the field with Rosecrans, Buell's successor, for three days; and though he won a victory, it was not complete, and the summer of 1863 found him again at Chattanooga. In the mean time, a Federal force under General Burnside passed through Cumberland Gap, and occupied Knoxville and much of East Tennessee, severing the direct line of rail communication from Richmond to the Southwest.

This condensed account of the Kentucky campaign, extending over many months, is given because of my personal intimacy with the commander, who apprised me of his plans. General Bragg died recently in Texas. I have rarely known a more conscientious, laborious man. Exacting of others, he never spared himself, but, conquering disease, showed a constant devotion to duty; and distinguished as were his services in the cause he espoused, they would have been far greater had he enjoyed the blessing of health.

Leaving Chattanooga, I proceeded to my destination, western Louisiana, and crossed the Mississippi at the entrance of Red River. Some miles below, in the Atchafalaya, I found a steamer, and learned that the Governor of the State was at Opelousas, which could be reached by descending the last river to the junction of the Bayou Courtableau, navigable at high water to the village of Washington, six miles north of Opelousas. Embarking on the steamer, I reached the junction at sunset, but the water in Courtableau was too low for steam navigation. As my family had sought refuge with friends in the vicinity of Washington, I was anxious to get on, and hired a boat, with four negro oarsmen, to take me up the bayou, twenty miles. The narrow stream was overarched by trees shrouded with Spanish moss, the universal parasite of Southern forests. Heavy rain fell, accompanied by vivid lightning, the flashes of which enabled us to find our way; and before dawn I had the happiness to embrace wife and children after a separation of fourteen months. Some hours later I reached Opelousas, and met the Governor, Thomas O. Moore, with whom I had served in our State Assembly. This worthy gentleman, a successful and opulent planter, had been elected Governor in 1860. He was a man of moderate temper and opinions, but zealously aided the Confederate cause after his State had joined it. Forced to leave New Orleans by the approach of Farragut's fleet, he brought my family with him, and was unwearied in kind attentions.

Melancholy indeed was the condition of the "District of Louisiana," to the command of which I was assigned.

Confederate authority had virtually ceased with the fall of New Orleans in the previous April. Fortifications at Barataria, Berwick's Bay, and other Gulf-coast points had been abandoned, the garrisons withdrawn, works dismantled, and guns thrown into the water. The Confederate Government had no soldiers, no arms or munitions, and no money, within the limits of the district. Governor Moore was willing to aid me to the extent of his ability, but, deprived by the loss of New Orleans and the lower river parishes of half the population and three fourths of the resources of his State, he could do little.

General Magruder had recently been assigned to command

in Texas, and General Holmes, the senior officer west of the
Mississippi, was far to the north in Arkansas.   To him I at once
reported my arrival and necessities.   Many days elapsed before
his reply was received, to the effect that he could give me no
assistance, as he meditated a movement against Helena on the
Mississippi River.   Without hope of aid from abroad, I addressed
myself to the heavy task of arousing public sentiment, apathetic
if not hostile from disaster and neglect, and the creation of some
means of defense.   Such was the military destitution that a regiment of cavalry could have ridden over the State, while innu-
merable rivers and bayous, navigable a large part of the year,
would admit Federal gunboats to the heart of every parish.

To understand subsequent operations in this region, one must
have some idea of its topography and river systems.

Washed on the east, from the Arkansas line to the Gulf of
Mexico, by the Mississippi, western Louisiana is divided into
two not very unequal parts by the Red River, which, entering
the State at its northwestern angle, near the boundaries of Texas
and Arkansas, flows southeast to the Mississippi through a broad,
fertile valley, then occupied by a population of large slave-own-
ers engaged in the culture of cotton.   From the southern slopes
of the Ozark Mountains in Central Arkansas comes the Washita River to unite with the Red, a few miles above the junction
of the latter with the Mississippi.   Preserving a southerly course,
along the eastern foot of the hills, the Washita enters the State
nearly a hundred miles west of the Mississippi, but the westerly
trend of the great river reduces this distance until the waters
meet.   The alluvion between these rivers, protected from inundation by levees along the streams, is divided by many bayous,
of which the Tensas, with its branch the Macon, is the most important.   These bayous drain the vast swamps into the Washita,
and, like this river, are in the season of floods open to steam
navigation.   Here was one of the great cotton-producing regions
of the South.   Estates of 5,000 acres and more abounded, and,
with the numerous slaves necessary to their cultivation, were
largely under the charge of overseers, while the proprietors resided in distant and more healthy localities.   Abundant facili-

ties for navigation afforded by countless streams superseded the necessity for railways, and but one line of some eighty miles existed. This extended from Monroe on the Washita to a point opposite Vicksburg on the Mississippi ; but the great flood of 1862 had broken the eastern half of the line. Finally, the lower Washita, at Trinity, where it receives the Tensas from the east and Little River from the west, takes the name of Black River. And it may be well to add that in Louisiana counties are called parishes, dikes levees, and streams bayous.

South of the Red River, population and industries change. The first is largely composed of descendants of French colonists, termed creoles, with some Spanish intermixed, and the sugar cane is the staple crop, changing as the Gulf is approached to rice. At the point where the united Red and Washita Rivers join the Mississippi, which here changes direction to the east, the Atchafalaya leaves it, and, flowing due south through Grand Lake and Berwick's Bay, reaches the Gulf at Atchafalaya Bay, two degrees west of its parent stream, and by a more direct course. Continuing the line of the Red and Washita, it not only discharges much of their waters, but draws largely from the Mississippi when this last is in flood. Midway between the Atchafalaya and the city of New Orleans, some eighty miles from either point, another outlet of the great river, the Bayou Lafourche, discharges into the Gulf after passing through a densely populated district, devoted to the culture of sugar cane and rice. A large lake, Des Allemands, collects the waters from the higher lands on the river and bayou, and by an outlet of the same name carries them to Barataria Bay. Lying many feet below the flood level of the streams, protected by heavy dikes, with numerous steam-engines for crushing canes and pumping water, and canals and ditches in every direction, this region resembles a tropical Holland. At the lower end of Lake Des Allemands passed the only line of railway in southern Louisiana, from a point on the west bank of the river opposite New Orleans to Berwick's Bay, eighty miles. Berwick's Bay, which is but the Atchafalaya after it issues from Grand Lake, is eight hundred yards wide, with great depth of water, and soon meets the Gulf in Atchafalaya Bay. A few miles above the railway terminus at Berwick's there enters from the west the Teche, loveliest of Southern streams. Navigable for more than a hundred miles, preserving at all seasons an equal breadth and depth, so gentle is its flow that it might be taken for a canal, did not the charming and graceful curves, by which it separates the undulating prairies of Attakapas from the alluvion of the Atchafalaya, mark it as the handiwork of Nature. Before the war, the Teche for fifty miles, from Berwick's Bay to New Iberia, passed through one field of sugar canes, the fertile and well-cultivated estates succeeding each other. The mansions of the opulent planters, as well as the villages of their slaves, were situated on the west bank of the bayou overlooking the broad, verdant prairie, where countless herds roamed. On the east bank, the dense forest had given way to fields of luxuriant canes; and to connect the two parts of estates, floating bridges were constructed, with openings in the center for the passage of steamers. Stately live oaks, the growth of centuries, orange groves, and flowers of every hue and fragrance surrounded the abodes of the *seigneurs;* while within, one found the grace of the *salon* combined with the healthy cheeriness of country life. Abundance and variety of game encouraged field sports, and the waters, fresh and salt, swarmed with fish. With the sky and temperature of Sicily, the breezes from prairie and Gulf were as health-giving as those that ripple the heather on Scotch moors. In all my wanderings, and they have been many and wide, I can not recall so fair, so bountiful, and so happy a land.

The upper or northern Teche waters the parishes of St. Landry, Lafayette, and St. Martin's—the Attakapas, home of the "Acadians." What the gentle, contented creole was to the restless, pushing American, that and more was the Acadian to the creole. In the middle of the past century, when the victories of Wolfe and Amherst deprived France of her Northern possessions, the inhabitants of Nouvelle Acadie, the present Nova Scotia, migrated to the genial clime of the Attakapas, where beneath the flag of the lilies they could preserve their allegiance, their traditions, and their faith. Isolated up to the time of the war, they spoke no language but their own *patois;* and, reading and writing not having come to them by nature, they were dependent for news on their curés and occasional peddlers, who tempted the women with *chiffons* and trinkets. The few slaves owned were humble members of the household, assisting in the cultivation of small patches of maize, sweet potatoes, and cotton, from which last the women manufactured the wonderful Attakapas *cotonnade,* the ordinary clothing of both sexes. Their little *cabanes* dotted the broad prairie in all directions, and it was pleasant to see the smoke curling from their chimneys, while herds of cattle and ponies grazed at will. Here, unchanged, was the French peasant of Fénelon and Bossuet, of Louis le Grand and his successor le Bien-Aimé. Tender and true were his traditions of la belle France, but of France before Voltaire and the encyclopædists, the Convention and the Jacobins—ere she had lost faith in all things, divine and human, save the *bourgeoisie* and *avocats.* Mounted on his pony, with lariat in hand, he herded his cattle, or shot and fished; but so gentle was his nature, that lariat and rifle seemed transformed into pipe and crook of shepherd. Light wines from the Médoc, native oranges, and home-made sweet cakes filled his largest conceptions of feasts; and violin and clarionet made high carnival in his heart.

On an occasion, passing the little hamlet of Grand Coteau, I stopped to get some food for man and horse. A pretty maiden of fifteen springs, whose parents were absent, welcomed me. Her lustrous eyes and long lashes might have excited the envy of "the dark-eyed girl of Cadiz." Finding her alone, I was about to retire and try my fortune in another house; but she insisted that she could prepare "monsieur un dîner dans un tour de main," and she did. Seated by the window, looking modestly on the road, while I was enjoying her repast, she sprang to her feet, clapped her hands joyously, and exclaimed: "V'là le gros Jean Baptiste qui passe sur son mulet avec *deux* bocals. Ah! nous aurons grand bal ce soir." It appeared that *one* jug of claret meant a dance, but *two* very high jinks indeed. As my hostess declined any remuneration for her trouble, I begged her to accept a pair of plain gold sleeve buttons, my only ornaments. Wonder, delight, and gratitude chased each other across the pleasant face, and the confiding little creature put up her rose-bud mouth. In an instant the homely room became as the bower of Titania, and I accepted the chaste salute with all the reverence of a subject for his Queen, then rode away with uncovered head so long as she remained in sight. Hospitable little maiden of Grand Coteau, may you never have graver fault to confess than the innocent caress you bestowed on the stranger!

It was to this earthly paradise, and upon this simple race, that the war came, like the tree of the knowledge of evil to our early parents.

Some weeks before I reached my new field, General Van Dorn, who commanded the Confederate forces east of the Mississippi, had successfully resisted a bombardment of Vicksburg by Federal gunboats, during which the Confederate ram Arkansas, descending the Yazoo River, passed through the enemy's fleet, inflicting some damage and causing much alarm, and anchored under the guns of Vicksburg. To follow up this success, Van Dorn sent General Breckenridge with a division against Baton Rouge, the highest point on the river above New Orleans then held by the Federals, and the Arkansas was to descend to coöperate in the attack. Breckenridge reached Baton Rouge at the appointed time, assaulted, and was repulsed after a severe action; but the Arkansas, disabled by an accident to her machinery, was delayed, and, learning of Breckenridge's failure, her commander ran her ashore on the west bank of the river a few miles above Baton Rouge, and destroyed her. Strengthening their garrison in this town, the Federals employed many steamers on the river between it and New Orleans, a hundred and twenty miles, armed vessels of Farragut's fleet guarding the stream. From time to time parties of infantry were landed to plunder and worry the peaceful inhabitants, though after the fall of New Orleans no Confederate forces had been on that part of the river, and no resistance was made by the people.

Two days were passed at Opelousas in consultation with Governor Moore, who transferred to me several small bodies of State troops which he had organized. Alexandria on the Red River, some seventy-five miles north of Opelousas, was the geographical center of the State and of steam navigation, and the proper place for the headquarters of the district. To escape the intense heat, I rode the distance in a night, and remained some days at Alexandria, engaged in the organization of necessary staff departments and in providing means of communication with different parts of the State. Great distances and the want of railway and telegraph lines made this last a heavy burden. Without trained officers, my presence was required at every threatened point, and I was seldom enabled to pass twenty-four consecutive hours at headquarters; but Adjutant Surget, of whom mention has been made, conducted the business of the district with vigor and discretion during my absence. Subsequently, by using an ambulance in which one could sleep, and with relays of mules, long distances were rapidly accomplished; and, like the Irishman's bird, I almost succeeded in being in two places at the same time.

Leaving Alexandria, I went south to visit the Lafourche and intervening regions. At Vermilionville, in the parish of Lafayette, thirty miles south of Opelousas, resided ex-Governor Mouton, a man of much influence over the creole and Acadian populations, and an old acquaintance. Desiring his aid to arouse public sentiment, depressed since the fall of New Orleans, I stopped to see him. Past middle age, he had sent his sons and kindrèd to the war, and was eager to assist the cause in all possible ways. His eldest son and many of his kinsmen fell in battle, his estate was diminished by voluntary contributions and wasted by plunder, and he was taken to New Orleans and confined for many weeks; yet he never faltered in his devotion, and preserved his dignity and fortitude.

In camp near New Iberia, seven and twenty miles south of Vermilionville, was Colonel Fournet, with a battalion of five companies raised in the parish, St. Martin's. The men were without instruction, and inadequately armed and equipped. Impressing on Fournet and his officers the importance of discipline and instruction, and promising to supply them with arms, I proceeded to the residence of Leclerc Fusilier, in the parish of St. Mary's, twenty miles below New Iberia. Possessor of great estates, and of a hospitable, generous nature, this gentleman had much weight in his country. His sons were in the army, and sixty years had not diminished his energy nor his enthusiasm. He desired to serve on my staff as volunteer aide, promising to join me whenever fighting was to be done; and he kept his promise. In subsequent actions on the Teche and Red River, the first gun seemed the signal for the appearance of Captain Fusilier, who, on his white pony, could be seen where the fight was the thickest, leading on or encouraging his neighbors. His corn bins, his flocks and herds, were given to the public service without stint; and no hungry, destitute Confederate was permitted to pass his door. Fusilier was twice captured, and on the first occasion was sent to Fortress Monroe, where he, with fifty other prisoners from my command, was embarked on the transport Maple Leaf for Fort Delaware. Reaching the capes of Chesapeake at nightfall, the prisoners suddenly attacked and overpowered the guard, ran the transport near to the beach in Princess Anne County, Virginia, landed, and made their way to Richmond, whence they rejoined me in Louisiana. Again taken, Fusilier escaped, while descending the Teche on a steamer, by springing from the deck to seize the overhanging branch of a live oak. The guard fired on him, but darkness and the rapid movement of the steamer were in his favor, and he got off unhurt.

I have dwelt somewhat on the characters of Mouton and Fusilier, not only because of their great devotion to the Confederacy, but because there exists a wide-spread belief that the creole race has become effete and nerveless. In the annals of time no breed has produced nobler specimens of manhood than these two; and while descendants of the French colonists remain on the soil of Louisiana, their names and characters should be reverenced as are those of Hampden and Sidney in England.

To Berwick's Bay, a hundred and seventy-five miles from

Alexandria. Here, on the eastern shore, was the terminus of the New Orleans and Opelousas railroad. A deep, navigable arm of the bay, called Bayou Bœuf, flows east of the station, which is on the island fronting the bay proper. Some engines and plant had been saved from the general wreck at New Orleans, and the line was operated from the bay to Lafourche crossing, thirty miles. The intervening territory constitutes the parish of Terrebonne, with fertile, cultivated lands along the many bayous, and low swamps between. From Lafourche crossing to Algiers, opposite New Orleans, is fifty miles ; and, after leaving the higher ground adjacent to the Lafourche, the line plunges into swamps and marshes, impassable except on the embankment of the line itself. Midway of the above points, the Bayou des Allemands, outlet of the large lake of the same name, is crossed ; and here was a Federal post of some two hundred men with two field guns. On the west bank of the Lafourche, a mile or two above the railway crossing, and thirty-two miles below Donaldsonville, where the bayou leaves the Mississippi, lies the town of Thibodeaux, the most considerable place of this region. Navigable for steamers, whenever the waters of its parent river are high, restrained from inundation by levees on both banks, the Lafourche flows through the fertile and populous parishes of Assumption and Lafourche, and, after a sinuous course of some ninety miles, reaches the Gulf to the west of Barataria Bay. Above Thibodeaux there were no bridges, and communication between the opposite banks was kept up by ferries.

One or two companies of mounted men, armed with fowling pieces, had been organized under authority from Governor Moore, and Colonel Waller's battalion of mounted riflemen had recently arrived from Texas. These constituted the Confederate army in this quarter.

CHAPTER VIII.

MENTION has been made of the plundering expeditions of the Federals, and the post at Bayou des Allemands was reported as the especial center from which raids on the helpless inhabitants were undertaken. I determined to attempt the surprise and capture of this post, which could be reached from the river at a point fifty miles below Donaldsonville. My estate was in the immediate vicinity of this point, and the roads and paths through plantations and swamps were well known to me. Colonel Waller was assigned to the duty, with minute instructions concerning roads and movements, and competent guides were furnished him. Moving rapidly by night, and, to escape observation, avoiding the road near the river, Waller with his Texans gained the enemy's rear, advanced on his camp, and, after a slight resistance, captured two companies of infantry and the guns. The captured arms and accouterments served to equip Waller's men, whose rifles were altered flintlocks and worthless, and the prisoners were sent to the Teche to be guarded by Fournet's Acadiens. This trifling success, the first in the State since the loss of New Orleans, attracted attention, and the people rejoiced at the capture of the Des Allemands garrison as might those of Greece at the unearthing of the accomplished and classic thief Cacus. Indeed, the den of that worthy never contained such multifarious "loot" as did this Federal camp. Books, pictures, household furniture, finger rings, ear rings, breastpins and other articles of feminine adornment and wear, attested the catholic taste and temper of these patriots.

Persuaded that the Federal commander at New Orleans,

General Benjamin F. Butler, was ignorant of the practices of his outlying detachments, I requested ex-Governor Wickliffe of Louisiana, a non-combatant, to visit that officer under a flag of truce and call his attention to the subject. Duty to the suffering population would force me to deal with perpetrators of such misdeeds as robbers rather than as soldiers. General Butler received Governor Wickliffe politely, invited him to dine, and listened attentively to his statements, then dismissed him without committing himself to a definite reply. However, the conduct complained of was speedily stopped, and, as I was informed, by orders from General Butler. This was the only intercourse I had with this officer during the war. Some months later he was relieved from command at New Orleans by General Banks, whose blunders served to endear him to President Lincoln, as did those of Villeroy to his master, the fourteenth Louis. When the good Scotch parson finished praying for all created beings and things, he requested his congregation to unite in asking a blessing for the "puir deil," who had no friends; and General Butler has been so universally abused as to make it pleasant to say a word in his favor. Not that he needs assistance to defend himself; for in the war of epithets he has proved his ability to hold his ground against all comers as successfully as did Count Robert of Paris with sword and lance.

Preservation of the abundant supplies of the Lafourche country, and protection of the dense population from which recruits could be drawn, were objects of such importance as to justify the attempt to secure them with inadequate means.

A few days after the Des Allemands affair, I was called to the north, and will for convenience anticipate events in this quarter during my absence. Minute instructions for his guidance were given to Colonel Waller. The danger to be guarded against while operating on the river was pointed out, viz.: that the enemy might, from transports, throw forces ashore above and below him, at points where the swamps in the rear were impassable; and this trap Waller fell into. Most of his men escaped by abandoning arms, horses, etc. Immunity from attack for some days had made them careless. Nothing compensates for absence of discipline; and the constant watchfulness, even when danger seems remote, that is necessary in war, can only be secured by discipline which makes of duty a habit.

Meanwhile, two skeleton regiments, the 18th Louisiana and Crescent, and a small battalion (Clack's) of infantry, with Semmes's and Ralston's batteries, reached me from east of the Mississippi, and were directed to the Lafourche. There also reported to me Brigadier Alfred Mouton, son of Governor Mouton, and a West Pointer. This officer had been wounded at Shiloh, and was now ordered to command on the Lafourche. His instructions were to make Thibodeaux his centre of concentration, to picket Bayou Des Allemands and Donaldsonville, thirty miles distant each, to secure early information of the enemy's movements, and to provide a movable floating bridge by which troops could cross the bayou, as the water was too low to admit steamers from the river. These same instructions had been given to the senior officer present before Mouton's arrival, but had been imperfectly executed. A feint on Des Allemands had induced the movement of nearly half the little force in that direction, and Mouton had scant time after he reached Thibodeaux to correct errors before the enemy was upon him.

In the last days of October the Federal General, Weitzel, brought up a force of some 4,000 from New Orleans, landed at Donaldsonville, and advanced down the Lafourche, on the west bank. There were Confederates on both sides of the bayou, but, having neglected their floating bridge, they could not unite. With his own, the 18th, the Crescent, Colonel McPheeters, and the four-gun battery of Captain Ralston—in all 500 men—Colonel Armand resisted Weitzel's advance at Labadieville, eight miles above Thibodeaux. The fighting was severe, and Armand only retired after his ammunition was exhausted; but he lost many killed and wounded, and some few prisoners. Colonel McPheeters was among the former, and Captains Ralston and Story among the latter. The loss of the Federals prevented Weitzel from attempting a pursuit; and Mouton, who deemed it necessary to retire across Berwick's Bay, was not interrupted in his movement. With his forces well in hand, Mouton would

8

have defeated Weitzel and retained possession of the Lafourche country. The causes of his failure to concentrate have been pointed out. Information of these untoward events reached me on the road from the north, and I arrived at Berwick's Bay as Mouton was crossing.

To return to the time of departure from the Lafourche. Several days were passed at New Iberia in attention to a matter of much interest. Some eight miles to the southwest of the village there rises from the low prairie and salt marsh, at the head of Vermilion Bay, an island of high land, near a thousand acres in extent. Connected with the mainland by a causeway of some length, the island was the property and residence of Judge Avery. A small bayou, Petit Anse, navigable for light craft, approached the western side and wound through the marsh to Vermilion Bay. Salt wells had long been known to exist on the island, and some salt had been boiled there. The want of salt was severely felt in the Confederacy, our only considerable source of supply being in southwestern Virginia, whence there were limited facilities for distribution. Judge Avery began to boil salt for neighbors, and, desiring to increase the flow of brine by deepening his wells, came unexpectedly upon a bed of pure rock salt, which proved to be of immense extent. Intelligence of this reached me at New Iberia, and induced me to visit the island. The salt was from fifteen to twenty feet below the surface, and the overlying soil was soft and friable. Devoted to our cause, Judge Avery placed his mine at my disposition for the use of the Government. Many negroes were assembled to get out salt, and a packing establishment was organized at New Iberia to cure beef. During succeeding months large quantities of salt, salt beef, sugar, and molasses were transported by steamers to Vicksburg, Port Hudson, and other points east of the Mississippi. Two companies of infantry and a section of artillery were posted on the island to preserve order among the workmen, and secure it against a sudden raid of the enemy, who later sent a gunboat up the Petit Anse to shell the mine, but the gunboat became entangled in the marsh and was impotent.

At Alexandria, where every effort was made to collect material, but without funds and among a depressed people, progress was slow. It was necessary to visit Monroe, the chief place of the important Washita country; and I was further impelled thereto by dispatches from Richmond advising me that Lieutenant-General Pemberton had been assigned to command of the country east of the Mississippi, and that it was important for me to meet him, in order to secure coöperation on the river. I rode the distance, *via* Monroe, to a point opposite Vicksburg, over two hundred miles, excepting forty miles east of Monroe, where the railway was in operation. The eastern half of the line, from Bayou Maçon to the Mississippi, had been broken up by the great flood of the previous spring.

Near Bayou Maçon was encamped Colonel Henry Grey with his recently organized regiment, the 28th infantry. Without much instruction and badly equipped, its material was excellent, and there were several officers of some experience, notably Adjutant Blackman, who had accompanied my old regiment, the 9th, to Virginia, where he had seen service. The men were suffering from camp diseases incident to new troops, and Colonel Grey was directed to move by easy marches to the Teche. In the low country between the Maçon and the Mississippi were some mounted men under Captain Harrison. Residents of this region, they understood the intricate system of swamps and bayous by which it is characterized, and furnished me guides to Vicksburg.

Vicksburg lies on the hills where the river forms a deep re-entering angle. The peninsula on the opposite or western bank is several miles in length, narrow, and, when the waters are up, impassable except along the river's bank. It was through this peninsula that the Federals attempted, by digging a canal, to pass their gunboats and turn the Vicksburg batteries. The position of the town with reference to approach from the west was marked by me at the time, and should be borne in mind.

General Pemberton, who was at Jackson, came to Vicksburg to meet me, and we discussed methods of coöperation. It was of vital importance to control the section of the Mississippi receiving the Red and Washita Rivers. By so doing connection would be preserved between the two parts of the Confederacy, and troops and supplies crossed at will. Port Hudson, some forty miles below the entrance of Red River, was as favorably situated as Vicksburg above : for there again the hills touched the river and commanded it. My operations on the Lafourche had induced the enemy to withdraw from Baton Rouge, fifteen miles below, and one or two heavy guns were already mounted at Port Hudson. Pemberton engaged to strengthen the position at once. As there were many steamers in the Red and Washita, I undertook to supply Vicksburg and Port Hudson with corn, forage, sugar, molasses, cattle, and salt; and this was done beyond the ability of the garrisons to store or remove them. Quantities of these supplies were lying on the river's bank when the surrenders of the two places occurred.

A Pennsylvanian by birth, Pemberton graduated from West Point in 1837, and was assigned to an artillery regiment. His first station was in South Carolina, and he there formed his early friendships. The storm of " nullification " had not yet subsided, and Pemberton imbibed the tenets of the Calhoun school. In 1843 or 1844 I met him for the first time on the Niagara frontier, and quite remember my surprise at his State-rights utterances, unusual among military men at that period. During the war with Mexico he was twice brevetted for gallantry in action. Later, he married a lady of Virginia, which may have tended to confirm his political opinions. At the beginning of civil strife he was in Minnesota, commanding a battalion of artillery, and was ordered to Washington. Arrived there with his command, he resigned his commission in the United States army, went to Richmond, and offered his sword to the Confederacy without asking for rank. Certainly he must have been actuated by principle alone ; for he had everything to gain by remaining on the Northern side.

In the summer of 1862 General Van Dorn, commanding east of the Mississippi, proclaimed martial law, which he explained to the people to be the will of the commander. Though a Mississippian by birth, such a storm was excited against Van

Dorn in that State that President Davis found it necessary to supersede him, and Pemberton was created a lieutenant-general for the purpose. Davis could have known nothing of Pemberton except that his military record was good, and it is difficult to foresee that a distinguished subordinate will prove incompetent in command. Errors can only be avoided by confining the selection of generals to tradespeople, politicians, and newspaper men without military training or experience. These are all great commanders *d'état*, and universally succeed. The incapacity of Pemberton for independent command, manifested in the ensuing campaign, was a great misfortune to the Confederacy, but did not justify aspersions on his character and motives. The public howled, gnashed its teeth, and lashed itself into a beautiful rage. He had joined the South for the express purpose of betraying it, and this was clearly proven by the fact that he surrendered on the 4th of July, a day sacred to the Yankees. Had he chosen any other day, his guilt would not have been so well established; but this particular day lacerated the tenderest sensibilities of Southern hearts. President Davis should have known all about it; and yet he made a pet of Pemberton. " Vox populi, vox diaboli."

Returned to Alexandria, I met my chief of artillery and ordnance, Major J. L. Brent, just arrived from the east with some arms and munitions, which he had remained to bring with him. This officer had served on the staff of General Magruder in the Peninsular and Richmond campaigns, after which, learning that I was ordered to Louisiana, where he had family connections, he applied to serve with me. Before leaving Richmond I had several interviews with him, and was favorably impressed.

A lawyer by profession, Major Brent knew nothing of military affairs at the outbreak of the war, but speedily acquainted himself with the technicalities of his new duties. Devoted to work, his energy and administrative ability were felt in every direction. Batteries were equipped, disciplined, and drilled. Leather was tanned, harness made, wagons built, and a little workshop, established at New Iberia by Governor Moore, became important as an arsenal of construction. The lack of paper for cartridges was embarrassing, and most of the country newspapers were stopped for want of material. Brent discovered a quantity of wall paper in the shops at Franklin, New Iberia, etc., and used it for cartridges; and a journal published at Franklin was printed on this paper. A copy of it would be "a sight" to Mr. Walter and the staff of the "Thunderer." The *esprit de corps* of Brent's artillery was admirable, and its conduct and efficiency in action unsurpassed. Serving with wild horsemen, unsteady and unreliable for want of discipline, officers and men learned to fight their guns without supports. True, Brent had under his command many brilliant young officers, whose names will appear in this narrative; but his impress was upon all, and he owes it to his command to publish an account of the services of the artillery in western Louisiana.

En route to Lafourche, I learned of the action at Labadieville, and hurried on to Berwick's Bay, which Mouton had just crossed, and in good time; for Federal gunboats entered from the Gulf immediately after. Their presence some hours earlier would have been uncomfortable for Mouton. It is curious to recall the ideas prevailing in the first years of the war about gunboats. To the wide-spread terror inspired by them may be ascribed the loss of Fort Donelson and New Orleans. *Omne ignotum pro magnifico;* and it was popularly believed that the destructive powers of these monsters were not to be resisted. Time proved that the lighter class of boats, called "tin-clads," were helpless against field guns, while heavy iron-clads could be driven off by riflemen protected by the timber and levees along streams. To fire ten-inch guns at skirmishers, widely disposed and under cover, was very like snipe-shooting with twelve-pounders; and in narrow waters gunboats required troops on shore for their protection.

Penetrated in all directions by watercourses navigable when the Mississippi was at flood, my "district" was especially exposed, and every little bayou capable of floating a cock-boat called loudly for forts and heavy guns. Ten guns, thirty-two- and twenty-four-pounders, of those thrown into the water at Barataria and Berwick's Bays after the surrender of New Orleans, had been recovered, and were mounted for defense.   To protect Red River against anything that might chance to run the batteries of Vicksburg and Port Hudson, two thirty-twos were placed in position on the south bank, thirty odd miles below Alexandria, where the high ground of Avoyelles Prairie touches the river; and for the same purpose two guns were mounted at Harrisonburg on the west bank of the Washita.   An abrupt hill approached the river at this point, and commanded it.

The presence of gunboats in Berwick's Bay made it necessary to protect the Atchafalaya also; for access to the Red and Washita could be had by it.   As yet, the waters were too low to navigate Grand Lake; but it was now November, and the winter flood must be expected.   Some twelve miles from St. Martinsville on the Teche was a large mound on the west bank of the Atchafalaya, called " Butte à la Rose."   A short distance above the point, where the river expands into Grand Lake, this " Butte " was the only place for many miles not submerged when the waters were up.   The country between it and the Teche was almost impassable even in the dry season—a region of lakes, bayous, jungle, and bog.   I succeeded in making my way through to inspect the position, the only favorable one on the river, and with much labor two twenty-fours were taken there and mounted.   Forts Beauregard on the Washita, De Russy on the Red, and Burton on the Atchafalaya, were mere water batteries to prevent the passage of gunboats, and served that purpose.   It was not supposed that they could be held against serious land attacks, and but fifty to a hundred riflemen were posted at each to protect the gunners from boats' crews.

During the floods of the previous spring many steamers had been brought away from New Orleans, and with others a powerful tow-boat, the Webb, now lying at Alexandria, and the Cotton.   This last, a large river steamer, was in the lower Teche in charge of Captain Fuller, a western steamboat man, and one of the bravest of a bold, daring class.   He desired to convert the Cotton into a gunboat, and was assisted to the extent of his means by Major Brent, who furnished two twenty-fours and a field piece for armament.   An attempt was made to protect the boilers and machinery with cotton bales and railway iron, of which we had a small quantity, and a volunteer crew was put on board, Fuller in command.

Midway between Berwick's Bay and Franklin, or some thirteen miles from each, near the Bisland estate, the high ground from Grand Lake on the east to Vermilion Bay on the west is reduced to a narrow strip of some two thousand yards, divided by the Teche. Here was the best position in this quarter for a small force; and Mouton, who had now ten guns and about thirteen hundred men, was directed to hold it, with scouts and pickets toward Berwick's. A floating bridge, of the kind described, was just above the position, and two others farther up stream afforded ready communication across the bayou. A light earthwork was thrown up from Grand Lake Marsh to the Teche, and continued west to the embankment of the uncompleted Opelousas Railway, which skirted the edge of Vermilion Marsh. The objection to this position was the facility of turning it by a force embarking at Berwick's, entering Grand Lake immediately above, and landing at Hutchin's, not far from Franklin, through which last passed the only line of retreat from Bisland. This danger was obvious, but the people were so depressed by our retreat from Lafourche that it was necessary to fight even with this risk.

Weitzel had followed slowly after Mouton, and now, in connection with gunboats, made little attacks on our pickets below Bisland; but I knew his force to be too small to attempt anything serious. In these affairs Fuller was always forward with the Cotton, though her boilers were inadequately protected, and she was too large and unwieldy to be handled in the narrow Teche. Meanwhile, I was much occupied in placing guns on the rivers at the points mentioned, getting out recruits for the two skeleton infantry regiments, consolidating independent companies, and other work of administration.

In the first days of January, 1863, Weitzel's force was increased to forty-five hundred men (see "Report on the Conduct of the War," vol. ii., p. 307); and on the 11th of the month, accompanied by gunboats, he advanced up the Teche and drove in

Mouton's pickets.   Left unprotected by the retreat of the pickets, the Cotton was assailed on all sides.   Fuller fought manfully, responding to the fire of the enemy's boats with his twenty-fours, and repulsing the riflemen on either bank with his field piece.   His pilots were killed and he had an arm broken, but he worked the wheel with his feet, backing up the bayou, as from her great length the boat could not be turned in the narrow channel.   Night stopped the enemy's advance, and Mouton, deeming his force too weak to cope with Weitzel, turned the Cotton across the bayou, and scuttled and burned her to arrest the further progress of the Federal boats.   Weitzel returned to Berwick's, having accomplished his object, the destruction of the Cotton, supposed by the Federals to be a formidable iron-clad.

Much disturbed by the intelligence of these events, as they tended still further to depress public sentiment and increase the dread of gunboats, I went to Bisland and tried to convince officers and men that these tin-clads could not resist the rapid fire of field guns, when within range.   At distances the thirty-pound Parrotts of the boats had every advantage, but this would be lost by bringing them to close quarters.   During my stay several movements from Berwick's were reported, and Mouton and I went down with a battery to meet them, hoping to illustrate my theory of the proper method of fighting gunboats; but the enemy, who intended nothing beyond annoyance, always retired before we could reach him.   Yet this gave confidence to our men.

The two twenty-fours removed from the wreck of the Cotton were mounted in a work on the west bank of the Teche, to command the bayou and road, and the line of breastworks was strengthened.   Some recruits joined, and Mouton felt able to hold the lines at Bisland against the force in his front.

In the last days of January, 1863, General Grant, with a large army, landed on the west bank of the Mississippi and began operations against Vicksburg, a fleet of gunboats under Admiral Porter coöperating with him.   The river was now in flood, and the Federals sought, by digging a canal through the narrow peninsula opposite Vicksburg, to pass their fleet below the place without exposing it to fire from the batteries. Many weeks were devoted to this work, which in the end was abandoned. In February the Federal gunboat Queen of the West, armed with a thirty-pound Parrott and five field guns, ran the batteries at Vicksburg and caused much alarm on the river below. The tow-boat Webb, before mentioned, had powerful machinery and was very fast, and I determined to use her as a ram and attempt the destruction of the Queen. A thirty-two-pounder, rifled and banded, was mounted forward, some cotton bales stuffed around her boilers, and a volunteer crew organized. Pending these preparations I took steamer at Alexandria and went down to Fort De Russy, and thence to Butte à la Rose, which at this season could only be reached by river. The little garrison of sixty men, with their two twenty-fours, had just before driven off some gunboats, attempting to ascend the Atchafalaya from Berwick's Bay. Complimenting them on their success and warning them of the presence of the Queen in our waters, I turned back, hoping to reach De Russy; but at Simmsport, on the west bank of the Atchafalaya, a mile or two below the point at which it leaves the Red, I learned that the Federal boat had passed up the latter river, followed by one of our small steamers captured on the Mississippi. Accompanied by Major Levy, an officer of capacity and experience, I took horse and rode across country to De Russy, thirty miles.

It was the 14th of February, a cold, rainy day; and as we emerged from the swamps of Deglaize on to the prairie of Avoyelles, the rain changed to sleet and hail, with a fierce north wind. Occasional gusts were so sharp that our cattle refused to face them and compelled us to halt. Suddenly, reports of heavy guns came from the direction of De Russy, five miles away. Spurring our unwilling horses through the storm, we reached the river as night fell, and saw the Queen of the West lying against the opposite shore, enveloped in steam. A boat was manned and sent over to take possession. A wounded officer, with a surgeon in charge, and four men, were found on board. The remainder of the crew had passed through the forest to the captured steamer below, embarked, and made off down river. A shot from De Russy had cut a steam pipe and the tiller rope, but in other respects the Queen was not materially injured. She was an ordinary river steamer, with her bow strengthened for ramming. A heavy bulwark for protection against sharp-shooters, and with embrasures for field guns, surrounded her upper deck.

Pushing on to Alexandria, I found the wildest alarm and confusion. The arrival of the Federal gunboat was momentarily expected, and the intelligence of her capture was hardly credited. The Webb was dispatched to overtake the escaped crew of the Queen, and the latter towed up to Alexandria for repairs. Entering the Mississippi, the Webb went up river, sighted the escaped steamer, and was rapidly overhauling her, when there appeared, coming down, a heavy iron-clad that had passed the Vicksburg batteries. This proved to be the Indianola, armed with two eleven-inch guns forward and two nine-inch aft, all in iron casemates. The Webb returned to De Russy with this information, which was forwarded to Alexandria. We had barely time to congratulate ourselves on the capture of the Queen before the appearance of the Indianola deprived us again of the navigation of the great river, so vital to our cause. To attempt the destruction of such a vessel as the Indianola with our limited means seemed madness; yet volunteers for the work promptly offered themselves.

Major Brent took command of the expedition, with Captain McCloskey, staff quartermaster, on the Queen, and Charles Pierce, a brave steamboatman, on the Webb. On the 19th of February Brent went down to De Russy with the Queen, mechanics still working on repairs, and there called for volunteer crews from the garrison. These were furnished at once, sixty for the Webb under Lieutenant Handy, seventy for the Queen, on which boat Brent remained. There were five and twenty more than desired; but, in their eagerness to go, many Texans and Louisianians smuggled themselves aboard. The fighting part of the expedition was soon ready, but there was difficulty about stokers. Some planters from the upper Red River had brought down their slaves to De Russy to labor on earthworks, but they positively refused to furnish stokers for the boats. It was a curious feature of the war that the Southern people would cheerfully send their sons to battle, but kept their slaves out of danger. Having exhausted his powers of persuasion to no purpose, Major Brent threw some men ashore, surrounded a gang of negroes at work, captured the number necessary, and departed. A famous din was made by the planters, and continued until their negroes were safely returned.

In the night of the 22d of February the expedition, followed by a tender, entered the Mississippi, and met a steamer from Port Hudson, with two hundred men, sent up by General Gardiner to destroy the Queen of the West, the capture of which was unknown. This, a frail river boat without protection for her boilers, could be of no service; but she followed Brent up the river, keeping company with his tender. On the 23d Natchez was reached, and here the formidable character of the Indianola was ascertained. While steaming up river in search of the enemy, the crews were exercised at the guns, the discharge of which set fire to the cotton protecting the boilers of the Queen. This was extinguished with difficulty, and showed an additional danger, to be guarded against by wetting the cotton thoroughly. Arrived in the afternoon of the 24th at a point sixty miles below Vicksburg, Brent learned that the Indianola was but a short distance ahead, with a coal barge lashed on each side. He determined to attack in the night, to diminish the chances of the enemy's fire. It was certain that a shell from one of the eleven- or nine-inch guns would destroy either of his boats.

At 10 P. M. the Indianola was seen near the western shore, some thousand yards distant, and the Queen, followed by the Webb, was driven with full head of steam directly upon her, both boats having their lights obscured. The momentum of the Queen was so great as to cut through the coal barge and indent the iron plates of the Indianola, disabling by the shock the engine that worked her paddles. As the Queen backed out the Webb dashed in at full speed, and tore away the remaining coal barge.   Both the forward guns fired at the Webb, but missed her.   Returning to the charge, the Queen struck the Indianola abaft the paddle box, crushing her frame and loosening some plates of armor, but received the fire of the guns from the rear casemates.   One shot carried away a dozen bales of cotton on the right side; the other, a shell, entered the forward port-hole on the left and exploded, killing six men and disabling two field pieces.   Again the Webb followed the Queen, struck near the same spot, pushing aside the iron plates and crushing timbers.   Voices from the Indianola announced the surrender, and that she was sinking.   As she was near the western shore, not far below Grant's army, Major Brent towed her to the opposite side, then in our possession, where, some distance from the bank, she sank on a bar, her gun deck above water.

Thus we regained control of our section of the Mississippi, and by an action that for daring will bear comparison with any recorded of Nelson or Dundonald.   Succeeding events at Vicksburg and Gettysburg so obscured this one, that in justice to the officers and men engaged it has seemed to me a duty to recount it.

Brent returned to Red River, with his boats much shattered by the fray; and before we could repair them, Admiral Farragut with several ships of war passed Port Hudson, and the navigation of the great river was permanently lost to us.   Of the brave and distinguished Admiral Farragut, as of General Grant, it can be said that he always respected non-combatants and property, and made war only against armed men.

In the second week of March a brigade of mounted Texans, with a four-gun battery, reached Opelousas, and was directed to Bisland on the lower Teche.   This force numbered thirteen hundred, badly armed; and to equip it exhausted the resources of the little arsenal at New Iberia.   Under Brigadier Sibley, it had made a campaign into New Mexico and defeated the Federals in some minor actions, in one of which, Valverde, the four guns had been captured.   The feeble health of Sibley caused his retirement a few days after he reached the Teche, and Colonel Thomas Green, a distinguished soldier, succeeded to the command of the brigade. The men were hardy and many of the officers brave and zealous, but the value of these qualities was lessened by lack of discipline. In this, however, they surpassed most of the mounted men who subsequently joined me, discipline among these "shining by its utter absence." Their experience in war was limited to hunting down Comanches and Lipans, and, as in all new societies, distinctions of rank were unknown. Officers and men addressed each other as Tom, Dick, or Harry, and had no more conception of military gradations than of the celestial hierarchy of the poets.

I recall an illustrative circumstance. A mounted regiment arrived from Texas, which I rode out to inspect. The profound silence in the camp seemed evidence of good order. The men were assembled under the shade of some trees, seated on the ground, and much absorbed. Drawing near, I found the colonel seated in the center, with a blanket spread before him, on which he was dealing the fascinating game of monte. Learning that I would not join the sport, this worthy officer abandoned his amusement with some displeasure. It was a scene for that illustrious inspector Colonel Martinet to have witnessed.

There also arrived from the east, in the month of March, 1863, to take command of the "Trans-Mississippi Department," Lieutenant-General E. Kirby Smith, which "department," including the States of Missouri, Arkansas, Louisiana, and Texas, and the Indian Territory, with claims on New Mexico, extended over some millions of square miles. The occupation of a large part of this region by the Federals would have spared General Smith some embarrassments, had he not given much of his mind to the recovery of his lost empire, to the detriment of the portion yet in his possession; and the substance of Louisiana and Texas was staked against the shadow of Missouri and northern Arkansas.

General E. Kirby Smith graduated from West Point in 1845, in time to see service in the war with Mexico. Resigning from the United States cavalry to join the Confederacy, he moved with General Joseph E. Johnston's forces from the Valley to reënforce Beauregard at Manassas, where he was wounded

while bringing up some troops to our left. Commanding in
eastern Tennessee in the summer of 1862, he led a force into
Kentucky through Cumberland Gap, to coöperate with Bragg.
At Richmond, Kentucky, a body of Federals was driven off,
and Smith moved north to Lexington and Frankfort; after
which his column was absorbed by Bragg's army. The senior
general west of the Mississippi, Holmes, was in Arkansas, where
he had accomplished nothing except to lose five thousand of his
best troops, captured at Arkansas Post by General Sherman.
It was advisable to supersede Holmes; and, though he proved
unequal to extended command, Smith, from his training and
services, seemed an excellent selection. General Smith remained for several weeks in Alexandria, when he was driven
away by the enemy's movements. The military situation of
my immediate command was explained to him.

To reopen the navigation of the Mississippi was the great
desire of the Federal Government, and especially of the Western people, and was manifested by declarations and acts. Grant
was operating against Vicksburg, and Banks would certainly
undertake the reduction of Port Hudson; but it was probable
that he would first clear the west bank of the Mississippi to
prevent interruption of his communications with New Orleans,
threatened so long as we had a force on the lower Atchafalaya
and Teche. Banks had twenty thousand men for the field,
while my force, including Green's Texans, would not exceed
twenty-seven hundred, with many raw recruits, and badly
equipped. The position at Bisland might be held against a
front attack, but could be turned by the way of Grand Lake.
With five thousand infantry I would engage to prevent the
investment of Port Hudson; and as such a reënforcement must
come from Holmes, and could not reach me for a month, I
hoped immediate orders would be issued.

On the 28th of March Weitzel, who had been quiet at Berwick's Bay for some time, sent the gunboat Diana, accompanied
by a land force, up the Teche to drive in our pickets. The
capture of the Queen of the West and destruction of the Indianola had impaired the prestige of gunboats, and the troops at

Bisland were eager to apply my theory of attacking them at close quarters. The enemy's skirmishers were driven off; a section of the "Valverde" battery, Captain Sayres, rapidly advanced; the fire of the gunboat was silenced in a moment, and she surrendered, with two companies of infantry on board. She was armed with a thirty-pounder Parrott and two field guns, and had her boilers protected by railway iron. Moved up to Bisland, her "Parrott" became a valuable adjunct to our line of defense.

CHAPTER IX.

INCREASED activity of the enemy at Berwick's Bay in the first days of April indicated an advance; and to guard against the danger from Grand Lake, Fuller, whose wounds in the Cotton affair were partially healed, was sent to Alexandria to complete repairs on the Queen and convert one or two other steamers into gunboats. It was hoped that he might harass the enemy on Grand Lake, delay the landing of troops, and aid the little garrison at Butte à la Rose in defending the Atchafalaya. Fuller was as energetic as brave, but the means at his disposal were very limited. Accompanied by a tender, he descended the Atchafalaya on the Queen, leaving orders for his steamers to follow as soon as they were armed. They failed to reach him, and his subsequent fate will be mentioned.

On the 10th of April the enemy had assembled at Berwick's sixteen thousand men under Weitzel, Emory, and Grover (" Report on the Conduct of the War," vol. ii., page 309). On the 12th Weitzel and Emory, twelve thousand strong, advanced up the Teche against Bisland, while Grover, with four thousand men, embarked on transports to turn our position by Grand Lake. Weitzel and Emory came in sight of our lines before nightfall, threw forward skirmishers, opened guns at long range, and bivouacked; and our scouts reported the movement on the lake. My dispositions were as follows: Mouton, with six hundred men and six guns, held the left from the lake to the Teche. The Diana in the bayou and two twenty-fours on the right bank guarded the stream and the main road; and sixteen hundred

9

men, with twelve guns, prolonged the line to the railway embankment on our extreme right, held by Green with his dismounted horsemen. One of Green's regiments, Colonel Reilly, the 2d Louisiana cavalry, Colonel Vincent, recently embodied, and a section of guns, were at Hutchin's Point on Grand Lake.

The cannonading ceased at dark, and when all was quiet I rode up to Franklin, thirteen miles, to look after my rear. A staff officer had been previously sent to direct the removal of stores from New Iberia, order down Clack's battalion, some ninety men, from the salt mines, and communicate with Fuller at Butte à la Rose; but the country around the Butte was flooded, and he was unable to reach it.

Above Franklin the Teche makes a great bend to the east and approaches Grand Lake at Hutchin's Point, where there was a shell bank, and a good road leading to the high ground along the bayou. The road to New Iberia leaves the Teche at Franklin to avoid this bend, and runs due north across the prairie. Just clear of the village it enters a small wood, through which flows a sluggish stream, the Bayou Yokely, crossed by a bridge. In the wood and near the stream the ground was low and boggy, impassable for wagons except on a causeway. The distance from Hutchin's Point to Yokely Bridge was less than that from Bisland; and this bridge, held by the enemy, made escape from the latter place impossible; yet to retreat without fighting was, in the existing condition of public sentiment, to abandon Louisiana.

I remained at Franklin until after midnight, when, learning from Reilly that no landing had been made at Hutchin's, I returned to Bisland. The enemy was slow in moving on the 13th, apparently waiting for the effect of his turning movement to be felt. As the day wore on he opened his guns, and gradually increased his fire until it became very heavy. Many of his field pieces were twenty-pounder Parrotts, to which we had nothing to reply except the Parrott on the Diana and the twenty-fours; and, as our supply of ammunition was small, Major Brent desired to reserve it for an emergency.

With the exception of Green's command, the troops on the

right of the Teche were raw, and had never been in action. As shot and shell tore over the breastwork behind which they were lying, much consternation was exhibited, and it was manifest that an assault, however feeble, would break a part of the line. It was absolutely necessary to give the men some *morale ;* and, mounting the breastwork, I made a cigarette, struck fire with my *briquet*, and walked up and down, smoking. Near the line was a low tree with spreading branches, which a young officer, Bradford by name, proposed to climb, so as to have a better view. I gave him my field glass, and this plucky youngster sat in his tree as quietly as in a chimney corner, though the branches around were cut away. These examples, especially that of Captain Bradford, gave confidence to the men, who began to expose themselves, and some casualties were suffered in consequence.

From the extreme right Colonel Green sent word that his corner was uncomfortably hot, and I found it so. The battery near him was cut up, its captain, Sayres, severely wounded, and Major Brent withdrew it. Green was assured that there were no places on our line particularly cool, and there was nothing to be done but submit to the pounding.

A heavy fire was concentrated on the twenty-fours and the Diana. Captain Semmes, son of Admiral Semmes of Alabama fame, and an officer of much coolness in action, had been detached from his battery and placed in command of the boat. A message from him informed me that the Diana was disabled. She was lying against the bank under a severe fire. The waters of the bayou seemed to be boiling like a kettle. An officer came to the side of the boat to speak to me, but before he could open his mouth a shell struck him, and he disappeared as suddenly as Harlequin in a pantomine. Semmes then reported his condition. Conical shells from the enemy's Parrotts had pierced the railway iron, killed and wounded several of his gunners and crew, and cut a steam pipe. Fortunately, he had kept down his fires, or escaping steam would have driven every one from the boat. It was necessary to take her out of fire for repairs. To lose even temporarily our best gun, the thirty-pounder, was hard, but there was no help for it.

During the day staff officers were frequently sent to Mouton to ascertain his condition; and, as the bridge over which they passed was in the line of fire directed on the Diana and the twenty-fours, the promenade was not a holiday affair.

Several times in the afternoon the enemy appeared to be forming for an assault; and after my men had become steady, I hoped an attack would be made, feeling confident of repulsing it.

Night brought quiet, and no report came from Reilly at Hutchin's. No news seemed good news; for I would have ample time to provide against a debarkation north of Hutchin's. The force at Bisland was in fine spirits. Protected by the breastwork, we had suffered but little; and the Diana was expected to resume her position before morning.

At 9 P. M. appeared Colonel Reilly to make the following report: The enemy had landed at Hutchin's, several thousand strong, with artillery, and advanced to the Teche, pushing our people back to and through Franklin. Reilly had left his command in camp below Franklin, toward Bisland, but thought the enemy had not reached the village at nightfall. Here was pleasant intelligence! There was no time to ask questions. I hoped to cut my way through, but feared the loss of wagons and material. Mouton was directed to withdraw from the left bank of the bayou, start the artillery and trains to Franklin, and follow with the infantry. Green, with his mounted men and a section of guns, was to form the rear guard; and Semmes was told to hurry his repairs and get the Diana to Franklin by dawn. As there was no means of removing the two twenty-fours, they were to be disabled. Leaving Major Brent to look after his artillery and Major Levy to superintend the prompt execution of orders, I rode for Franklin, taking Reilly with me. Reaching his camp, three miles from the town, I found the men sleeping and the trains parked, though the enemy was so near at hand. The camp was aroused, the troops were ordered under arms, and Reilly left to move up at once, with his trains following.

Two hours after midnight, and the village of Franklin was

as silent as the grave. Beyond the last houses, toward New Iberia, a faint light from some camp fires could be seen. Were the Federals in possession of the road? Approaching the fires cautiously, I saw a sentinel walking his post, and, as he passed between me and the light, marked his ragged Confederate garb. Major Clack had reached this point after dark, and intended to resume his march to Bisland in the morning. He speedily got his little band under arms, and in the darkness we beat the wood to our right. Not a picket nor scout was found, and Yokely Causeway and Bridge were safe. From the farther edge of the wood, in open fields, Federal camp fires were visible. It was a wonderful chance. Grover had stopped just short of the prize. Thirty minutes would have given him the wood and bridge, closing the trap on my force. Reilly, with his own and Vincent's regiments of horse and the two guns, came up. The guns were placed on the road near the Teche, with orders to stand fast. Reilly and Vincent dismounted their men, sent horses well to the rear, and formed line in the wood to the left of the guns, with Clack to the left of Vincent.

The first light of dawn made objects visible and aroused the Federals, some two hundred yards distant. Advancing rapidly from the wood, our line poured in a fire and rushed forward with a shout. Taken by surprise, the Federals fell back, leaving a battery on their right exposed. To prevent the sleepy gunners from opening, I rode straight on the guns, followed by my staff and four mounted couriers, and the gunners made off. All this was easy enough. Surprise and the uncertain light had favored us; but broad day exposed our weakness, and the enemy threw forward a heavy line of skirmishers. It was necessary for us to regain the wood, now four hundred yards to the rear. Officers behaved admirably in seconding my efforts to encourage and steady their men and keep them well in hand. Our two guns on the road fired rapidly and effectively, but the Federals came on in numbers, and their fire began to tell. Reilly was killed, Vincent wounded in the neck, and many others went down. At this moment the peculiar whistle of a Parrott shell was heard, and Semmes appeared with the Diana.

The enemy's advance was arrested; Gray's infantry from Bisland came up; the wood was occupied; Mouton with the remaining infantry arrived, and all danger was over. Green, in command of the rear guard, showed great vigor, and prevented Emory and Weitzel from pressing the trains. Besides the twenty-fours mentioned, one gun of Cornay's battery, disabled in the action of the 13th, was left at Bisland, and with these exceptions every wagon, pot, or pan was brought off. Two months later these guns were recaptured, much to the delight of our men.

The trains over Yokely Bridge and on the road to New Iberia, Mouton skillfully withdrew from Grover's front as Green entered Franklin from below. To facilitate this, Semmes was directed to work the Diana's gun to the last moment, then get ashore with his crew, and blow up the boat. With his usual coolness Semmes carried out his instructions, but, remaining too long near the Diana to witness the explosion he had arranged, was captured.

The object sought in holding on to Bisland was attained. From this time forward I had the sympathy and support of the people, and my troops were full of confidence. Our retreat to Opelousas, by New Iberia and Vermilionville, was undisturbed, Green with his horse keeping the enemy in check. Indeed, the pursuit was without energy or vigor. The first defensible position was at the Bayou Vermilion, thirty miles south of Opelousas. Here, after an action of some warmth, the enemy was held back until night and the bridge destroyed. From Opelousas the infantry, by easy marches, moved to and up the valley of the Red River, where supplies were abundant. The country was open, and the great superiority of his numbers enabled the enemy to do as he liked. Mouton, with Green's horse, marched west of Opelousas. It was hoped that he could find subsistence between that place and the Mermentou River, and be in position to fall on the enemy's rear and capture any small force left on the Teche. I supposed that the Federal army, after reaching Alexandria, would turn to the east, cross the Mississippi, and invest Port Hudson; and this supposition proved to be correct.

Meantime, accompanied by a tender, Fuller on the Queen

entered Grand Lake on the 13th, expecting his two armed steamers to follow. On the morning of the 14th the Federal gunboats from Berwick's Bay appeared, and Fuller, dispatching the tender up the Atchafalaya to hasten his steamers, prepared for action, as he doubtless would have done in presence of Admiral Farragut's fleet. A shell set fire to the Queen, and Fuller with his crew was captured. On the 20th the enemy's gunboats, assisted by four companies of infantry, captured Butte à la Rose with two twenty-four-pounders and sixty men. Semmes, Fuller, and the prisoners taken from the Queen and at the Butte, were on the transport Maple Leaf with Captain Fusilier, and escaped in the manner related, excepting Fuller, who from wounds received in his last action was unable to walk. Remaining in charge of the Maple Leaf until his friends were ashore, he restored her to the Federals, was taken to Fort Delaware, and died in prison. A braver man never lived.

The Federal army reached Opelousas on the 20th of April, and remained there until the 5th of May, detained by fear of Mouton's horse to the west. Unfortunately, this officer was forced by want of supplies to move to the Sabine, more than a hundred miles away, and thrown out of the game for many days.

In the "Report on the Conduct of the War," vol. ii., pp. 309 and 310, the Federal General Banks makes the following statements: "During these operations on the Teche we captured over twenty-five hundred prisoners and twenty-two guns; destroyed three gunboats and eight steamers"; and further: "A dispatch from Governor Moore to General Taylor was intercepted, in which Taylor was directed to fall back into Texas." At the time, my entire force in western Louisiana was under three thousand, and it is rather startling to learn that we were all captured. Two twenty-fours and one field gun were abandoned at Bisland, and two twenty-fours lost at Butte à la Rose. We scuttled and burnt the Cotton at Bisland, and blew up the Diana (captured from the enemy) at Franklin. The Queen (also captured) was destroyed in action on Grand Lake. The Federals caught two small steamers, the Ellen and Cornie, in the Atchafalaya, and we destroyed two in the Teche. The other four reported by General Banks must have come from the realm of the multitude of prisoners and guns. It also appears from the intercepted dispatch of Governor Moore that major-generals of the Confederate army were under the orders of State governors —an original discovery.

The delay of the Federals at Opelousas gave abundant time to remove our stores from Alexandria. General Kirby Smith, the new departmental commander, was advised to retire to Shreveport, two hundred miles up Red River, where, remote from danger or disturbance, he could organize his administration. Threatened in rear, Fort De Russy was untenable; so the place was dismantled and the little garrison withdrawn. On the 16th of April Admiral Porter with several gunboats had passed the Vicksburg batteries, and the abandonment of De Russy now left the Red River open to him. He reached Alexandria on the 9th of May, a few hours in advance of Banks's army. From the 8th to the 11th of the same month some of his gunboats bombarded Fort Beauregard, on the Washita, but were driven off by the garrison under Colonel Logan.

At this time I was sorely stricken by domestic grief. On the approach of the enemy to Alexandria my family embarked on a steamer for Shreveport. Accustomed to the gentlest care, my good wife had learned to take action for herself, insisting that she was unwilling to divert the smallest portion of my time from public duty. A moment to say farewell, and she left with our four children, two girls and two boys, all pictures of vigorous health. Before forty-eight hours had passed, just as she reached Shreveport, scarlet fever had taken away our eldest boy, and symptoms of the disease were manifest in the other children. The bereaved mother had no acquaintance in Shreveport, but the Good Samaritan appeared in the person of Mr. Ulger Lauve, a resident of the place, who took her to his house and showed her every attention, though he exposed his own family to great danger from contagion. The second boy died a few days later. The two girls, older and stronger, recovered. I was stunned by this intelligence, so unexpected, and it was well perhaps that the absorbing character of my duties left no time for the indulgence of private grief; but it was sad to think of the afflicted mother, alone with her dead and dying, deprived of the consolation of my presence. Many days passed before we met, and then but for an hour.

My infantry, hardly a thousand strong, with the trains, had marched to Natchitoches and camped, and some mounted scouts to observe the enemy were kept in the vicinity of Alexandria.

On page 309 of the "Report" before quoted, General Banks says: "A force under Generals Weitzel and Dwight pursued the enemy nearly to Grand Ecore, so thoroughly dispersing his forces that he was unable to reorganize a respectable army until July." A party of Federal horse crossed Cane River at Monette's Ferry, forty miles below Grand Ecore, and chased a mounted orderly and myself about four miles, then turned back to Alexandria; but I maintain that the orderly and I were not dispersed, for we remained together to the end.

The Federal army withdrew from Alexandria on the 13th of May, and on the 23d crossed the Mississippi and proceeded to invest Port Hudson; whereupon I returned by steamer to Alexandria, directing the infantry at Natchitoches to march back to the Teche to unite with Mouton. Having obtained supplies on the Sabine, Mouton and Green, the latter promoted to brigadier for gallant conduct, returned to the Teche country, but arrived too late to cut off the enemy, who with large plunder had crossed to the east side of Berwick's Bay, where he had fortifications and gunboats.

At Alexandria a communication from General Kirby Smith informed me that Major-General Walker, with a division of infantry and three batteries, four thousand strong, was on the march from Arkansas, and would reach me within the next few days; and I was directed to employ Walker's force in some attempt to relieve Vicksburg, now invested by General Grant, who had crossed the Mississippi below on the 1st of May.

The peculiar position of Vicksburg and the impossibility of approaching it from the west bank of the Mississippi have been stated, and were now insisted upon. Granting the feasibility of traversing the narrow peninsula opposite the place, seven miles in length and swept by guns afloat on both sides, what would be gained? The problem was to withdraw the garrison, not to reënforce it; and the correctness of this opinion was proved by the fact that Pemberton could not use the peninsular route to send out messengers.

On the other hand, I was confident that, with Walker's force, Berwick's Bay could be captured, the Lafourche overrun, Banks's communication with New Orleans interrupted, and that city threatened. Its population of two hundred thousand was bitterly hostile to Federal rule, and the appearance of a Confederate force on the opposite bank of the river would raise such a storm as to bring General Banks from Port Hudson, the garrison of which could then unite with General Joseph Johnston in the rear of General Grant. Too late to relieve Port Hudson, I accomplished all the rest with a force of less than three thousand of all arms.

Remonstrances were of no avail. I was informed that all the Confederate authorities in the east were urgent for some effort on our part in behalf of Vicksburg, and that public opinion would condemn us if we did not *try to do something*. To go two hundred miles and more away from the proper theatre of action in search of an indefinite *something* was hard; but orders are orders. Time was so important that I determined to run the risk of moving Walker by river, though the enemy could bring gunboats into the lower Red and Washita, as well as into the Tensas, and had some troops in the region between this last and the Mississippi. Steamers were held in readiness, and as soon as Walker arrived his command was embarked and taken up the Tensas. I went on in advance to give notice to the boats behind of danger; for, crowded with troops, these would have been helpless in the event of meeting an enemy.

Without interference, a point on the Tensas opposite Vicksburg was reached and the troops disembarked. Here Captain Harrison's mounted men, previously mentioned, met us. For safety the steamers were sent down the Tensas to its junction with the Washita, and up the last above Fort Beauregard; and bridges were thrown over the Tensas and Maçon to give communication with the terminus of the Monroe Railway.

Walker rapidly advanced to the village of Richmond, midway between the Tensas and Mississippi, some twelve miles from each, where he surprised and captured a small Federal party. At Young's Point, ten miles above Vicksburg, on the west bank of the river, the enemy had a fortified camp, and a second one four miles above Young's, both occupied by negro troops. Holding one brigade in reserve at the point of separation of the roads, Walker sent a brigade to Young's and another to the camp above. Both attacks were made at dawn, and, with the loss of some scores of prisoners, the negroes were driven over the levee to the protection of gunboats in the river.

Fifteen miles above Vicksburg the Yazoo River enters the Mississippi from the east, and twenty-five miles farther up Steele's Bayou connects the two rivers. Before reaching the Mississippi the Yazoo makes a bend to the south, approaching the rear of Vicksburg. The right of Grant's army rested on this bend, and here his supplies were landed, and his transports were beyond the reach of annoyance from the west bank of the Mississippi.

As foreseen, our movement resulted, and could result, in nothing. Walker was directed to desist from further efforts on the river, and move to Monroe, where steamers would be in readiness to return his command to Alexandria, to which place I pushed on in advance. Subsequently, General Kirby Smith reached Monroe direct from Shreveport, countermanded my orders, and turned Walker back into the region east of the Tensas, where this good soldier and his fine division were kept idle for some weeks, until the fall of Vicksburg. The time wasted on these absurd movements cost us the garrison of Port Hudson, nearly eight thousand men; but the pressure on General Kirby Smith to *do something* for Vicksburg was too strong to be resisted.

At Alexandria I found three small regiments of Texan horse, just arrived. Together they numbered six hundred and fifty, and restored the loss suffered in action and in long marches by the forces on the Teche. Colonel (afterward brigadier) Major, the senior officer, was ordered to move these regiments to Morgan's Ferry on the Atchafalaya; and by ambulance, with relays of mules, I reached Mouton and Green on the lower Teche in a few hours.

The Federals had a number of sick and convalescent at Berwick's Bay, but the effective force was small. Some works strengthened their positions, and there was a gunboat anchored in the bay. Mouton and Green were directed to collect small boats, skiffs, flats, even sugar-coolers, in the Teche; and the importance of secrecy was impressed upon them. Pickets were doubled to prevent communication with the enemy, and only a few scouts permitted to approach the bay. Returning north to Morgan's Ferry, I crossed the Atchafalaya with Major's command, and moved down the Fordoche and Grosse-Tête, bayous draining the region between the Atchafalaya and Mississippi. A short march brought us near the Fausse Rivière, an ancient bed of the Mississippi, some miles west of the present channel, and opposite Port Hudson.

Halting the command on the Fordoche, I rode out to the estate of an acquaintance on Fausse Rivière, whence the noise of battle at Port Hudson could be heard. Two ladies of the family, recently from New Orleans, told me that the Federal force left in the city would not exceed a thousand men; that a small garrison occupied a work near Donaldsonville, where the Lafourche leaves the Mississippi, and with this exception there were no troops on the west bank of the river. From our position on the Fordoche to the Bayou Bœuf, in rear of the Federal camp at Berwick's Bay, was over a hundred miles. The route followed the Grosse-Tête to Plaquemine on the Mississippi, and to escape observation Plaquemine must be passed in the night. Below this point there was an interior road that reached the Lafourche some distance below Donaldsonville. Minute instructions and guides were given to Major.

It was now the 19th of June, and he was expected to reach the Bœuf on the morning of the 23d. The necessity of punctuality was impressed on him and his officers, as I would attack

Berwick's at dawn on the 23d, and their coöperation was required to secure success. Indeed, their own safety depended
on promptness. The men carried rations, with some forage,
and wagons were sent back across the Atchafalaya. Major
moved in time to pass Plaquemine, twenty odd miles, before
midnight, and I hastened to Mouton's camp below Bisland,
reaching it in the afternoon of the 22d.

Fifty-three small craft, capable of transporting three hundred men, had been collected. Detachments for the boats were
drawn from Green's brigade and the 2d Louisiana horse. Major
Hunter of Baylor's Texans was placed in command, with Major
Blair of the 2d Louisiana as second. After nightfall Hunter embarked his men, and paddled down the Teche to the Atchafalaya
and Grand Lake. Fortunately, there was no wind; for the
slightest disturbance of the lake would have swamped his *fleet*.
He had about twelve miles to make, and was expected to reach
before daylight the northeast end of the island, a mile from
Berwick's and the railway terminus, where he was instructed to
lie quiet until he heard General Green's guns from the west
side of the bay, then rush on the rear of the Federal works.
During the night Green placed a battery opposite the gunboat
and railway station, and deployed five hundred dismounted men
along the shores of the bay, here eight hundred yards wide.
The battery was run up by hand, and every precaution to secure silence taken. At dawn of the 23d (June, 1863) our guns
opened on the gunboat, and speedily drove it away. Fire was
then directed on the earthwork, where the enemy, completely
surprised, had some heavy pieces with which he attempted to
reply. A shout was heard in his rear, and Hunter with his
party came rushing on. Resistance ceased at once; but before
Hunter closed in, a train of three engines and many carriages
escaped from the station toward the Bœuf, seven miles away.
I crossed in a " pirogue " with Green, and sent back two flats
and several skiffs found on the east side for his men, who used
them to get over, their horses swimming alongside.

It was a scene of the wildest excitement and confusion.
The sight of such quantities of "loot" quite upset my hungry

followers. Wandering through the station and warehouse, filled with stores, a Texan came upon a telegraphic instrument, clicking in response to one down the line. Supposing this to be some infernal machine for our destruction, he determined to save his friends at the risk of his own life, and smashed the instrument with his heavy boots; then rushed among his comrades, exclaiming: "Boys! they is trying to blow us up. I seen the triggers a-working, but I busted 'em."

Mouton now crossed with some infantry, and order was restored; and Green, who had brought over several scores of horses, mounted his men and followed the rail toward the Bœuf. Before reaching it he heard the noise of the train; then, firing and moving forward, found the train stopped, and Major, up to time, in possession of the bridge. The capture of the train was of importance, as it enabled us to operate the thirty miles of rail between Berwick's and the Lafourche.

In the combined movements described, Green and Major had set out from points more than a hundred miles apart, the latter marching through a region in possession or under control of the enemy, while the boat expedition of Hunter passed over twelve miles of water; yet all reached their goal at the appointed time. Although every precaution had been taken to exclude mistakes and insure coöperation, such complete success is not often attained in combined military movements; and I felt that sacrifices were due to Fortune.

In his rapid march from the Fordoche Major captured seventy prisoners and burned two steamers at Plaquemine. He afterward encountered no enemy until he reached Thibodeaux, near which place, at Lafourche Crossing, there was a stockade held by a small force to protect the railway bridge. Colonel Pyron, with two hundred men, was detached to mask or carry this stockade, and Major passed on to the Bœuf. Pyron's attack was repulsed with a loss of fifty-five killed and wounded, Pyron among the latter; but the enemy, after destroying the bridge, abandoned the post and three guns and retired to New Orleans.

The spoils of Berwick's were of vast importance. Twelve

guns, thirty-twos and twenty-fours (among which were our old friends from Bisland), seventeen hundred prisoners, with many small arms and accouterments, and great quantities of quartermaster's, commissary, ordnance, and medical stores, fell into our hands. For the first time since I reached western Louisiana I had supplies, and in such abundance as to serve for the Red River campaign of 1864. Three fourths of the prisoners were sick and convalescent men left here, as well as the stores, by General Banks, when he marched up the Teche in April. Excepting those too ill to be moved, the prisoners were paroled and sent to New Orleans under charge of their surgeons.

I was eager to place batteries on the Mississippi to interrupt Banks's communication with New Orleans; but the passage of Berwick's Bay consumed much time, though we worked night and day. We were forced to dismount guns and carriages and cross them piecemeal in two small flats, and several days elapsed before a little steamer from the upper Teche could be brought down to assist. It must be remembered that neither artillery nor wagons accompanied Major's march from the Fordoche.

On the 24th General Green, with Major's men and such of his own as had crossed their horses, marched for Donaldsonville, sixty-five miles, and General Mouton, with two regiments of infantry, took rail to Thibodeaux and sent pickets down the line to Bayou Des Allemands, twenty-five miles from New Orleans. Our third regiment of infantry remained at the bay, where Major Brent was at work mounting the captured guns on the southern end of the island and on the western shore opposite. Gunboats could stop the crossing, and entrance from the Gulf was open. While we might drive off "tin-clads" the enemy had boats capable of resisting field guns, and it is remarkable that, from the 23d of June to the 22d of July, he made no attempt to disturb us at Berwick's Bay.

General Green reached the vicinity of Donaldsonville on the 27th, and found an earthwork at the junction of the Lafourche and Mississippi. This work, called Fort Butler, had a ditch on three sides, and the river face was covered by gunboats in the stream. The garrison was reported to be from two

to three hundred negro troops.   After some correspondence
with Mouton, Green determined to assault the place, and drew
around it five hundred of his men in the night of the 27th.
Two hours before dawn of the 28th Colonel Joseph Phillipps
led his regiment, two hundred strong, to the attack.   Darkness
and ignorance of the ground caused much blundering.   The
levee above the fort was mistaken for the parapet, and some
loss was sustained from the fire of gunboats.   Changing direction, Phillipps came upon the ditch, unknown to him as to
Green, who had been deceived by false information.   The ditch
passed, Phillipps mounted the parapet and fell dead as he
reached the top.   An equally brave man, Major Ridley, worthy
of his leader, followed, and, calling on his men to come, jumped
into the work.   Frightened by his appearance, the enemy abandoned the parapet; but finding that Ridley was alone, returned
and captured him.   A dozen men would have carried the place;
but the ditch afforded protection from fire, and the men, disheartened by Phillipps's death, could not be induced to leave it.
Indeed, the largest part of our loss, ninety-seven, was made up
of these men, who remained in the ditch until daylight and surrendered.

The above statements are taken from the report of Major
Ridley, made after he was exchanged.   The affair was unfortunate.   Open to fire from vessels on the river, Fort Butler was
of no value to us, and the feeble garrison would have remained
under cover; but, like the Irishman at Donnybrook, Green's
rule was to strike an enemy whenever he saw him—a most com-
mendable rule in war, and covering a multitude of such small
errors as the attack on Fort Butler.

Meantime I was detained at Berwick's Bay, engaged in hurrying over and forward artillery and arranging to transport the
more valuable stores into the interior.   It was not, however,
until near the end of the first week in July that I succeeded in
placing twelve guns on the river below Donaldsonville.   Fire
was opened, one transport destroyed and several turned back.
Gunboats attempted to dislodge us, but were readily driven
away by the aid of Green's men, dismounted and protected by

the levee. For three days the river was closed to transports, and our mounted scouts were pushed down to a point opposite Kenner, sixteen miles above New Orleans. A few hours more, and the city would have been wild with excitement; but in war time once lost can not be regained. The unwise movement toward Vicksburg retarded operations at Berwick's and on the river, and Port Hudson fell. During the night of the 10th of July intelligence of its surrender on the previous day reached me, and some hours later the fall of Vicksburg on the 4th was announced.

An iron-clad or two in Berwick's Bay, and the road at Plaquemine held by troops, supported by vessels in the river, would close all egress from the Lafourche, and the enemy could make arrangements to bag us at his leisure; while Grant's army and Porter's fleet, now set free, might overrun the Washita and Red River regions and destroy Walker's division, separated from me by a distance of more than three hundred miles. The outlook was not cheerful, but it was necessary to make the best of it, and at all hazards save our plunder. Batteries and outposts were ordered in to the Lafourche; Green concentrated his horse near Donaldsonville, the infantry moved to Labadieville to support him, and Mouton went to Berwick's, where he worked night and day in crossing stores to the west side of the bay.

On the 13th of July Generals Weitzel, Grover, and Dwight, with six thousand men, came from Port Hudson, disembarked at Donaldsonville, and advanced down the Lafourche. Ordering up the infantry, I joined Green, but did not interfere with his dispositions, which were excellent. His force, fourteen hundred, including a battery, was dismounted and in line. As I reached the field the enemy came in sight, and Green led on his charge so vigorously as to drive the Federals into Donaldsonville, capturing two hundred prisoners, many small arms, and two guns, one of which was the field gun lost at Bisland. The affair was finished too speedily to require the assistance of the infantry.

Undisturbed, we removed not only all stores from Berwick's, but many supplies from the abundant Lafourche country, in-

10

cluding a large herd of cattle driven from the prairies of Opelousas by the Federals some weeks before. On the 21st of July.
we ran the engines and carriages on the railway into the bay,
threw in the heavy guns, and moved up the Teche, leaving
pickets opposite Berwick's. Twenty-four hours thereafter the
enemy's scouts reached the bay. The timidity manifested after
the action of the 13th may be ascribed to the fertile imagination of the Federal commander, General Banks, which multiplied my force of less than three thousand of all arms into nine
or twelve thousand.

In the "Report on the Conduct of the War," vol. ii., pages
313 and 314, General Banks states :

"Orders had been sent to Brashear City [Berwick's] to remove all stores, but to hold the position, with the aid of gunboats, to the last. The enemy succeeded in crossing Grand Lake
by means of rafts, and surprised and captured the garrison,
consisting of *about three hundred men*. The enemy, greatly
strengthened in numbers, then attacked the works at Donaldsonville, on the Mississippi, which were defended by a garrison
of two hundred and twenty-five men, including convalescents,
commanded by Major J. D. Bullen, 28th Maine volunteers.
The attack was made on the morning of the 28th of June, and
lasted until daylight. The garrison made a splendid defense,
killing and wounding more than their own number, and capturing as many officers and nearly as many men as their garrison numbered. The enemy's troops were under the command
of General Green of Texas, and consisted of the Louisiana
troops under General Taylor and five thousand Texas cavalry,
making a force of nine to twelve thousand in that vicinity.

"The troops engaged in these different operations left but
four hundred men for the defense of New Orleans. Upon the
surrender of Port Hudson it was found that the enemy had
established batteries below, on the river, cutting off our communication with New Orleans, making it necessary to send a
large force to dislodge them. On the 9th of July seven transports, containing all my available force, were sent below against
the enemy in the vicinity of Donaldsonville. The country was

speedily freed from his presence, and Brashear City [Berwick's] was recaptured on the 22d of July."

Here are remarkable statements. Fourteen hundred men and the vast stores at Berwick's (Brashear City) are omitted, as is the action of the 13th of July with "all my [his] available force. . . . The country was speedily freed from his [my] presence, and Brashear City reoccupied," though I remained in the country for eleven days after the 9th, and had abandoned Brashear City twenty-four hours before the first Federal scout made his appearance. The conduct of Major J. D. Bullen, 28th Maine volunteers, with two hundred and twenty-five negroes, "including convalescents," appears to have surpassed that of Leonidas and his Spartans; but, like the early gods, modern democracies are pleased by large utterances.

While we were engaged in these operations on the Lafourche, a movement of Grant's forces from Natchez was made against Fort Beauregard on the Washita. The garrison of fifty men abandoned the place on the 3d of September, leaving four heavy and four field guns, with their ammunition, to be destroyed or carried off by the enemy.

CHAPTER X.

RECENT events on the Mississippi made it necessary to concentrate my small force in the immediate valley of Red River. Indeed, when we lost Vicksburg and Port Hudson, we lost not only control of the river but of the valley from the Washita and Atchafalaya on the west to Pearl River on the east. An army of forty odd thousand men, with all its material, was surrendered in the two places, and the fatal consequences were felt to the end of the struggle. The policy of shutting up large bodies of troops in fortifications, without a relieving army near at hand, can not be too strongly reprobated. Vicksburg should have been garrisoned by not more than twenty-five hundred men, and Port Hudson by a thousand. These would have been ample to protect the batteries against a sudden *coup*, and forty thousand men added to General Joseph Johnston's force would have prevented the investment of the places, or at least made their loss of small moment.

After wasting three months in ineffectual attempts to divert the channel of the Mississippi, General Grant ran gunboats and transports by the batteries, and crossed the river below. Instead of meeting this movement with every available man, Pemberton detached General Bowen with a weak division, who successfully resisted the Federal advance for many hours, vainly calling the while for reënforcements. Pemberton then illustrated the art of war by committing every possible blunder. He fought a series of actions with fractions against the enemy's masses, and finished by taking his defeated fragments into the Vicksburg trap. It may be stated, however, that, had he acted wisely and kept out of Vicksburg, he would have been quite as much hounded as he subsequently was.

Grant's error in undertaking an impossible work cost him three months' time and the loss by disease of many thousands of his men. The event showed that he could as readily have crossed the river below Vicksburg at first as at last; but, once over, he is entitled to credit for promptly availing himself of his adversary's mistakes and vigorously following him. The same may be said of his first success at Fort Donelson on the Cumberland. The terror inspired by gunboats in the first year of the war has been alluded to; and at Fort Donelson General Grant had another potent ally. The two senior Confederate generals, politicians rather than warriors, retired from command on the approach of the enemy. One can imagine the effect of such conduct, unique in war, on the raw troops left behind. General Buckner, an educated soldier, was too heavily handicapped by his worthy superiors to make a successful defense, and General Grant secured an easy victory. "Among the blind, the one-eyed are kings."

General Grant's first essay at Belmont failed, and at Shiloh he was out-manœuvred and out-fought by Sidney Johnston, and, indeed, he was saved from destruction by Johnston's death. Before he moved against Bragg at Missionary Ridge, the latter had detached Longstreet with a third of his force, while he (Grant) reënforced Thomas with most of the Vicksburg army and two strong corps under Hooker from the east. The historian of the Federal Army of the Potomac states that, in reply to a question of General Meade, Grant said: "I never manœuvre"; and one has but to study the Virginia campaign of 1864, and imagine an exchange of resources by Grant and Lee, to find the true place of the former among the world's commanders. He will fall into the class represented by Marshal Villars and the Duke of Cumberland.

Genius is God-given, but men are responsible for their acts; and it should be said of General Grant that, as far as I am aware, he made war in the true spirit of a soldier, never by deed or word inflicting wrong on non-combatants. It would be to the credit of the United States army if similar statements could be made of Generals Sherman and Sheridan.

Released at length from the swamps of the Tensas, where it had suffered from sickness, Walker's division of Texas infantry joined me in the early autumn, and was posted to the north of Opelousas. Major-General J. G. Walker served as a captain of mounted rifles in the war with Mexico. Resigning from the United States army to join the Confederacy, he commanded a division at the capture of Harper's Ferry in 1862, and in the subsequent battle of Antietam; after which he was transferred to Arkansas. Seconded by good brigade and regimental officers, he had thoroughly disciplined his men, and made them in every sense soldiers; and their efficiency in action was soon established.

On the 29th of September Green, with his horse and a part of Mouton's brigade of Louisiana infantry, crossed the Atchafalaya at Morgan's Ferry, and attacked and routed the enemy on the Fordoche, capturing four hundred and fifty prisoners and two guns. Green lost a hundred in killed and wounded; the enemy, who fought under cover, less than half that number.

In October the Federals moved a large force of all arms up the Teche, their advance reaching the Courtableau. I concentrated for a fight, but they suddenly retired to the Bayou Bourbeau, three miles south of Opelousas, where they left a considerable body under General Burbridge. On the 3d of November Green, reënforced by three regiments of Walker's division, was ordered to attack them, and they were beaten with the loss of six hundred prisoners. This was the first opportunity I had had of observing the admirable conduct of Walker's men in action. Green's pursuit was stopped by the approach of heavy masses of the enemy from the south, who seemed content with the rescue of Burbridge, as they retired at once to the vicinity of New Iberia, fifty miles away. Green followed with a part of his horse, and kept his pickets close up; but one of his regiments permitted itself to be surprised at night, on the open prairie near New Iberia, and lost a hundred men out of a hundred and twenty-five. So much for want of discipline and over-confidence. General Banks's report mentions this capture, but is silent about Bourbeau.

The prisoners taken at the Bourbeau were marched to the Red River, where supplies could be had. The second day after the action, *en route* for Alexandria in an ambulance, I turned out of the road on to the prairie to pass the column, when I observed an officer, in the uniform of a colonel, limping along with his leg bandaged. Surprised at this, I stopped to inquire the reason, and was told that the colonel refused to separate from his men. Descending from the ambulance, I approached him, and, as gently as possible, remonstrated against the folly of walking on a wounded leg. He replied that his wound was not very painful, and he could keep up with the column. His regiment was from Wisconsin, recruited among his neighbors and friends, and he was very unwilling to leave it. I insisted on his riding with me, for a time at least, as we would remain on the road his men were following. With much reluctance he got into the ambulance, and we drove on. For some miles he was silent, but, avoiding subjects connected with the war, I put him at ease, and before Alexandria was reached we were conversing pleasantly. Impressed by his bearing and demeanor, I asked him in what way I could serve him, and learned that he desired to send a letter to his wife in Wisconsin, who was in delicate health and expecting to be confined. She would hear of the capture of his regiment, and be uncertain as to his fate. " You shall go to the river to-night," I replied, "catch one of your steamers, and take home the assurance of your safety. Remain on parole until you can send me an officer of equal rank, and I will look to the comfort of your men and have them exchanged at the earliest moment." His manly heart was so affected by this as to incapacitate him from expressing his thanks.

During the administration of Andrew Johnson a convention met in the city of Philadelphia which, at the earnest instance of the President, I attended. The gallant Wisconsin colonel was also there to lend his assistance in healing the wounds of civil strife. My presence in the city of *brotherly love* furnished an occasion to a newspaper to denounce me as " a rebel who, with hands dripping with loyal blood, had the audacity to show myself in a loyal community." Whereupon my Wisconsin friend, accompanied by a number of persons from his State, called on me to express condemnation of the article in question, and was ready, with the slightest encouragement, to make the newspaper office a hot place. This was the difference between brave soldiers and non-fighting politicians, who grew fat by inflaming the passions of sectional hate.

The ensuing winter of 1863–4 was without notable events. Control of the Mississippi enabled the enemy to throw his forces upon me from above and below Red River, and by gunboats interfere with my movements along this stream; and as soon as the Lafourche campaign ended, steps were taken to provide against these contingencies. Twenty miles south of Alexandria a road leaves the Bœuf, an effluent of Red River, and passes through pine forest to Burr's Ferry on the Sabine. Twenty odd miles from the Bœuf this road intersects another from Opelousas to Fort Jesup, an abandoned military post, thence to Pleasant Hill, Mansfield, and Shreveport. At varying distances of twelve to thirty miles the valley of the Red River is an arc, of which this last-mentioned road is the chord, and several routes from the valley cross to ferries on the Sabine above Burr's. But the country between the Bœuf and Pleasant Hill, ninety miles, was utterly barren, and depots of forage, etc., were necessary before troops could march through it. With great expenditure of time and labor depots were established, with small detachments to guard them; and events proved that the time and labor were well bestowed.

Movements of the Federals along the west coast of Texas in November induced General Kirby Smith to withdraw from me Green's command of Texas horse, and send it to Galveston. This left me with but one mounted regiment, Vincent's 2d Louisiana, and some independent companies, which last were organized into two regiments—one, on the Washita, by Colonel Harrison, the other, on the Teche, by Colonel Bush; but they were too raw to be effective in the approaching campaign. Mouton's brigade of Louisiana infantry could be recruited to some extent; but the Texas infantry received no recruits, and was weakened by the ordinary casualties of camp life, as well as by the action of the Shreveport authorities. The commander of the "Trans-Mississippi Department" displayed much ardor in the establishment of bureaux, and on a scale proportioned rather to the extent of his territory than to the smallness of his force. His staff surpassed in numbers that of Von Moltke during the war with France; and, to supply the demands of bureaux and staff, constant details from the infantry were called for, to the great discontent of the officers in the field. Hydrocephalus at Shreveport produced atrophy elsewhere. Extensive works for defense were constructed there, and heavy guns mounted; and, as it was known that I objected to fortifications beyond mere water batteries, for reasons already stated, the chief engineer of the "department" was sent to Fort De Russy to build an iron-casemated battery and other works. We shall see what became of De Russy.

In the winter there joined me from Arkansas a brigade of Texas infantry, numbering seven hundred muskets. The men had been recently dismounted, and were much discontented thereat. Prince Charles Polignac, a French gentleman of ancient lineage, and a brigadier in the Confederate army, reported for duty about the same time, and was assigned to command this brigade. The Texans swore that a Frenchman, whose very name they could not pronounce, should never command them, and mutiny was threatened. I went to their camp, assembled the officers, and pointed out the consequences of disobedience, for which I should hold them accountable; but promised that if they remained dissatisfied with their new commander *after an action*, I would then remove him. Order was restored, but it was up-hill work for General Polignac for some time, notwithstanding his patience and good temper. The incongruity of the relation struck me, and I thought of sending my monte-dealing Texas colonel to Paris, to command a brigade of the Imperial Guard.

In the first weeks of 1864 the enemy sent a gunboat expedition up the Washita, and Polignac's brigade, with a battery, was moved to Trinity to meet it. The gunboats were driven off, and Polignac, by his coolness under fire, gained the confidence of his men, as he soon gained their affections by his care and attention. They got on famously, and he made capital soldiers out of them. General Polignac returned to Europe in 1865, and as he had shown great gallantry and talent for war while serving with me, I hoped that he might come to the front during the struggle with Germany; but he belonged to that race of historic gentry whose ancestors rallied to the white plume of Henry at Ivry, and followed the charge of Condé at Rocroy. Had he been a shopkeeper or scribbling attorney, he might have found favor with the dictator who ruled France.

All the information received during the months of January and February, 1864, indicated a movement against me in the early spring; and in the latter month it was ascertained that Porter's fleet and a part of Sherman's army from Vicksburg would join Banks's forces in the movement, while Steele would coöperate from Little Rock, Arkansas. This information was communicated to department headquarters, and I asked that prompt measures should be taken to reënforce me; but it was "a far cry" to Shreveport as to "Lochow," and the emergency seemed less pressing in the rear than at the front.

The end of February found my forces distributed as follows: Harrison's mounted regiment (just organized), with a four-gun battery, was in the north, toward Monroe; Mouton's brigade near Alexandria; Polignac's at Trinity on the Washita, fifty-five miles distant; Walker's division at Marksville and toward Simmsport on the Atchafalaya, with two hundred men under Colonel Byrd detached to assist the gunners at De Russy, which, yet unfinished, contained eight heavy guns and two field pieces. Walker had three companies of Vincent's horse on the east side of the Atchafalaya, watching the Mississippi. The remainder of Vincent's regiment was on the Teche.

Increased activity and concentration at Berwick's Bay, and a visit of Sherman to New Orleans to confer with Banks, warned me of the impending blow; and on the 7th of March Polignac was ordered to move at once to Alexandria, and thence, with

Mouton's brigade, to the Bœuf, twenty-five miles south.   Harrison was directed to get his regiment and battery to the west bank of the Washita, gather to him several independent local companies of horse, and report to General Liddel, sent to command on the north bank of Red River, whence he was to harass the enemy's advance up that stream.   Vincent was ordered to leave flying scouts on the Teche and move his regiment, with such men as Bush had recruited, to Opelousas, whence he afterward joined me on the Burr's Ferry road.   At Alexandria steamers were loaded with stores and sent above the falls, and everything made ready to evacuate the place.   These arrangements were not completed a moment too soon.

On March 12th Admiral Porter, with nineteen gunboats, followed by ten thousand men of Sherman's army, entered the mouth of Red River.   (These numbers are from Federal official reports.)   On the 13th, under cover of a part of the fleet, the troops debarked at Simmsport, on the Atchafalaya near the Red, other vessels ascending the latter stream, and on the 14th, under command of General A. J. Smith, marched to De Russy, thirty miles, which they reached about 5 P.M.   As stated, the work was incomplete, and had time been given me would have been abandoned.   Attacked in the rear, the garrison surrendered after losing ten killed and wounded.   Byrd's two hundred men were in rifle pits on the river below, where gunboats, under Commander Phelps, were removing obstructions in the channel.   A number of Byrd's men and a few gunners escaped to the swamps and rejoined their commands ; but we lost a hundred and eighty-five prisoners, eight heavy guns, and two field pieces.   Thus much for our Red River Gibraltar.

Cut off from direct communication by the sudden appearance of the enemy on the 12th, the three mounted companies east of the Atchafalaya were forced to cross at Morgan's Ferry, below Simmsport, and did not rejoin Walker until the 15th. This officer was thereby left without means of information ; but, judging correctly of the numbers of the enemy by a personal observation of his transports and fleet, he fell back from his advanced position to the Bœuf, forty miles, where he was united with Mouton and Polignac. His division at this time was reduced to some thirty-three hundred muskets, too weak to make head against A. J. Smith's column.

On the afternoon of the 15th of March the advanced boats of Porter's fleet reached Alexandria, whence all stores had been removed ; but, by the mismanagement of a pilot, one steamer was grounded on the falls and had to be burned.

In the "Report on the Conduct of the War," vol. ii., page 192, Colonel J. S. Clarke, aide-de-camp to General Banks, states that Banks's army in this campaign was twenty-eight thousand strong, eighteen thousand under Franklin, ten thousand under A. J. Smith. General Steele, operating from Arkansas, reports his force at seven thousand ; and the number of gunboats given is taken from the reports of Admiral Porter to the Secretary of the Navy.

To meet Porter and A. J. Smith, Major-General Franklin had left the lower Teche on the 13th for Alexandria, with eighteen thousand men. My entire force on the south side of Red River consisted of fifty-three hundred infantry, five hundred horse, and three hundred artillerymen ; and Liddel, on the north, had about the same number of horse and a four-gun battery. From Texas, if at all, the delayed reënforcements must come, and it was vital to cover the roads from the Sabine.

From the Bœuf, on the 16th, I marched on the Burr's Ferry road to Carroll Jones's, which was reached on the evening of the 18th. Here, where the Burr's Ferry and Natchitoches roads separated, was a depot of forage, and I camped.

Polignac's and the Louisiana brigade, under Colonel Gray, were united in a division for General Mouton. Vincent's horse, from Opelousas, joined on the 19th, and on the following day was sent forward to the Bayou Rapides, twelve miles, where it skirmished with the enemy's horse from Alexandria, twenty miles below. At dawn of the 21st Edgar's battery, four guns, was sent to strengthen Vincent, and posted in a strong position near James's Store, where it overlooked and commanded the valley.

Meanwhile, couriers were dispatched to the Sabine to inform

approaching reënforcements of my position, and direct them on to the Fort Jesup road. The 21st proved to be a cold, rainy day, with gusts of wind. Toward evening the sound of Edgar's guns was heard. Fearing a surprise during the night, Captain Elgee of my staff was sent to withdraw the battery and warn Vincent of the necessity of vigilance; but the enemy had been too prompt. Vincent's pickets found their fires more agreeable than outposts. At nightfall the battery and a number of the horse were captured, as was Captain Elgee, who rode up just after the event. We lost the four guns, with their caissons, and two hundred men. Vincent, with the remainder of his command escaped. In truth, my horse was too ill disciplined for close work. On the 22d we marched to Beaseley's, twelve miles, and remained until the 29th, hoping that reënforcements would reach us. Beaseley's was a depot of forage, and covered roads to Fort Jesup and Natchitoches; and a cross road reached the Red River valley at a point twenty-five miles below the latter place, by which some supplies were obtained. As no reënforcements arrived, and the enemy was moving up the river, the troops were ordered to Pleasant Hill via Fort Jesup, forty miles, and I went to Natchitoches, thirty miles. Here, on the night of the 30th, I met Colonel McNeill's regiment of Texas horse, numbering two hundred and fifty men, of whom fifty were without arms; and the following morning Colonel Herbert came in, with a hundred and twenty-five of his three hundred and fifty men unarmed. These were a part of Green's command, and the first reënforcements received.

The enemy's advance reached Natchitoches, by the river road, on the 31st, and McNeill and Herbert were directed to fall back slowly toward Pleasant Hill, thirty-six miles. I remained in the town until the enemy entered, then rode four miles to Grand Ecore, where, in the main channel of Red River, a steamer was awaiting me. Embarking, I went up river to Blair's Landing, forty miles by the windings of the stream, whence was a road, sixteen miles, to Pleasant Hill. Four miles from Blair's was Bayou Pierre, a large arm of the river, crossed by a ferry. At Pleasant Hill, on the 1st of April, Walker and

Mouton, with their infantry divisions, artillery, and trains joined me, as did Green with his staff. From the latter I learned that De Bray's regiment of cavalry, with two batteries and trains, was in march from Fort Jesup. As the enemy was moving from Natchitoches, and could strike the Jesup road across country, De Bray was ordered to push forward his artillery and wagons, and look well to his right. He reached Pleasant Hill after dark. The enemy attempted to impede the march, but was driven off, with a loss of five wounded to De Bray. During the day our horse, toward Natchitoches, had some skirmishing.

It appeared that General Major, with the remainder of Green's horse, could not get up before the 6th, and he was directed to cross the Sabine at Logansport and march to Mansfield, twenty miles in my rear. This insured his march against disturbance; and, to give him time, I halted two days at Pleasant Hill, prepared for action. But the enemy showed no disposition to advance seriously, and on the 4th and 5th the infantry moved to Mansfield, where on the following day Major, with his horse and Buchell's regiment of cavalry, joined. General Major was sent to Pleasant Hill to take charge of the advance.

De Bray's and Buchell's regiments have been spoken of as *cavalry* to distinguish them from mounted infantry, herein called *horse*. They had never before left their State (Texas), were drilled and disciplined, and armed with sabers. Buchell's regiment was organized in the German settlement of New Braunfels. The men had a distinct idea that they were fighting for their adopted country, and their conduct in battle was in marked contrast to that of the Germans whom I had encountered in the Federal army in Virginia. Colonel Buchell had served in the Prussian army, and was an instructed soldier. Three days after he joined me, he was mortally wounded in action, and survived but a few hours. I sat beside him as his brave spirit passed away. The old "Fatherland" sent no bolder horseman to battle at Rossbach or Gravelotte.

During this long retreat of two hundred miles from the banks of the Atchafalaya to Mansfield, I had been in correspondence with General Kirby Smith at Shreveport, and always expressed my intention to fight as soon as reënforcements reached me. General Kirby Smith thought that I would be too weak to meet the enemy, even with all possible reënforcements, and suggested two courses: one, to hold the works at Shreveport until he could concentrate a force to relieve me; the other, to retire into Texas and induce the enemy to follow us.

My objection to the first suggestion was, that it would result in the surrender of the troops and Shreveport, as it would be impossible to raise a new force for their relief; and to the second, that its consequences would be quite as disastrous as a defeat, as it would be an abandonment of Louisiana and southern Arkansas. The men from these States might be expected to leave us, and small blame to them; while from the interior of Texas we could give no more aid to our brethren on the east of the Mississippi than from the Sandwich Islands. General Kirby Smith did not insist on the adoption of either of his own suggestions, nor express an approval of mine; but when Mansfield was reached, a decision became necessary.

Three roads lead from this place to Shreveport, the Kingston, Middle, and Keachi. The distance by the first, the one nearest to the valley of Red River, is thirty-eight miles; by the second, forty; and by the third, forty-five. From Keachi, five and twenty miles from Mansfield and twenty from Shreveport, roads cross the Sabine into Texas. Past Mansfield, then, the enemy would have three roads, one of which would be near his fleet on the river, and could avail himself of his great superiority in numbers. This was pointed out to the " Aulic Council " at Shreveport, but failed to elicit any definite response.

On the 21st of March there had reached Shreveport, from Price's command in Arkansas, two brigades of Missouri infantry and two of Arkansas, numbering together forty-four hundred muskets. These troops I had repeatedly asked for, but they were retained at Shreveport until the afternoon of the 4th of April, when they marched to Keachi, and reported to me from that place on the morning of the 6th. Supplies were far from abundant in the vicinity of Mansfield; and as I might at any moment receive an order to retire to Keachi, they were directed to remain there for the present. Green, now promoted to major-general, was placed in command of all the horse, with Brigadiers Bee, Major, and Bagby under him.

On the morning of the 7th of April, Major, from Pleasant Hill, reported the enemy advancing in force; whereupon Green went to the front. Later in the day the southerly wind brought such distinct sounds of firing to Mansfield as to induce me to join Green. Riding hard, I suddenly met some fifty men from the front, and reined up to speak to them; but, before I could open my mouth, received the following rebuke from one of the party for a bad habit: "General! if you won't curse us, we will go back with you." I bowed to the implied homily, rode on, followed by the men, and found Green fighting a superior force of horse. Putting in my little reënforcement, I joined him, and enjoyed his method of managing his wild horsemen; and he certainly accomplished more with them than any one else could have done. After some severe work, the enemy's progress was arrested, and it became evident that Green could camp that night at a mill stream seven miles from Pleasant Hill, a matter of importance.

The roads in this region follow the high ridge dividing the drainage of Red River from that of the Sabine, and water is very scarce. Between Pleasant Hill and Mansfield but two streams are found, the one above mentioned, and a smaller, seven miles nearer to the latter place. For twenty miles from Pleasant Hill toward Natchitoches there was little or no water; and at Pleasant Hill itself we had exhausted the wells and reduced the store in cisterns during our stay. This, as it affected movements and positions of troops, should be borne in mind.

Leaving Green, I returned to Mansfield, stopping on the road to select my ground for the morrow. This was in the edge of a wood, fronting an open field eight hundred yards in width by twelve hundred in length, through the center of which the road to Pleasant Hill passed. On the opposite side of the field was a fence separating it from the pine forest, which, open on the higher ground and filled with underwood on the lower, spread over the country. The position was three miles in front of Mansfield, and covered a cross-road leading to the Sabine. On either side of the main Mansfield-Pleasant Hill road, at two miles' distance, was a road parallel to it and connected by this Sabine cross-road.

General Churchill, commanding the Missouri-Arkansas troops at Keachi, was ordered to march for Mansfield at dawn of the 8th, and advised that a battle was impending. My medical director was instructed to prepare houses in the village for hospitals, and quartermasters were told to collect supplies and park surplus wagons. An officer with a small guard was selected to preserve order in the town, and especially among the wagoners, always disposed to " stampede." Walker and Mouton were ordered to move their divisions in the morning, ready for action, to the position selected; and a staff officer was sent to Green, with instructions to leave a small force in front of the enemy, and before dawn withdraw to the appointed ground. These arrangements made, a dispatch was sent to General Kirby Smith at Shreveport, informing him that I had returned from the front, found the enemy advancing in force, and would give battle on the following day, April 8, 1864, unless positive orders to the contrary were sent to me. This was about 9 P. M. of the 7th.

My confidence of success in the impending engagement was inspired by accurate knowledge of the Federal movements, as well as the character of their commander, General Banks, whose measure had been taken in the Virginia campaigns of 1862 and since.

On the morning of the 7th of April Admiral Porter left Grand Ecore with six gunboats and twenty transports, on which last were embarked some twenty-five hundred troops. The progress of these vessels up the river was closely watched by an officer of my staff, who was also in communication with General Liddel on the north side. Banks began his movement from Grand Ecore to Pleasant Hill on the 6th, with an estimated force of twenty-five thousand. Though lateral roads existed, his column marched by the main one, and in the following order:

11

Five thousand mounted men led the advance, followed by a large wagon train and much artillery. Infantry succeeded, then more wagons and artillery, then infantry again. In the afternoon of the 7th I knew that the front and rear of his column were separated by a distance of twenty miles.

My troops reached the position in front of Sabine cross-road at an early hour on the 8th, and were disposed as follows: On the right of the road to Pleasant Hill, Walker's infantry division of three brigades, with two batteries; on the left, Mouton's, of two brigades and two batteries. As Green's men came in from the front, they took position, dismounted, on Mouton's left. A regiment of horse was posted on each of the parallel roads mentioned, and De Bray's cavalry, with McMahon's battery, held in reserve on the main road. Dense forest prevented the employment of much artillery, and, with the exception of McMahon's, which rendered excellent service, none was used in the action.

I had on the field fifty-three hundred infantry, three thousand horse, and five hundred artillerymen—in all, eight thousand eight hundred men, a very full estimate. But the vicious dispositions of the enemy made me confident of beating all the force he could concentrate during the day; and on the morrow Churchill, with forty-four hundred muskets, would be up.

The forenoon of the 8th wore on as the troops got into position. Riding along the line, I stopped in front of the Louisiana brigade of Mouton's division, and made what proved to be an unfortunate remark to the men: " As they were fighting in defense of their own soil I wished the Louisiana troops to draw the first blood." But they were already inflamed by many outrages on their homes, as well as by camp rumors that it was intended to abandon their State without a fight. At this moment our advanced horse came rushing in, hard followed by the enemy. A shower of bullets reached Mouton's line, one of which struck my horse, and a body of mounted men charged up to the front of the 18th Louisiana. A volley from this regiment sent them back with heavy loss. Infantry was reported in the wood opposite my left. This was a new disposition of the enemy, for on the 6th and 7th his advance consisted of horse alone; and to meet it, Mouton was strengthened by moving Randall's brigade of Walker's from the right to the left of the road. To cover this change, skirmishers were thrown forward and De Bray's regiment deployed in the field.

The enemy showing no disposition to advance, at 4 P. M. I ordered a forward movement of my whole line. The ardor of Mouton's troops, especially the Louisianians, could not be restrained by their officers. Crossing the field under a heavy fire of artillery and small arms, the division reached the fence, paused for a moment to draw breath, then rushed into the wood on the enemy. Here our loss was severe. General Mouton was killed, as were Colonels Armand, Beard, and Walker, commanding the 18th, Crescent, and 28th Louisiana regiments of Gray's brigade. Major Canfield of the Crescent also fell, and Lieutenant-Colonel Clack of the same regiment was mortally wounded. As these officers went down, others, among whom Adjutant Blackman was conspicuous, seized the colors and led on the men. Polignac's brigade, on the left of Gray's, also suffered heavily. Colonel Noble, 17th Texas, with many others, was killed. Polignac, left in command by the death of Mouton, displayed ability and pressed the shattered division steadily forward. Randall, with his fine brigade, supported him on the right; while Major's dismounted men, retarded by dense wood, much to the impatience of General Green, gradually turned the enemy's right, which was forced back with loss of prisoners and guns.

On the right of the main road General Walker, with Waul's and Scurry's brigades, encountered but little resistance until he had crossed the open field and entered the wood. Finding that he outflanked the enemy's left, he kept his right brigade, Scurry's, advanced, and swept everything before him.

The first Federal line, consisting of all the mounted force and one division of the 13th army corps, was in full flight, leaving prisoners, guns, and wagons in our hands. Two miles to the rear of the first position, the 2d division of the 13th corps was brought up, but was speedily routed, losing guns and prisoners; and our advance continued. Near sunset, four miles from our original position, the 19th army corps was found, drawn up on a ridge overlooking a small stream. Fatigued, and disordered by their long advance through dense wood, my men made no impression for a time on this fresh body of troops; but possession of the water was all-important, for there was none other between this and Mansfield. Walker, Green, and Polignac led on their weary men, and I rode down to the stream. There was some sharp work, but we persisted, the enemy fell back, and the stream was held, just as twilight faded into darkness.

Twenty-five hundred prisoners, twenty pieces of artillery, several stands of colors, many thousands of small arms, and two hundred and fifty wagons were the fruits of victory in the battle of Mansfield. Eight thousand of the enemy, his horse and two divisions of infantry, had been utterly routed, and over five thousand of the 19th corps driven back at sunset. With a much smaller force on the field, we invariably outnumbered the enemy at the fighting point; and foreseeing the possibility of this, I was justified in my confidence of success. The defeat of the Federal army was largely due to the ignorance and arrogance of its commander, General Banks, who attributed my long retreat to his own wonderful strategy.

Night put an end to the struggle along the little stream, and my troops camped by the water.

A dispatch was sent to General Kirby Smith, at Shreveport, to inform him of the result of the day's fighting, and of my intention to push the enemy on the following morning. Leaving instructions for Green, with all the mounted force, to pursue at dawn, I rode to Mansfield to look after our wounded and meet Churchill. The precautions taken had preserved order in the village throughout the day. Hospitals had been prepared, the wounded brought in and cared for, prisoners and captured property disposed of. Churchill came and reported his command in camp, four miles from Mansfield, on the Keachi road; and he was directed to prepare two days' rations, and march toward Pleasant Hill at 3 A. M.

Sitting by my camp fire to await the movement of Churchill's column, I was saddened by recollection of the many dead, and the pleasure of victory was turned to grief as I counted the fearful cost at which it had been won. Of the Louisianians fallen, most were acquaintances, many had been neighbors and friends; and they were gone. Above all, the death of gallant Mouton affected me. He had joined me soon after I reached western Louisiana, and had ever proved faithful to duty. Mod, dest, unselfish, and patriotic, he showed best in action, always leading his men. I thought of his wife and children, and of his father, Governor Mouton, whose noble character I have attempted to portray.

Churchill's march disturbed these solemn reveries, and I returned to the front, where Walker and Green were awaiting the approaching day. The horse, with a battery, moved early to Pleasant Hill, fourteen miles, leaving Walker and Polignac to follow Churchill's column as soon as it had passed. I rode with Green, and we found many stragglers, scattered arms, and burning wagons, showing the haste of the enemy's retreat. The mill stream, seven miles distant, was reached, then the vicinity of Pleasant Hill, before a shot was fired. A short mile in front of the latter place the enemy was found; and as our rapid advance had left the infantry far to the rear, feints were made to the right and left to develop his position and strength.

The village of Pleasant Hill occupies part of a plateau, a mile wide from east to west, along the Mansfield and Fort Jesup road. The highest ground, called College Hill, is on the west, and here enters a road from the Sabine, which, sixteen miles to the east, strikes the Red River at Blair's Landing; while, from the necessity of turning Spanish Lake, the distance to Natchitoches and Grand Ecore is thirty-six miles. The Federal fleet, with accompanying troops, was now many miles above Blair's, which by river is forty-five miles above Grand Ecore. Driven from Pleasant Hill to the latter place, the Federal forces would be widely separated, and might be destroyed in detail. Though it appeared to be the enemy's intention to continue his retreat, as he was known to be moving back his trains, yet if undisturbed he might find courage to attempt a junction with his fleet at Blair's Landing; and I did not wish to lose the advantage of the *morale* gained by success on the previous day.

Our reconnoissance showed that the Federal lines extended across the open plateau, from College Hill on their left to a wooded height on the right of the road to Mansfield. Winding along in front of this position was a gully cut by winter rains, but now dry, and bordered by a thick growth of young pines, with fallen timber interspersed. This was held by the enemy's advanced infantry, with his main line and guns on the plateau. Separating the gully and thicket from the forest toward Mansfield was an open field, several hundred yards wide near the road, but diminishing in width toward the west. Here the Federal commander had concentrated some eighteen thousand, including A. J. Smith's force, not engaged on the previous day.

My plan of attack was speedily determined. Orders were sent to the infantry to fill canteens at the mill stream, and to the trains to park there. Shortly after midday the infantry appeared, Churchill in advance; but a glance showed that his men were too much exhausted to attack. They had marched forty-five miles, and were thoroughly jaded. Walker's and Polignac's divisions had been heavily engaged on the previous day, and all were suffering from heat and thirst. Accordingly, two hours were given to the troops to lie down and rest.

At 3 P. M. Churchill, with two batteries and three regiments of horse, was directed to move to the right and turn the enemy's left. His route was through the forest for two miles to the road coming from the Sabine. The enemy's left outflanked, he was to attack from the south and west, keeping his regiments of horse well to his right, and Walker would attack on his left. This was explained to Churchill, and Mr. T. J. Williams, formerly sheriff of De Soto parish, and acquainted with every road in the vicinity, was sent with him as a guide. On Walker's left, near the road from Mansfield, Major Brent had twelve guns in the wood, with four on the road, where were posted Buchell's and De Bray's cavalry, under General Bee, and Polignac's division, the last in reserve. In the wood on the left of the road from Mansfield, Major, with two brigades of horse dismounted, was to drive back the enemy's skirmishers, turn his right, and gain the road to Blair's Landing. As no offensive movement by the enemy was anticipated, he would be turned on both flanks, subjected to a concentric fire, and overwhelmed. Though I had but twelve thousand five hundred men against eighteen thousand in position, the *morale* was greatly in our favor, and intelligent execution of orders was alone necessary to insure success.

At 4.30 P. M. Churchill was reported to be near the position whence he would attack; and, to call off attention, Major Brent advanced his twelve guns into the field, within seven hundred yards of the enemy's line, and opened fire. Soon thereafter the sound of Churchill's attack was heard, which the cheers of his men proved to be successful. Walker at once led forward his division by echelons of brigades from his right, Brent advanced his guns, and Major turned the enemy's right and gained possession of the road to Blair's. Complete victory seemed assured when Churchill's troops suddenly gave way, and for a time arrested the advance of Walker and Major.

The road from the Sabine reached, Churchill formed his line with the two Missouri brigades, General Parsons on the right, and the two Arkansas, General Tappan, on the left. Advancing three fourths of a mile through the forest, he approached the enemy's line, and found that he had not gained ground enough to outflank it. Throwing forward skirmishers, he moved by the right flank until the Missouri brigades were on the right of the Sabine road, the regiments of horse being farther to the right. Churchill should have placed his whole command on the right of the Sabine road, and he would have found no difficulty in successfully executing his orders. In his official report he states "that had my [his] line extended a half mile more to the right, a brilliant success would have been achieved"; and he gives as the reason for not so disposing his force that he judged, from information furnished by his guides, the enemy's left to be already outflanked.

The attack ordered, the Missourians threw themselves on the enemy, drove him from the gully and thicket, mounted the plateau, broke an opposing line, captured and sent to the rear three hundred prisoners, got possession of two batteries, the horses of which had been killed, and reached the village. Here a Federal brigade, left by Churchill's error on his right, attacked them in flank and rear, while their rapid charge had put three hundred yards between them and the Arkansas brigades, delayed by the gully. The enemy's reserve was thrust into this opening and advanced in front. Finding themselves assaulted on all sides, the Missourians retreated hastily, and in repassing the gully and thicket fell into much confusion. Colonel Hardiman, commanding the horse, checked the enemy, and Parsons rallied his men on the line first formed by Churchill. The Arkansas brigades had forced the gully and mounted the plateau as the Missourians retreated, whereupon they fell back, their left brigade (Gause's) running into Walker's right (Scurry's) and impeding its advance. Gause imagined that Scurry had fired on him; but as his entire loss in the action amounted to but fifteen killed and fifty-nine wounded, out of eleven hundred men, there appears little ground for this belief. Churchill's two batteries followed the Missourians, and with much difficulty reached the plateau, where they opened an effective fire. When the infantry retreated three carriages broke down in the attempt to get through the thicket and fallen timber, and the guns were lost. Night ended the conflict on this part of the field, and both sides occupied their original positions. We brought off three hundred prisoners, but lost three guns and one hundred and seventy-nine prisoners from Churchill's command. Out of two thousand men, the Missourians lost three hundred and thirty-one in killed and wounded, and the Arkansas brigades, of equal strength, one hundred and forty-two.

Within a few minutes of the time when our whole line became engaged, an officer came to inform me that General Walker was wounded. Directing Polignac to move up his division and hold it in readiness, I left General Green in charge of the center and hastened to Walker, whose division was now fully engaged in the wood. I found him suffering from a contusion in the groin, and ordered him to retire, which he unwillingly did. Here it was that our right gave way in the manner described. Scurry's brigade of Walker's, disordered by the sudden retreat upon it of Gause, was heavily pressed by the enemy. Scurry and his men struggled gallantly, but required immediate relief; and to give it, Waul and Randall on their left were ordered to drive back the line fronting them. Never was order more thoroughly executed. Leading on their fine brigades with skill and energy, these officers forced back the Federals and relieved Scurry.

Meanwhile, the fire of Brent's guns had overpowered a Federal battery posted on the plateau in front of the road from Mansfield. The confusion attending the withdrawal of this battery, coupled with the fierce attack of Waul and Randall, led General Green to believe that the enemy was retreating, and he ordered Bee to charge with his two regiments of cavalry, Buchell's and De Bray's. Bee reached the plateau, where he was stopped by a heavy fire from infantry, in the wood on both sides of the road. Some men and horses went down, Buchell was mortally wounded, and Bee and De Bray slightly. The charge was premature and cost valuable lives, but was of use in moral effect. I returned to the road as Bee, with coolness and pluck, withdrew. Brent advanced his guns close up to the opposing line, Polignac attacked on Randall's left with his reduced but stubborn division, and Green urged on his dismounted horsemen, cleared the wood from the Mansfield to the Blair's Landing road, and at nightfall held the position previously occupied by the Federal battery.

Severe fighting continued in the dense thicket, where Polignac, Randall, Waul, and Scurry were steadily driving back the enemy. Approaching twilight obscured the wood, but resistance in front was becoming feeble, and, anxious to reach the village, I urged on our men. As Randall and Waud gained ground to the front, they became separated by a ravine in which was concealed a brigade of Federals. Isolated by the retreat of their friends, these troops attempted to get out. Fired on from both sides of the ravine, a part of them appeared on the field in front of Brent's guns, to be driven back by grape. With heavy loss they at length succeeded in escaping through the thicket. A letter from the commander was subsequently captured, wherein he denounces the conduct of his superiors who abandoned him to his fate. However true the allegation, it is doubtful if his brigade could have rendered more service elsewhere. The suddenness of its appearance stopped our forward movement, and a cry arose that we were firing on our own people. The thickening gloom made it impossible to disabuse the troops of this belief, and I ordered them to withdraw to the open field. The movement was made slowly and in perfect order, the men forming in the field as they emerged from the thicket. The last light of day was fading as I rode along the line, and the noise of battle had ceased.

Churchill came to report the result of his attack, and seemed much depressed. I gave such consolation as I could, and directed him to move his command to the mill stream, seven miles to the rear, where he would find his trains and water. A worthy, gallant gentleman, General Churchill, but not fortunate in war.

The mill stream was the nearest water to be had, and I was compelled to send the troops back to it. The enemy made no attempt to recover the ground from which his center and right had been driven. Bee picketed the field with his cavalry, his forage wagons were ordered up from the mill stream, and it was hoped that water for his two regiments could be found in the wells and cisterns of the village. Sounds of retreat could be heard in the stillness of the night. Parties were sent on the field to care for the wounded, and Bee was ordered to take up the pursuit toward Grand Ecore at dawn, to be followed by the horse from the mill stream as soon as water and forage had been supplied. These dispositions for the morning made, worn out by fatigue and loss of sleep, I threw myself on the ground, within two hundred yards of the battle field, and sought rest. The enemy retreated during the night, leaving four hundred wounded, and his many dead unburied. On the morning of the 10th Bee pursued for twenty miles before he overtook his rear guard, finding stragglers and burning wagons and stores, evidences of haste.

In the two actions of Mansfield and Pleasant Hill my loss in killed and wounded was twenty-two hundred. At Pleasant Hill we lost three guns and four hundred and twenty-six prisoners, one hundred and seventy-nine from Churchill's, and two hundred and forty-seven from Scurry's brigade at the time it was so nearly overwhelmed. The Federal loss in killed and wounded exceeded mine, and we captured twenty guns and twenty-eight hundred prisoners, not including stragglers picked up after the battle. The enemy's campaign for conquest was defeated by an inferior force, and it was doubtful if his army and fleet could escape destruction.

These were creditable results, yet of much less importance than those that would have been accomplished but for my blunder at Pleasant Hill. Instead of intrusting the important attack by my right to a subordinate, I should have conducted it myself and taken Polignac's division to sustain it. True, this would have removed my reserve from the center and line of retreat, and placed it on a flank; but I was confident that the enemy had no intention of resuming the offensive, and should have acted on that conviction. All this flashed upon me the instant I learned of the disorder of my right. Herein lies the vast difference between genius and commonplace: one anticipates errors, the other discovers them too late.

The foregoing account of Churchill's attack at Pleasant Hill, hidden from me by intervening wood, is taken from his official report and the reports of his subordinates; and I will now supplement it by some extracts from the testimony given by General Francis Fessenden of the Federal army. On pages 94 and 95 of the second volume of the "Report on the Conduct of the War," the following appears:

"In the afternoon we were changed, from a position in the woods in front of Pleasant Hill, to a position in rear of a deep ditch near the town. We were placed behind this ditch, in open ground, and practically held the left of the front line; and my regiment was on the left.   I think it was not expected that an attack would be made by the enemy in that direction.   The attack was expected by the road which led in by the right center of the army.   Instead of that, however, the enemy came around through the woods, and about half-past 5 o'clock drove in our skirmishers, and made a very fierce attack on the brigade I was in—Colonel Benedict's brigade.   The brigade fell back under the attack a great deal broken up, and my regiment was separated from the other three regiments which went off in another direction.   I had fallen back still further to the left, as I knew there was a brigade of troops in there to protect our left flank and rear from attack in that direction.   My regiment being the last of the brigade to fall back, the enemy had already advanced so far after the other three regiments that I could not fall back where they did.   I therefore fell back in another direction, rallying my regiment and forming on the right of the brigade referred to; and that brigade, my regiment, and another brigade, which I think had been brought up under General Emory, made an attack upon the enemy's column, which had advanced some distance, and drove them back with great loss.   We continued to advance, and drove them a mile or more, so completely off the field that there was no other attack made by the enemy in that direction.

"That night we fell back again, marching all night and all the next morning, until we reached the camping ground at the end of our first day's march from Grand Ecore.   I ought to state here that in that attack of the enemy on our left the brigade commander, Colonel Benedict, was killed, and I then assumed command of the brigade.   We remained at Grand Ecore some eight or nine days, where we built intrenchments to a certain extent—rifle pits.   I think the whole army threw up a kind of temporary work in front."

General Fessenden's statements accord with the reports of Churchill and his officers, and in other respects are accurate.

On page 62 of the volume quoted from, General A. L. Lee, commanding mounted division of Banks's army, testifies:

"The next morning (9th of April) I was ordered by General Banks to detach one thousand cavalry to act as scouts and skirmishers, and to take the remainder of my division, and take whatever was left of the detachment of the 13th army corps and some negro troops that were there, and take the trains and the majority of the artillery of the army to Grand Ecore. It was thought that the enemy would get between us and Grand Ecore. I started about 11 o'clock with this train, and with six or eight batteries of artillery, and reached Grand Ecore the next day. The battle of the 9th of April commenced just as I was leaving. The next day at night the main army had reached Grand Ecore and joined me there. General Banks impressed on me very strongly that, in sending me back from Pleasant Hill just as the fight was commencing, it was of the greatest importance to save what material we had left. Early the next morning, when I was distant from Pleasant Hill eighteen miles, I received a dispatch from General Banks. I have not the dispatch with me, but it was to this effect: that they had whipped the enemy terribly; that Price was killed, also two or three other rebel generals whom he named, but who have since recovered; and that I was to send back the subsistence trains for such and such troops. I was very much puzzled by that order, and immediately sent a staff officer back for more specific instructions. But he had not been gone more than half an hour when a staff officer of General Banks arrived with an order to me, with which he had left in the night, for me to continue pressing on with the whole train to Grand Ecore, and with instructions if any wagons broke down to burn them, not stop to fix anything, but get everything into Grand Ecore as quickly as I could, and look out very carefully on the flanks."

There can be no question of the correctness of these statements of General A. L. Lee.

The following quotations from the reports of Admiral Porter to the Secretary of the Navy are taken from page 239, and succeeding pages of the same volume:

"FLAG-SHIP CRICKET, GRAND ECORE, *April* 14, 1864.

"The army here has met with a great defeat, no matter what the generals try to make of it. With the defeat has come demoralization, and it will take some time to reorganize and make up the deficiencies in killed and prisoners. The whole affair has been seriously mismanaged. It was well we came up, for I am convinced the rebels would have attacked this broken army at Grand Ecore had we not been here to cover them. I do not think our army would be in a condition to resist them. I must confess that I feel a little uncertain how to act. I could not leave this army now without disgracing myself forever; and, when running a risk in their cause, I do not want to be deserted. One of my officers has already been asked 'If we would not burn our gunboats as soon as the army left?' speaking as if a gunboat was a very ordinary affair, and could be burned with indifference. I inclose two notes I received from Generals Banks and Stone. There is a faint attempt to make a victory out of this, but two or three such victories would cost us our existence."

Again, on page 166 of the same volume appears this dispatch from Lieutenant-General Grant, at Culpepper, Virginia, to General Halleck, Chief of Staff, at Washington:

"You can see from General Brayman's dispatch to me something of General Banks's disaster."

Concerning the battle of Pleasant Hill General Banks reports (page 326):

"The whole of the reserves were now ordered up, and in turn we drove the enemy, continuing the pursuit until night compelled us to halt. The battle of the 9th was desperate and sanguinary. The defeat of the enemy was complete, and his loss in officers and men more than double that sustained by our forces. There was nothing in the immediate position and condition of the two armies to prevent a forward movement the next morning, and orders were given to prepare for an advance. But representations subsequently received from General Franklin and all the general officers of the 19th corps, as to the condition of their respective commands for immediate active operations against the enemy, caused a suspension of this order, and a conference of the general officers was held in the evening, in which it was determined to retire upon Grand Ecore the following day. The reasons urged for this course were: 1. That the absence of water made it absolutely necessary to advance or retire without delay. General Emory's command had been without rations for two days, and the train, which had been turned to the rear during the battle, could not be put in condition to move forward upon the single road through dense woods, in which it stood, without great difficulty and much loss of time."

Again, on page 13, General Banks states:

"The enemy was driven from the field. It was as clear a rout as it was possible for any army to suffer. After consulting with my officers, I concluded, against my own judgment, to fall back to Grand Ecore and reorganize. We held the field of battle. Our dead were buried. The wounded men were brought in and placed in the best hospitals we could organize, and surgeons were left with them, with provisions, medicines, and supplies; and at daybreak we fell back to Grand Ecore."

Here the proportion of fiction to fact surpasses that of sack to bread in Sir John's tavern bill; and it may be doubted if a mandarin from the remotest province of the Celestial Empire ever ventured to send such a report to Peking. General Fessenden's testimony, given above, shows that the army marched during the night of the 9th, and continued to Grand Ecore, where it intrenched; and General A. L. Lee's, that the main army joined him at that place on the evening of the 10th. Twenty of the thirty-six miles between Pleasant Hill and Grand Ecore were passed on the 10th by my cavalry before the rear of the enemy's column was seen; yet General Banks officially reports that his army left Pleasant Hill at daybreak of the 10th. Homeric must have been the laughter of his troops when this report was published.

CHAPTER XI.

From my resting-place on the ground at Pleasant Hill, after the battle of the 9th, I was aroused about 10 P. M. by General Kirby Smith, just arrived from Shreveport. This officer disapproved of further pursuit of Banks, except by a part of our mounted force, and ordered the infantry back to Mansfield. He was apprehensive that the troops on the transports above would reach Shreveport, or disembark below me and that place. In addition, Steele's column from Arkansas caused him much uneasiness, and made him unwilling for my troops to increase their distance from the capital of the "Trans-Mississippi Department." It was pointed out that the water in Red River was falling, and navigation becoming more and more difficult; that I had a staff officer watching the progress of the fleet, which was not accompanied by more than three thousand men, too few to attempt a landing, and that they would certainly hear of Banks's defeat and seek to rejoin him at Grand Ecore. As to Steele he was more than a hundred miles distant from Shreveport, harassed by Price's force; he must learn of Banks's misfortune, and, leading but a subsidiary column, would retire to Little Rock. Banks, with the remains of his beaten army, was before us, and the fleet of Porter, with barely water enough to float upon. We had but to strike vigorously to capture or destroy both. But it was written that the sacrifices of my little army should be wasted, and, on the morning of the 10th, I was ordered to take all the infantry and much of the horse to Mansfield.

The Bayou Pierre, three hundred feet wide and too deep to ford, leaves the Red River a few miles below Shreveport, and after a long course, in which it frequently expands into lakes, returns to its parent stream three miles above Grand Ecore, dividing the pine-clad hills on the west from the alluvion of the river on the east. Several roads lead from the interior to landings on the river, crossing Bayou Pierre by ferries. One from Pleasant Hill to Blair's Landing, sixteen miles, has been mentioned. Another led from Mansfield to Grand Bayou Landing, eighteen miles. Dispatches from Captain McCloskey informed me that the enemy's fleet had passed this last place on the morning of the 9th, pushing slowly up river, impeded by low water. Feeling assured that intelligence of Banks's defeat would send the fleet back to Grand Ecore, and hoping to cut off its commucation, at dawn of the 11th I sent General Bagby, with a brigade of horse and a battery, from Mansfield to Grand Bayou landing. Before reaching the ferry at Bayou Pierre, he ascertained that the fleet had turned back on the afternoon of the 10th. There was a pontoon train at Shreveport that I had in vain asked for, and Bagby experienced great delay in crossing Bayou Pierre by means of one small flat. The fleet, descending, passed Grand Bayou Landing at 10 o'clock A. M. of the 11th, some hours before Bagby reached the river; and he pushed on toward Blair's Landing, where he arrived on the night of the 12th, after the close of Green's operations of that day.

General Green, from Pleasant Hill, had been directing the movements of our advanced horse, a part of which, under Bee, was in front of Grand Ecore and Natchitoches. Advised of the movements of the enemy's fleet, he, with seven hundred and fifty horse and two batteries, left Pleasant Hill for Blair's Landing at 6 o'clock P. M. on the 11th. As in the case of Bagby, he was delayed at Bayou Pierre, and, after hard work, only succeeded in crossing three guns and a part of his horse before the fleet came down on the 12th. Green attacked at once, and leading his men in his accustomed fearless way, was killed by a discharge of grape from one of the gunboats. Deprived of their leader, the men soon fell back, and the fleet reached Grand

12

Ecore without further molestation from the west bank. The enemy's loss, supposed by our people to have been immense, was officially reported at seven on the gunboats and fifty on the transports. *Per contra,* the enemy believed that our loss was stupendous; whereas we had scarcely a casualty except the death of General Green, an irreparable one. No Confederate went aboard the fleet and no Federal came ashore; so there was a fine field of slaughter in which the imagination of both sides could disport itself.

With facilities for crossing the Pierre at hand, the fleet, during the 11th and 12th, would have been under the fire of two thousand riflemen and eighteen guns and suffered heavily, especially the transports, crowded with troops. As it was, we accomplished but little and lost General Green.

Like Mouton, this officer had joined me at an early period of my service in western Louisiana. Coming to me with the rank of colonel, his conspicuous services made it my pleasant duty to recommend him for promotion to brigadier and major-general. Upright, modest, and with the simplicity of a child, danger seemed to be his element, and he rejoiced in combat. His men adored him, and would follow wherever he led; but they did not fear him, for, though he scolded at them in action, he was too kind-hearted to punish breaches of discipline. In truth, he had no conception of the value of discipline in war, believing that all must be actuated by his own devotion to duty. His death was a public calamity, and mourned as such by the people of Texas and Louisiana. To me he was a tried and devoted friend, and our friendship was cemented by the fact that, through his Virginia mother, we were related by blood. The great Commonwealth, whose soil contains his remains, will never send forth a bolder warrior, a better citizen, nor a more upright man than Thomas Green.

The brigade of horse brought by General Green to Louisiana, and with which he was so long associated, had some peculiar characteristics. The officers such as Colonels Hardiman, Baylor, Lane, Herbert, McNeill, and others, were bold and enterprising. The men, hardy frontiersmen, excellent riders, and skilled riflemen, were fearless and self-reliant, but discharged their duty as they liked and when they liked. On a march they wandered about at will, as they did about camp, and could be kept together only when a fight was impending. When their arms were injured by service or neglect, they threw them away, expecting to be supplied with others. Yet, with these faults, they were admirable fighters, and in the end I became so much attached to them as to be incapable of punishing them.

After the affair at Blair's Landing on the 12th, the horse returned to Pleasant Hill, and thence joined Bee in front of Grand Ecore, where Banks had his army concentrated behind works, with gunboats and transports in the river, Bee occupying the town of Natchitoches, four miles away. On the morning of the 13th General Kirby Smith visited me at Mansfield. Relieved of apprehension about the fleet, now at Grand Ecore, he expressed great anxiety for the destruction of Steele's column. I was confident that Steele, who had less than ten thousand men and was more than a hundred miles distant from Shreveport, would hear of Banks's disaster and retreat; but General Kirby Smith's views differed from mine. I then expressed my willingness to march, with the main body of the infantry, to join Price in Arkansas, and serve under his command until Steele's column was destroyed or driven back; insisting, however, that in the event of Steele's retreat I should be permitted to turn on Banks and Porter, to complete the work of Mansfield and Pleasant Hill. The destruction of the Federal army and capture of the fleet, helpless alone by reason of low and falling water in Red River, were the legitimate fruits of those victories, and I protested with all possible earnestness against a policy that would fail to reap them. After this conversation General Kirby Smith returned to Shreveport, leaving me under the impression that my last proposition was acceded to. The loss of valuable time incurred by a wild-goose chase after Steele was most annoying, but I was hopeful it might be recovered. To get the fleet down to Alexandria and over the falls at that place would require much time in the low condition of the water; and Banks's army was so much demoralized by defeat that Bee found no difficulty in restraining its movements with his horse.

At dawn of the 14th Walker's and Churchill's divisions of infantry, with their artillery, prepared for an active campaign, marched for Shreveport, forty miles. The same day Polignac's infantry division, reduced to some twelve hundred muskets, was sent toward Grand Ecore to strengthen the horse in front of the enemy. On the evening of the 15th I reached Shreveport, and had a short interview with General Kirby Smith, who informed me that Steele had begun his retreat from a point a hundred and ten miles distant, but that he hoped to overtake him, and would personally direct the pursuit. I was further informed that my presence with the troops was not desired, and that I would remain in nominal command of Shreveport, but might join the force near Grand Ecore if I thought proper. All this with the curt manner of a superior to a subordinate, as if fearing remonstrance. General Kirby Smith marched north of Shreveport on the 16th, and three days thereafter I received a dispatch from his "chief of staff" informing me that the pontoon train, asked for in vain when it would have been of priceless value, would be sent back from his army and placed at my disposition. Doubtless General Kirby Smith thought that a pontoon train would supply the place of seven thousand infantry and six batteries.

I remained at Shreveport three days, occupied with reports and sending supplies to my little force near Grand Ecore, toward which I proceeded on the 19th of April. Major-General Wharton, who had gained reputation as a cavalry officer in the Confederate Army of Tennessee, accompanied me. He had reported for duty at Shreveport on the 18th, and was assigned to the command of the horse to replace the lamented Green. We reached Polignac's camp, in the vicinity of Grand Ecore, ninety odd miles from Shreveport, on the evening of the 21st, and learned that the enemy had threatened an advance during the day. This convinced me of his intention to retreat, and an officer was sent to General Bee to warn him.

Cane River leaves the main channel of the Red below Grand

Ecore, and, passing by Natchitoches, returns to the Red after a winding course of sixty miles. Except at the season of floods, it is not navigable; but the alluvion through which it flows is very productive, while the pine forest immediately to the west is sterile. Bee, under instructions, occupied the valley of Cane River with his horse, and had been ordered to keep his pickets close to Grand Ecore and Natchitoches, draw his forage from plantations along the river, and, when the enemy retreated toward Alexandria, fall back before him to Monette's Ferry, which he was expected to hold. Monette's Ferry, forty miles below Natchitoches, was on the only practicable road to Alexandria. Here the river made a wide, deep ford, and pine-clad hills rose abruptly from the southern bank. On the left, looking toward Natchitoches, were hills and impassable lakes, easily held against any force. On the right, hills, rugged and pine-clad, extended eight miles to the point at which Cane River reënters the Red. The distance from Monette's to Alexandria is thirty-five miles, of which fourteen is through wooded hills. Roads led west to Carroll Jones's and Beaseley's, twelve and thirty miles respectively; and on these roads Bee was directed to keep his trains.

Concerning the position at Monette's General Banks reports: "The army marched from Grand Ecore on the morning of the 22d of April. To prevent the occupation of Monette's Bluff, on Cane River, a strong position commanding the only road leading across the river to Alexandria, or to prevent the concentration of the enemy's forces at that point, it became necessary to accomplish the evacuation without his knowledge." As before stated, the threatened advance of the 21st convinced me that the enemy's retreat was imminent, and so I advised Bee; but there was not time to send General Wharton to him after I reached Polignac's camp. Bee had two thousand horse and four batteries, and, after several days to examine and prepare his ground, might well be expected to hold it with tenacity.

Immediately after the battle of Pleasant Hill I had sent Vincent, with his own and Bush's regiments of Louisiana horse, to threaten Alexandria and drive out small parties of the enemy from the Attakapas and Teche regions. Subsequently, a brigade of Texas horse, seven hundred strong, under Brigadier William Steele, joined me, and was now with Polignac.

As anticipated, the enemy left Grand Ecore during the night of the 21st and marched without halting to Cloutierville, thirty-two miles. With Steele's brigade, Wharton drove his rear guard from Natchitoches on the morning of the 22d, capturing some prisoners, and continued the pursuit to the twenty-four-mile ferry. On the 23d, after a sharp action, he pushed the enemy's rear below Cloutierville, taking some score of prisoners. Polignac's infantry joined that evening, and covered a road leading through the hills from Cloutierville to Beaseley's. If Bee stood firm at Monette's, we were in position to make Banks unhappy on the morrow, separated as he was from the fleet, on which he relied to aid his demoralized forces. But Bee gave way on the afternoon of the 23d, permitting his strong position to be forced at the small cost to the enemy of less than four hundred men, and suffering no loss himself. Then, instead of attacking the great trains, during their fourteen miles' march through the forest, and occupying with artillery McNutt's Hill, a high bluff twenty miles from Alexandria and commanding the road thither in the valley, he fell back at once to Beaseley's, thirty miles. Before this mistake could be rectified, the enemy crossed at Monette's, burning many wagons at the ford, and passed below McNutt's Hill. General Bee had exhibited much personal gallantry in the charge at Pleasant Hill, but he was without experience in war, and had neglected to study the ground or strengthen his position at Monette's. Leaving Mansfield for Shreveport on the 15th, under orders from General Kirby Smith, I only got back to the front on the night of the 21st, too late to reach Monette's or send Wharton there.

It was very disheartening, but, persuaded that the enemy could not pass the falls at Alexandria with his fleet, I determined to stick to him with my little force of less than forty-five hundred of all arms. It was impossible to believe that General Kirby Smith would continue to persist in his inexplicable policy, and fail to come, ere long, to my assistance.

On the 26th Bee's horse, from Beaseley's, joined Steele's at

McNutt's Hill; and together, under Wharton, they attacked the enemy in the valley and drove him, with loss of killed and prisoners, to the immediate vicinity of Alexandria.

When General Banks retreated so hastily from Grand Ecore, Admiral Porter was laboring to get his fleet down to Alexandria. In a communication to the Secretary of the Navy from his flag-ship below Grand Ecore, he says (" Report on the Conduct of the War," vol. ii., pages 234–5) :

" I soon saw that the army would go to Alexandria again, and we would be left above the bars in a helpless condition. The vessels are mostly at Alexandria, above the falls, excepting this one and two others I kept to protect the Eastport. The Red River is falling at the rate of two inches a day. If General Banks should determine to evacuate this country, the gunboats will be cut off from all communication with the Mississippi. It cannot be possible that the country would be willing to have eight iron-clads, three or four other gunboats, and many transports sacrificed without an effort to save them. It would be the worst thing that has happened this war."

The Eastport, the most formidable iron-clad of the Mississippi squadron, grounded on a bar below Grand Ecore. Three tinclad gunboats and two transports remained near to assist in getting her off; and, to prevent this, some mounted riflemen were sent, on the morning of the 26th, to coöperate with Liddel's raw levies on the north bank of the river. These forced the enemy to destroy the Eastport, and drove away the gunboats and transports. Our loss in the affair was two killed and four wounded. Meantime, to intercept the gunboats and transports on their way down, Colonel Caudle of Polignac's division, with two hundred riflemen and Cornay's four-gun battery, had been posted at the junction of Cane and Red Rivers, twenty miles below. At 6 o'clock P. M. of the 26th the leading gunboat and one transport came down. Our fire speedily crippled and silenced the gunboat, and a shot exploded the boiler of the transport. Under cover of escaping steam the gunboat drifted out of fire, but the loss of life on the transport was fearful. One hundred dead and eighty-seven severely scalded, most of whom subsequently died, were brought on shore.   These unfortunate creatures were negroes, taken from plantations on the river above.   The object of the Federals was to remove negroes from their owners; but for the lives of these poor people they cared nothing, or, assuredly, they would not have forced them, on an unprotected river steamer, to pass riflemen and artillery, against which gunboats were powerless.   On the following day, the 27th, the two remaining gunboats and transport attempted to pass Caudle's position; and the former, much cut up, succeeded, but the transport was captured.   Colonel Caudle had one man wounded, and the battery one killed—its commander, Captain Cornay, who, with Mouton, Armand, and many other creoles, proved by distinguished gallantry that the fighting qualities of the old French breed had suffered no deterioration on the soil of Louisiana.

The following extracts from the report of Admiral Porter well exhibit the efficiency of Caudle and Cornay in this affair:

"FLAG-SHIP CRICKET, OFF ALEXANDRIA, *April* 28, 1864.

"When rounding the point, the vessels in close order and ready for action, we descried a party of the enemy with artillery on the right bank, and we immediately opened fire with our bow guns.   The enemy immediately returned it with a *large number of cannon, eighteen in all,* every shot of which struck this vessel. The captain gave orders to stop the engines.   I corrected this mistake, and got headway on the vessel again, but not soon enough to avoid the pelting showers of shot and shell which the enemy poured into us, every shot going through and through us, clearing all our decks in a moment.   I took charge of the vessel, and, *as the battery was a very heavy one,* I determined to pass it, which was done under the heaviest fire I ever witnessed. Seeing that the Hindman did not pass the batteries, the Juliet disabled, and that one of the pump boats (transport) had her boiler exploded by a shot, I ran down to a point three or four miles below.   Lieutenant-Commander Phelps had two vessels in charge, the Juliet and Champion (transport), which he wished to get through safely.   He kept them out of range until he could partially repair the Juliet, and then, starting under a heavy fire, he make a push by. Unfortunately the pump boat (Champion) was disabled and set fire to. The Hindman had her wheel ropes cut away, and drifted past, turning round and round, and getting well cut up in going by. The Juliet was cut to pieces in hull and machinery; had fifteen killed and wounded. I inclose the report of Lieutenant-Commander Phelps, from the time of his first misfortune until his arrival at this place (Alexandria), where I now am with all the fleet, but very much surprised that I have any left, considering all the difficulties encountered. I came up here with the river on the rise, and water enough for our largest vessels; and even on my way up to Shreveport from Grand Ecore the water rose, while it commenced falling where I left the largest gunboats. Falling or not, I could not go back while in charge of the transports and material on which *an army of thirty thousand men depended.*"

This is high testimony to the fighting capacity of two hundred riflemen and four guns, two twelve-pounder smooth-bores and two howitzers, all that Admiral Porter's three gunboats had to contend with. It proves the utter helplessness of gunboats in narrow streams, when deprived of the protection of troops on the banks. Even the iron-clads, with armor impenetrable by field guns, were readily driven off by sharpshooters, who, under cover, closed their ports or killed every exposed man.

On the 24th Liddel, from the north bank of Red River, dashed into Pineville, opposite Alexandria, killed and captured a score of the enemy's party, and drove the remainder over the river.

On the 27th Admiral Porter's fleet was lying above the falls, now impassable, and Banks's army, over twenty thousand strong, was in and around Alexandria behind earthworks. Such was the condition to which this large force had been reduced by repeated defeat, that we not only confined it to its works, driving back many attacks on our advanced positions, but I felt justified in dividing my little command in order to blockade the river below, and cut off communication with the Mississippi. Wharton's horse was divided into three parts, each a thousand strong, and accompanied by artillery. The first, under Steele, held the river and Rapides roads, above and west of Alexandria; the second, under Bagby, the Bœuf road to the south of that place; while Major, with the third, was sent to Davide's Ferry, on the river, twenty-five miles below. Polignac's infantry, twelve hundred muskets, was posted on the Bœuf within supporting distance of the two last. Liddel's seven hundred newly-organized horse, with four guns, was of little service beyond making feints to distract the enemy.

Major reached his position on the 30th, and on the following day, the 1st of May, captured and sunk the transport Emma. On the 3d he captured the transport City Belle, on her way up to Alexandria, with the 120th Ohio regiment on board. All the officers and two hundred and seventy-six men were taken, with many killed and wounded. On the evening of the 4th the gunboats Covington and Signal, each mounting eight heavy guns, with the transport Warner, attempted to pass. The Covington was blown up by her crew to escape capture, but the Signal and Warner surrendered. Four guns, two three-inch rifled and two howitzers, were engaged in this action with the Covington and Signal. They were run up to the river's bank by hand, the howitzers above, the three-inch rifles below the gunboats, which, overpowered by the rapid fire, moved back and forth until one surrendered and the other was destroyed, affording a complete illustration of the superiority of field guns to gunboats in narrow streams. There was no further attempt to pass Major's position, and Federal communication with the Mississippi was closed for fifteen days.

During these operations the enemy was engaged night and day in the construction of a dam across the Red River, to enable him to pass his fleet over the falls; and the following extracts from the report of Admiral Porter to the Secretary of the Navy well exhibit the condition of affairs in and around Alexandria ("Report on the Conduct of the War," vol. ii., page 250):

"Flag-ship Cricket, Alexandria, *April* 28, 1864.

"Sir: I have written you an account of the operations of the fleet in these waters, but take the liberty of writing to you confidentially the true state of affairs. I find myself blockaded by a fall of three feet of water, three feet four inches being the amount now on the falls. Seven feet being required to get over, no amount of lightening will accomplish the object. I have already written to you how the whole state of things has been changed by a too blind carelessness on the part of our military leader, and our retreat back to Alexandria from place to place has so demoralized General Banks's army that the troops have no confidence in anybody or anything. Our army is now all here, with the best general (Franklin) wounded and unfit for duty in the field. General Banks seems to hold no communication with any one, and it is impossible for me to say what he will do. I have no confidence in his promises, as he asserted in a letter, herein inclosed, that he had no intention of leaving Grand Ecore, when he had actually already made all his preparations to leave. The river is crowded with transports, and every gunboat I have is required to convoy them. I have to withdraw many light-draughts from other points on the Mississippi to supply demands here. In the mean time the enemy are splitting up into parties of two thousand, and bringing in the artillery (with which we have supplied them) to blockade points below here; and what will be the upshot of it all I can not foretell. I know that it will be disastrous in the extreme, for this is a country in which a retreating army is completely at the mercy of an enemy. Notwithstanding that the rebels are reported as coming in from Washita, with heavy artillery to plant on the hills opposite Alexandria, no movement is being made to occupy the position, and I am in momentary expectation of hearing the rebel guns open on the transports on the town side; or if they go down or come up the river, it will be at the risk of destruction. Our light-clads can do nothing against hill batteries. I am in momentary expectation of seeing this army retreat, when the result will be disastrous. Unless instructed by the Government, I do not think that General

Banks will make the least effort to save the navy here. The following vessels are above the falls and command the right of the town : Mound City, Louisville, Pittsburgh, Carondelet, Chillicothe, Osage, Neosho, Ozark, Lexington, and Fort Hindman. At this moment the enemy have attacked our outposts, and driven in our indifferent cavalry, which came up numbering six thousand, and have brought nothing but calamity in their train. Our whole army is cooped up in this town, while a much inferior force is going rampant about the country, making preparations to assail our helpless transports, which, if caught filled with men, would be perfect slaughter-houses. Quick remedies are required, and I deem it my duty to lay the true state of affairs before you. If left here by the army, I will be obliged to destroy this fleet to prevent it falling into the enemy's hands. I can not conceive that the nation will permit such a sacrifice to be made, when men and money can prevent it. We have fought hard for the opening of the Mississippi, and have reduced the naval forces of the rebels in this quarter to two vessels. If we have to destroy what we have here, there will be material enough to build half a dozen iron-clads, and the Red River, which is now of no further dread to us, will require half the Mississippi squadron to watch it. I am apprehensive that the turrets of the monitors will defy any efforts we can make to destroy them. Our prestige will receive a shock from which it will be long in recovering ; and if the calamities I dread should overtake us, the annals of this war will not present so dire a one as will have befallen us."

Thus Admiral Porter, who even understates the facts.

In vain had all this been pointed out to General Kirby Smith, when he came to me at Pleasant Hill in the night after the battle. Granted that he was alarmed for Shreveport, sacred to him and his huge staff as Benares, dwelling-place of many gods, to the Hindoo ; yet, when he marched from that place on the 16th of April against Steele, the latter, already discomfited by Price's horse, was retreating, and, with less than a third of Banks's force at Grand Ecore, was then further from Shreveport than was Banks. To pursue a retreating foe, numbering six thousand men, he took over seven thousand infantry, and left me twelve hundred to operate against twenty odd thousand and a powerful fleet. From the evening of the 21st of April, when I returned to the front near Grand Ecore, to the 13th of May, the day on which Porter and Banks escaped from Alexandria, I kept him advised of the enemy's movements and condition. Couriers and staff officers were sent to implore him to return and reap the fruits of Mansfield and Pleasant Hill, whose price had been paid in blood. Not a man was sent me; even the four-gun battery with Liddell on the north of the river was, without my knowledge, withdrawn toward Arkansas. From first to last, General Kirby Smith seemed determined to throw a protecting shield around the Federal army and fleet.

In all the ages since the establishment of the Assyrian monarchy no commander has possessed equal power to destroy a cause. Far away from the great centers of conflict in Virginia and Georgia, on a remote theatre, the opportunity of striking a blow decisive of the war was afforded. An army that included the strength of every garrison from Memphis to the Gulf had been routed, and, by the incompetency of its commander, was utterly demoralized and ripe for destruction. But this army was permitted to escape, and its 19th corps reached Chesapeake Bay in time to save Washington from General Early's attack, while the 13th, 16th, and 17th corps reënforced Sherman in Georgia. More than all, we lost Porter's fleet, which the falling river had delivered into our hands; for the protection of an army was necessary to its liberation, as without the army a dam at the falls could not have been constructed. With this fleet, or even a portion of it, we would have at once recovered possession of the Mississippi, from the Ohio to the sea, and undone all the work of the Federals since the winter of 1861. Instead of Sherman, Johnston would have been reënforced from west of the Mississippi, and thousands of absent men, with fresh hope, would have rejoined Lee. The Southern people might have been spared the humiliation of defeat, and the countless woes and wrongs inflicted on them by their conquerors.

It was for this that Green and Mouton and other gallant spirits fell! It was for this that the men of Missouri and Arkansas made a forced march to die at Pleasant Hill! It was for this that the divisions of Walker and Polignac had held every position intrusted to them, carried every position in their front, and displayed a constancy and valor worthy of the Guards at Inkermann or Lee's veterans in the Wilderness! For this, too, did the handful left, after our brethren had been taken from us, follow hard on the enemy, attack him constantly at any odds, beat off and sink his gunboats, close the Red River below him and shut up his army in Alexandria for fifteen days! Like "Sister Ann" from her watch tower, day after day we strained our eyes to see the dust of our approaching comrades arise from the north bank of the Red. Not a camp follower among us but knew that the arrival of our men from the North would give us the great prize in sight. Vain, indeed, were our hopes. The commander of the "Trans-Mississippi Department" had the power to destroy the last hope of the Confederate cause, and exercised it with all the success of Bazaine at Metz.

"The affairs of mice and men aft gang aglee," from sheer stupidity and pig-headed obstinacy. General Kirby Smith had publicly announced that Banks's army was too strong to be fought, and that the proper policy was either to defend the works protecting Shreveport, or retreat into Texas. People do not like to lose their reputations as prophets or sons of prophets. Subsequently, it was given out that General Kirby Smith had a wonderful plan for the destruction of the enemy, which I had disturbed by rashly beating his army at Mansfield and Pleasant Hill; but this plan, like Trochu's for the defense of Paris, was never disclosed—undoubtedly, because *c'était le secret de Polichinelle*.

After many days of energetic labor, the enemy on the 13th of May succeeded in passing his fleet over the falls at Alexandria, evacuated the place, and retreated down the river, the army, on the south bank, keeping pace with the fleet. Admiral Porter, in his report to the Secretary of the Navy, gives a graphic account of the passage of the falls, and under date of May 19th, says: " In my report in relation to the release of the gunboats from their unpleasant position above the falls, I did not think it prudent to mention that I was obliged to destroy eleven thirty-two-pounders, not having time to haul them from above the falls to Alexandria, the army having moved and drawn in all their pickets. For the same reason I also omitted to mention that I was obliged to take off the iron from the sides of the Pook gunboats and from the Ozark, to enable them to get over."

To harass the retreat, the horse and artillery, on the river above Alexandria, were directed to press the enemy's rear, and the remaining horse and Polignac's infantry to intercept his route at Avoyelles Prairie. During the 14th, 15th, and 16th he was constantly attacked in front, rear, and right flank; and on the 17th Wharton charged his rear near Mansura, capturing many prisoners, while Colonel Yager, with two regiments of horse, cut in on the wagon train at Yellow Bayou, killed and drove off the guard, and destroyed much property. Meanwhile Liddell, on the north bank of the Red, followed the fleet and kept up a constant fire on the transports. But for the unfortunate withdrawal of his battery, before alluded to, he could have destroyed many of these vessels. On the 18th we attacked the enemy at Yellow Bayou, near Simmsport, and a severe engagement ensued, lasting until night. We held the field, on which the enemy left his dead, but our loss was heavy, four hundred and fifty-two in killed and wounded; among the former, Colonel Stone, commanding Polignac's old brigade. Polignac, in charge of division, was conspicuous in this action. The following day, May 19, 1864, the enemy crossed the Atchafalaya and was beyond our reach. Here, at the place where it had opened more than two months before, the campaign closed.

The army I had the honor to command in this campaign numbered, at its greatest strength, about thirteen thousand of all arms, including Liddell's force on the north bank of Red River; but immediately after the battle of Pleasant Hill it was reduced to fifty-two hundred by the withdrawal of Walker's and Churchill's divisions. Many of the troops marched quite four hundred miles, and from the 5th of April to the 18th of May not a day passed without some engagement with the enemy, either on land or river. Our total loss in killed, wounded, and missing was three thousand nine hundred and seventy-six; that of the enemy, nearly three times this number.

From the action at Yellow Bayou on the 18th of May, 1864, to the close of the war in the following year, not a shot was fired in the "Trans-Mississippi Department." Johnston was forced back to Atlanta and relieved from command, and Atlanta fell. Not even an effective demonstration was made toward Arkansas and Missouri to prevent troops from being sent to reënforce Thomas at Nashville, and Hood was overthrown. Sherman marched unopposed through Georgia and South Carolina, while Lee's gallant army wasted away from cold and hunger in the trenches at Petersburg. Like Augustus in the agony of his spirit, the sorely pressed Confederates on the east of the Mississippi asked, and asked in vain: "Varus! Varus! Where are our legions?"

The enemy's advance, fleet and army, reached Alexandria on the 16th of March, but he delayed sixteen days there and at Grand Ecore. My first reënforcements, two small regiments of horse, joined at Natchitoches on the 31st; but the larger part of Green's force came in at Mansfield on the 6th of April, Churchill's infantry reaching Keachi the same day. Had Banks pushed to Mansfield on the 5th instead of the 8th of April, he would have met but little opposition; and, once at Mansfield, he had the choice of three roads to Shreveport, where Steele could have joined him.

Judging from the testimony given to the Congressional Committee on the Conduct of the War, cotton and elections seem to have been the chief causes of delay. In the second volume of "Report" may be found much crimination and recrimination between the Navy and Army concerning the seizure of cotton. Without attempting to decide the question, I may observe that Admiral Porter informs the Secretary of the Navy of "the capture from the rebels of three thousand bales of cotton on the Washita river, and two thousand on the Red, all of which I have sent to Cairo"; while General Banks testifies that he "took from western Louisiana ten thousand bales of cotton and twenty thousand beef cattle, horses, and mules." From this, the Army appears to have surpassed the navy to the extent of five thousand bales of cotton and the above-mentioned number of beef cattle, etc.   Whether Admiral Porter or General Banks was the more virtuous, the unhappy people of Louisiana were deprived of "cakes and ale."

In his enthusiasm for art the classic cobbler forgot his last; but "all quality, pride, pomp, and circumstance of glorious war" could not make General Banks forget his politics, and he held elections at Alexandria and Grand Ecore.   The General describes with some unction the devotion of the people to the "Union," which was and was to be, to them, "the fount of every blessing."

Says General Banks in his report : " It became necessary to accomplish the evacuation [of Grand Ecore] without the enemy's knowledge.   The conflagration of a portion of the town at the hour appointed for the movement partially frustrated the object."   And further on : " Rumors were circulated freely throughout the camp at Alexandria, that upon the evacuation of the town it would be burned, and a considerable portion of the town was destroyed."   Evidently, these burnings were against the orders of General Banks, who appears to have lost authority over some of his troops.   Moreover, in their rapid flight from Grand Ecore to Monette's Ferry, a distance of forty miles, the Federals burned nearly every house on the road.   In pursuit, we passed the smoking ruins of homesteads, by which stood weeping women and children.   Time for the removal of the most necessary articles of furniture had been refused.   It was difficult to restrain one's inclination to punish the ruffians engaged in this work, a number of whom were captured ; but they asserted, and doubtless with truth, that they were acting under orders.

From the universal testimony of citizens, I learned that

13

General Banks and the officers and men of the 19th corps, Eastern troops, exerted themselves to prevent these outrages, and that the perpetrators were the men of General A. J. Smith's command from Sherman's army. Educated at West Point, this General Smith had long served in the regular army of the United States, and his men were from the West, whose brave sons might well afford kindness to women and babes. A key to their conduct can be found in the " Memoirs " of General W. T. Sherman, the commander who formed them, and whose views are best expressed in his own words.

The city of Atlanta, from which the Confederates had withdrawn, was occupied by Slocum's corps of Sherman's army on the 2d of September, 1864. In vol. ii. of his " Memoirs," page 111, General Sherman says : " I was resolved to make Atlanta a pure military garrison or depot, with no civil population to influence military measures. I gave notice of this purpose as early as the 4th of September, to General Halleck, in a letter concluding with these words : ' If the people raise a howl against my barbarity and cruelty, I will answer that war is war, and not popularity-seeking. If they want peace, they and their relations must stop the war.' " On pages 124–6 appears the correspondence of General Sherman with the mayor and councilmen of Atlanta concerning the removal of citizens, in which the latter write : " We petition you to reconsider the order requiring them to leave Atlanta. It will involve in the aggregate consequences appalling and heartrending. Many poor women are in an advanced state of pregnancy, others now having young children, and whose husbands for the greater part are either in the army, prisoners, or dead. Some say, ' I have such a one sick at my house ; who will wait on them when I am gone ? ' Others say, ' What are we to do ? we have no house to go to, and no means to buy, build, or rent any ; no parents, relatives, or friends to go to.' This being so, how is it possible for the people still here, mostly women and children, to find shelter ? And how can they live through the winter in the woods ? " To this General Sherman replies : " I have your letter of the 11th, in the nature of a petition to revoke my orders removing all the inhabitants from Atlanta. I have read it carefully, and give full credit to your statements of the distress that will be occasioned, and yet shall not revoke my orders, because *they were not intended to meet the humanities of the case.* You might as well appeal against the thunderstorm as against these terrible hardships of war. They are inevitable; and the only way the people of Atlanta can hope once more to live in peace and quiet at home is to stop the war, which can only be done by admitting that it began in error and is perpetuated in pride." Again, on page 152 is Sherman's telegram to General Grant : " Until we can repopulate Georgia, it is useless for us to occupy it; but the utter destruction of its roads, houses, and people will cripple their military resources. I can make this march, and make Georgia howl." It could hardly be expected that troops trained by this commander would respect *the humanities.*

CHAPTER XII.

PROSTRATED by two years of constant devotion to work—work so severe, stern, and exacting as to have prevented me from giving the slightest attention to my family, even when heavily afflicted—and persuaded that under existing administration nothing would be accomplished in the "Trans-Mississippi Department," a month after the close of the Red River campaign I applied for relief from duty. After several applications this was granted, and with my wife and two surviving children I retired to the old Spanish-French town of Natchitoches. The inhabitants, though impoverished by the war, had a comfortable house ready for my family, to which they invited me, with all the warmth of Southern hearts and all the good taste of the Latin race. Here I remained for several weeks, when information of my promotion to lieutenant-general came from Richmond, with orders to report for duty on the east side of the Mississippi. The officers of my staff, who had long served with me, desired and were permitted to accompany me, with the exception of Brent, now colonel of artillery, who could not be spared. Colonel Brent remained in west Louisiana until the close of the war, attaining the rank of brigadier. Of his merit and services I have already written.

The Red River campaign of 1864 was the last Federal campaign undertaken for political objects, or intrusted·to political generals. Experience taught the Washington Government that its enormous resources must be concentrated, and henceforth unity of purpose and action prevailed. Posts on the Mississippi between Memphis and New Orleans were strengthened, intervening spaces closely guarded by numerous gunboats, and parties thrown ashore to destroy all boats that could be found. Though individuals, with precaution, could cross the great river, it was almost impossible to take over organized bodies of troops or supplies, and the Confederates on the west were isolated. The Federal Government now directed its energies against Richmond and Atlanta.

Upon what foundations the civil authorities of the Confederacy rested their hopes of success, after the campaign of 1864 fully opened, I am unable to say; but their commanders in the field, whose rank and position enabled them to estimate the situation, fought simply to afford statesmanship an opportunity to mitigate the sorrows of inevitable defeat.

A grand old oak, on the east bank of the Black River, the lower Washita, protected my couch; and in the morning, with two guides, the faithful Tom following, I threaded my way through swamp and jungle to the Mississippi, which was reached at sunset. A light canoe was concealed some distance from the river bank, and after the short twilight faded into night this was borne on the shoulders of the guides, and launched. One of the guides embarked to paddle, and Tom and I followed, each leading a horse. A gunboat was lying in the river a short distance below, and even the horses seemed to understand the importance of silence, swimming quietly alongside of our frail craft. The eastern shore reached, we stopped for a time to rub and rest the cattle, exhausted by long-continued exertion in the water; then pushed on to Woodville, some five and twenty miles east. This, the chief town of Wilkison county, Mississippi, was in telegraphic communication with Richmond, and I reported my arrival to the war office. An answer came, directing me to take command of the department of Alabama, Mississippi, etc., with the information that President Davis would shortly leave Richmond to meet me at Montgomery, Alabama. While awaiting telegram, I learned of the fall of Atlanta and the forts at the entrance of Mobile Bay. My predecessor in the department to the command of which telegraphic orders had just assigned me was General Bishop Polk, to whom I accord all his titles; for in him, after a sleep of several centuries, was awakened the church militant. Before he joined Johnston in northern Georgia, Polk's headquarters were at Meridian, near the eastern boundary of Mississippi, where the Mobile and Ohio Railway, running north, is crossed by the Vicksburg, Jackson, and Selma line, running east. To this point I at once proceeded, *via* Jackson, more than a hundred miles northeast of Woodville. Grierson's and other "raids," in the past summer, had broken the New Orleans and Jackson Railway, so that I rode the distance to the latter place. It was in September, and the fierce heat was trying to man and beast. The open pine forests of southern Mississippi obstruct the breeze, while affording no protection from the sun, whose rays are intensified by reflection from the white, sandy soil. Jackson reached, I stopped for an hour to see the Governor of Mississippi, Clarke, an old acquaintance, and give instructions to Brigadier Wirt Adams, the local commander; then took rail to Meridian, eighty miles, where I found the records of the department left by General Polk, as well as several officers of the general staff. These gentlemen had nothing especial to do, and appeared to be discharging that duty conscientiously; but they were zealous and intelligent, and speedily enabled me to judge of the situation. Major-General Maury, in immediate command at Mobile, and the senior officer in the department before my arrival, had ordered General Forrest with his cavalry to Mobile in anticipation of an attack. Forrest himself was expected to pass through Meridian that evening, *en route* for Mobile.

Just from the Mississippi river, where facilities for obtaining information from New Orleans were greater than at Mobile, I was confident that the enemy contemplated no immediate attack on the latter place. Accordingly, General Maury was informed by telegraph of my presence, that I assumed command of the department, and would arrest Forrest's movement. An hour later a train from the north, bringing Forrest in advance of his troops, reached Meridian, and was stopped; and the General, whom I had never seen, came to report. He was a tall, stalwart man, with grayish hair, mild countenance, and slow and homely of speech. In few words he was informed that I considered Mobile safe for the present, and that all our energies must be directed to the relief of Hood's army, then west of Atlanta. The only way to accomplish this was to worry Sherman's communications north of the Tennessee river, and he must move his cavalry in that direction at the earliest moment.

To my surprise, Forrest suggested many difficulties and asked numerous questions: how he was to get over the Tennessee; how he was to get back if pressed by the enemy; how he was to be supplied; what should be his line of retreat in certain contingencies; what he was to do with prisoners if any were taken, etc. I began to think he had no stomach for the work; but at last, having isolated the chances of success from causes of failure with the care of a chemist experimenting in his laboratory, he rose and asked for Fleming, the superintendent of the railway, who was on the train by which he had come. Fleming appeared—a little man on crutches (he had recently broken a leg), but with the energy of a giant—and at once stated what he could do in the way of moving supplies on his line, which had been repaired up to the Tennessee boundary. Forrest's whole manner now changed. In a dozen sharp sentences he told his wants, said he would leave a staff officer to bring up his supplies, asked for an engine to take him back north twenty miles to meet his troops, informed me he would march with the dawn, and hoped to give an account of himself in Tennessee.

Moving with great rapidity, he crossed the Tennessee river, captured stockades with their garrisons, burned bridges, destroyed railways, reached the Cumberland River below Nashville, drove away gunboats, captured and destroyed several transports with immense stores, and spread alarm over a wide region. The enemy concentrated on him from all directions, but he eluded or defeated their several columns, recrossed the Tennessee, and brought off fifteen hundred prisoners and much spoil. Like Clive, Nature made him a great soldier; and he was without the former's advantages. Limited as was Clive's education, he was a Porson of erudition compared with Forrest, who read with difficulty. In the last weeks of the war he was much with me, and told me the story of his life. His father, a poor trader in negroes and mules, died when he was fifteen years of age, leaving a widow and several younger children dependent on him for support. To add to his burden, a posthumous infant was born some weeks after the father's death. Continuing the paternal occupations in a small way, he continued to maintain the family and give some education to the younger children. His character for truth, honesty, and energy was recognized, and he gradually achieved independence and aided his brethren to start in life. Such was his short story up to the war.

Some months before the time of our first meeting, with two thousand men he defeated the Federal General Sturgis, who had five times his force, at Tishimingo; and he repeated his success at Okalona, where his opponent, General Smith, had even greater odds against him. The battle of Okalona was fought on an open plain, and Forrest had no advantage of position to compensate for great inferiority of numbers; but it is remarkable that he employed the tactics of Frederick at Leuthen and Zorndorf, though he had never heard these names. Indeed, his tactics deserve the closest study of military men. Asked after the war to what he attributed his success in so many actions, he replied: "Well, I *got there first with the most men.*" Jomini could not have stated the key to the art of war more concisely. I doubt if any commander since the days of lion-hearted Richard has killed as many enemies with his own hand as Forrest. His word of command as he led the charge was unique: "Forward, men, and *mix* with 'em!" But, while cutting down many a foe with long-reaching, nervous arm, his keen eye watched the whole fight and guided him to the weak spot. Yet he was a tender-hearted, kindly man. The accusations of his enemies that he murdered prisoners at Fort Pillow and elsewhere are absolutely false. The prisoners captured on his expedition into Tennessee, of which I have just written, were negroes, and he carefully looked after their wants himself, though in rapid movement and fighting much of the time. These negroes told me of Mass Forrest's kindness to them. After the war I frequently met General Forrest, and received many evidences of attachment from him. He has passed away within a month, to the regret of all who knew him. In the States of Alabama, Mississippi, and Tennessee, to generations yet unborn, his name will be a "household word."

Having devoted several hours at Meridian to the work mentioned, I took rail for Mobile, a hundred and forty miles. This town of thirty thousand inhabitants is situated on the west bank of the Alabama (here called Mobile) River, near its entrance into Mobile Bay, which is five-and-twenty miles long by ten broad. A month before my arrival Admiral Farragut had captured Fort Morgan at the eastern mouth of the bay, after defeating the Confederate fleet under Admiral Buchanan, who was severely wounded in the action. Two or three of Buchanan's vessels had escaped, and were in charge of Commodore Farrand near Mobile. The shallow waters of the bay were thickly planted with torpedoes, and many heavy guns were mounted near the town, making it safe in front. Mobile had excellent communications with the interior. The Alabama, Tombigby, and Black Warrior Rivers afforded steam navigation to central Alabama and eastern Mississippi, while the Mobile and Ohio Railway reached the northern limit of the latter State. Supplies from the fertile "cane-brake" region of Alabama and the prairies of eastern Mississippi were abundant. Before they abandoned Pensacola, the Confederates had taken up fifty miles of rails from the Pensacola and Montgomery line, and used them to make a connection between the latter place and Blakeley, at the eastern head of the bay, opposite Mobile. From the known dispositions of the Federal forces, I did not think it probable that any serious attempt on Mobile would be made until spring. Already in possession of Fort Morgan and Pensacola, thirty miles east of the first, and the best harbor on the Gulf, the enemy, when he attacked, would doubtless make these places his base. It was important, then, to look to defensive works on the east side of the bay, and such works were vigorously pushed at Blakeley, above mentioned, and at Spanish Fort, several miles south. I had no intention of standing a siege in Mobile, but desired to hold the place with a small force, so as to compel the employment of an army to reduce it; and for this its situation was admirably adapted. The Mobile River, forty miles long, and formed by the Alabama and Tombigby, is but the estuary at the head of Mobile Bay, silted up with detritus by the entering streams. Several miles wide, it incloses numerous marshy islands in its many channels. These features make its passage difficult, while the Mobile and Ohio Railway, trending to the west as it leaves the town to gain the high land above the valley, affords a ready means for the withdrawal of a limited force.

The officer commanding at Mobile was well qualified for his task. Major-General D. H. Maury, nephew to the distinguished Matthew Maury, formerly of the United States navy, graduated from West Point in time to serve in the war with Mexico, where he was wounded. A Virginian, he resigned from the United States cavalry to share the fortunes of his State. Intelligent, upright, and devoted to duty, he gained the respect and confidence of the townspeople, and was thereby enabled to supplement his regular force of eight thousand of all arms with a body of local militia. It was a great comfort to find an able officer in this responsible position, who not only adopted my plans, but improved and executed them. General Maury had some excellent officers under him, and the sequel will show how well they discharged their duty to the end.

From Mobile to Meridian, and after some days to Selma, ninety miles east. The railway between these last places had been recently laid down, and was very imperfect. There was no bridge over the Tombigby at Demopolis, and a steam ferry was employed. East of Demopolis, the line passed through the canebrake country, a land of fatness. The army of Lee, starving in the trenches before Richmond and Petersburg, could have been liberally supplied from this district but for lack of transportation.

Here it may be asserted that we suffered less from inferiority of numbers than from want of mechanical resources. Most of the mechanics employed in the South were Northern men, and returned to their section at the outbreak of war. The loss of

New Orleans, our only large city, aggravated this trouble, and we had no means of repairing the long lines of railway, nor the plant. Even when unbroken by raids, wear and tear rendered them inefficient at an early period of the struggle. This had a more direct influence on the sudden downfall of the Confederacy than is generally supposed.

Selma, a place of some five thousand people, is on the north bank of the Alabama River, by which it has steam communication with Mobile and Montgomery, forty miles above on the opposite bank. In addition to the railway from Meridian, there was a line running to the northeast in the direction of Dalton, Georgia, the existing terminus of which was at Blue Mountain, a hundred and odd miles from Selma; and, to inspect the line, I went to Blue Mountain. This, the southern limit of the Alleghanies, which here sink into the great plain of the gulf, was distant from the Atlanta and Chattanooga Railway, Sherman's only line of communication, sixty miles. A force operating from Blue Mountain would approach this line at a right angle, and, drawing its supplies from the fertile country near Selma, would cover its own communications while threatening those of an enemy from Atlanta to Chattanooga. On this account the road might be of importance.

Returning to Selma, I stopped at Talladega, on the east bank of the Coosa River, the largest affluent of the Alabama, and navigable by small steamers to Rome, Georgia. Here I met Brigadier Daniel Adams, in local command, and learned much of the condition of the surrounding region. After passing Chattanooga the Tennessee River makes a great bend to the South, inclosing a part of Alabama between itself and the Tennessee State line; and in this district was a small Confederate force under Brigadier Roddy, which was enabled to maintain an exposed position by knowledge of the country. General Adams thought he could procure wire enough to establish communication with Roddy, or materially shorten the courier line between them; and, as this would duplicate my means of getting news, especially of Forrest, he was directed to do so. I had no knowledge of Hood's plans or condition, saving that he had been defeated and was

southwest of Atlanta; but if he contemplated operations on
Sherman's communications, which was his true policy, he must
draw supplies from Selma, as much of the country between the
Tennessee and Alabama Rivers was sterile and sparsely populated.
Accordingly, I moved my headquarters to Selma and ordered
the collection of supplies there, and at Talladega; then took
steamer for Montgomery, to meet the General Assembly of Alabama, called in extra session in view of the crisis produced by
Hood's defeat and the fall of Atlanta.   Just as the steamer was
leaving Selma, I received dispatches from Forrest, announcing
his first success after crossing the Tennessee river.   Traveling
alone, or with one staff officer, and unknown to the people, I had
opportunities of learning something of the real state of public
sentiment in my new department.   Citizens were universally
depressed and disheartened.   Sick and wounded officers and
men from Hood's army were dissatisfied with the removal of
Johnston from command, and the subsequent conduct of affairs.
From conversations in railway carriages and on river steamers I
had gathered this, and nothing but this, since my arrival.

Reaching Montgomery in the morning, I had interviews
with the Governor and leading members of the Assembly, who
promised all the assistance in their power to aid in the defense
of the State.   The Governor, Watts, who had resigned the
office of Attorney-General of the Confederacy to accept his
present position, was ever ready to coöperate with me.

Late in the afternoon a dispatch was received from President Davis, announcing his arrival for the following morning.
He came, was received by the State authorities, visited the Capitol, addressed the Assembly, and then received leading citizens;
all of which consumed the day, and it was ten o'clock at night
when he took me to his chamber, locked the door, and said we
must devote the night to work, as it was imperative for him to
return to Richmond the next morning.   He began by saying
that he had visited Hood and his army on his way to Montgomery, and was gratified to find officers and men in excellent
spirits, not at all depressed by recent disasters, and that he
thought well of a movement north toward Nashville.   I ex-

pressed surprise at his statement of the condition of Hood's army, as entirely opposed to the conclusions forced on me by all the evidence I could get, and warned him of the danger of listening to narrators who were more disposed to tell what was agreeable than what was true. He readily admitted that persons in his position were exposed to this danger. Proceeding to discuss the suggested movement toward Nashville, I thought it a serious matter to undertake a campaign into Tennessee in the autumn, with troops so badly equipped as were ours for the approaching winter. Every mile the army marched north, it was removing farther from supplies, and no reënforcements were to be hoped for from any quarter. Besides, Sherman could control force enough to garrison Chattanooga and Nashville, and, if time were allowed him to accumulate supplies at Atlanta by his one line of rail, could abandon everything south of Chattanooga, and with fifty thousand men, in the absence of Hood's army, march where he liked. The President asked what assistance might be expected from the trans-Mississippi. I replied, none. There would not be another gun fired there; for the Federals had withdrawn their troops to concentrate east of the river. The difficulty of bringing over organized bodies of men was explained, with the addition of their unwillingness to come. The idea prevailed that the States west of the Mississippi had been neglected by the Government, and this idea had been encouraged by many in authority. So far from desiring to send any more men to the east, they clamored for the return of those already there. Certain senators and representatives, who had bitterly opposed the administration at Richmond, talked much wild nonsense about setting up a government west of the Mississippi, uniting with Maximilian, and calling on Louis Napoleon for assistance. The President listened attentively to this, and asked, "What then?" I informed him of the work Forrest was doing, pointed out the advantages of Blue Mountain as a base from which to operate, and suggested that Hood's army be thrown on Sherman's line of railway, north of Atlanta. As Johnston had been so recently removed from command, I would not venture to recommend his return, but believed that our chances would be increased by the assignment of Beauregard to the army. He still retained some of the early popularity gained at Sumter and Manassas, and would awaken a certain enthusiasm. Apprehending no immediate danger for Mobile, I would strip the place of everything except gunners and join Beauregard with four thousand good troops. Even the smallest reënforcement is inspiriting to a defeated army, and by seizing his railway we would force Sherman to battle. Granting we would be whipped, we could fall back to Blue Mountain without danger of pursuit, as the enemy was chained to his line of supply, and we certainly ought to make the fight hot enough to cripple him for a time and delay his projected movements. At the same time, I did not disguise my conviction that the best we could hope for was to protract the struggle until spring. It was for statesmen, not soldiers, to deal with the future.

The President said Beauregard should come, and, after consultation with Hood and myself, decide the movements of the army; but that he was distressed to hear such gloomy sentiments from me. I replied that it was my duty to express my opinions frankly to him, when he asked for them, though there would be impropriety in giving utterance to them before others; but I did not admit the gloom. In fact, I had cut into this game with eyes wide open, and felt that in staking life, fortune, and the future of my children, the chances were against success. It was not for me, then, to whimper when the cards were bad; that was the right of those who were convinced there would be no war, or at most a holiday affair, in which everybody could display heroism. With much other talk we wore through the night. In the morning he left, as he purposed, and I returned to Selma. My next meeting with President Davis was at Fortress Monroe, under circumstances to be related.

Some days at Selma were devoted to accumulation of supplies, and General Maury was advised that he must be prepared to forward a part of his command to that place, when a message from Beauregard informed me that he was on the way to Blue Mountain and desired to meet me there. He had not seen

Hood, whose army, after an ineffectual attack on Altoona, had left Sherman's line of communication, moved westward, and was now some fifteen miles to the north of Blue Mountain. Having told me this, Beauregard explained the orders under which he was acting. To my disappointment, he had not been expressly assigned to command Hood's army, but to the general direction of affairs in the southwest. General Maury, a capable officer, was at Mobile; Forrest, with his cavalry division, I had sent into Tennessee; and a few scattered men were watching the enemy in various quarters—all together hardly constituting a command for a lieutenant-general, my rank. Unless Beauregard took charge of Hood's army, there was nothing for him to do except to command me. Here was a repetition of 1863. Then Johnston was sent with a roving commission to command Bragg in Tennessee, Pemberton in Mississippi, and others in sundry places. The result was that he commanded nobody, and, when Pemberton was shut up in Vicksburg, found himself helpless, with a handful of troops, at Jackson. To give an officer discretion to remove another from command of an army in the field is to throw upon him the responsibility of doing it, and this should be assumed by the government, not left to an individual.

However, I urged on Beauregard the considerations mentioned in my interview with President Davis, that Sherman had detached to look after Forrest, was compelled to keep garrisons at many points from Atlanta to Nashville, and, if forced to action fifty or sixty miles north of the former place, would be weaker then than we could hope to find him later, after he had accumulated supplies. I mentioned the little reënforcement we could have at once from Mobile, my readiness to take any command, division, brigade, or regiment to which he might assign me, and, above all, the necessity of prompt action. There were two persons present, Colonel Brent, of Beauregard's staff, and Mr. Charles Villeré, a member of the Confederate Congress from Louisiana. The former said all that was proper for a staff officer in favor of my views; the latter, Beauregard's brother-in-law, warmly urged their adoption. The General ordered his horse, to visit Hood, and told me to await intelligence from him. On his return from Hood, he informed me that the army was moving to the northwest, and would cross the Tennessee river near the Muscle Shoals. As this plan of campaign had met the sanction of President Davis, and Hood felt confident of success, he declined to interfere. I could not blame Beauregard ; for it was putting a cruel responsibility on him to supersede a gallant veteran, to whom fortune had been adverse. There was nothing to be said and nothing to be done, saving to discharge one's duty to the bitter end. Hood's line of march would bring him within reach of the Mobile and Ohio Railway in northern Mississippi, and supplies could be sent him by that road. Selma ceased to be of importance, and my quarters were returned to Meridian. Forrest, just back from Tennessee, was advised of Hood's purposes and ordered to coöperate. Maury was made happy by the information that he would lose none of his force, and the usual routine of inspections, papers, etc., occupied the ensuing weeks.

My attention was called about this time to the existence of a wide-spread evil. A practice had grown up of appointing provost-marshals to take private property for public use, and every little post commander exercised the power to appoint such officials. The land swarmed with these vermin, appointed without due authority, or self-constituted, who robbed the people of horses, mules, cattle, corn, and meat. The wretched peasants of the middle ages could not have suffered more from the " free companies" turned loose upon them. Loud complaints came up from State governors and from hundreds of good citizens. I published an order, informing the people that their property was not to be touched unless by authority given by me and in accordance with the forms of law, and they were requested to deal with all violators of the order as with highwaymen. This put an end to the tyranny, which had been long and universally submitted to.

The readiness of submission to power displayed by the American people in the war was astonishing. Our British forefathers transmitted to us respect for law and love of liberty founded upon it; but the influence of universal suffrage seemed to have destroyed all sense of personal manhood, all conception of individual rights. It may be said of the South, that its people submitted to wrong because they were engaged in a fierce struggle with superior force; but what of the North, whose people were fighting for conquest? Thousands were opposed to the war, and hundreds of thousands to its conduct and objects. The wonderful vote received by McClellan in 1864 showed the vast numbers of the Northern minority; yet, so far from modifying in the smallest degree the will and conduct of the majority, this multitude of men dared not give utterance to their real sentiments; and the same was true of the South at the time of secession. Reformers who have tried to improve the morals of humanity, discoverers who have striven to alleviate its physical conditions, have suffered martyrdom at its hands. Years upon years have been found necessary to induce the masses to consider, much less adopt, schemes for their own advantage. A government of numbers, then, is not one of virtue or intelligence, but of force, intangible, irresistible, irresponsible—resembling that of Cæsar depicted by the great historian, which, covering the earth as a pall, reduced all to a common level of abject servitude. For many years scarce a descendant of the colonial gentry in the Eastern States has been elected to public office. To-day they have no existence even as a social force and example. Under the baleful influence of negro suffrage it is impossible to foretell the destiny of the South. Small wonder that pure democracies have ever proved ready to exchange " Demos " for some other tyrant.

Occasional visits for inspection were made to Mobile, where Maury was strengthening his defenses. On the east side of the bay, Blakeley and Spanish Fort were progressing steadily, as I held that the enemy would attack there, tempted by his possession of Pensacola and Fort Morgan. Although this opinion was justified in the end, hope may have had some influence in its formation; for we could meet attack from that quarter better than from the west, which, indeed, would have speedily driven us from the place. The loss of the Mobile and Ohio

14

railway would have necessitated the withdrawal of the garrison across the bay, a difficult operation, if pressed by superior force.

The Confederate Congress had enacted that negro troops, captured, should be restored to their owners. We had several hundreds of such, taken by Forrest in Tennessee, whose owners could not be reached ; and they were put to work on the fortifications at Mobile, rather for the purpose of giving them healthy employment than for the value of the work. I made it a point to visit their camps and inspect the quantity and quality of their food, always found to be satisfactory. On one occasion, while so engaged, a fine-looking negro, who seemed to be leader among his comrades, approached me and said : " Thank you, Massa General, they give us plenty of good victuals ; but how you like our work ? " I replied that they had worked very well. " If you will give us guns we will fight for these works, too. We would rather fight for our own white folks than for strangers." And, doubtless, this was true. In their dealings with the negro the white men of the South should ever remember that no instance of outrage occurred during the war. Their wives and little ones remained safe at home, surrounded by thousands of faithful slaves, who worked quietly in the fields until removed by the Federals. This is the highest testimony to the kindness of the master and the gentleness of the servant ; and all the dramatic talent prostituted to the dissemination of falsehood in " Uncle Tom's Cabin " and similar productions can not rebut it.

About the middle of November I received from General Lee, now commanding the armies of the Confederacy, instructions to visit Macon and Savannah, Georgia, if I could leave my department, and report to him the condition of affairs in that quarter, and the probabilities of Sherman's movements, as the latter had left Atlanta. I proceeded at once, taking rail at Montgomery, and reached Macon, *via* Columbus, Georgia, at dawn. It was the bitterest weather I remember in this latitude. The ground was frozen and some snow was falling. General Howell Cobb, the local commander, met me at the station and took me to his house, which was also his office. Arrived there, horses appeared, and Cobb said he supposed that I would desire to ride out and inspect the fortifications, on which he had been at work all night, as the enemy was twelve miles north of Macon at noon of the preceding day. I asked what force he had to defend the place. He stated the number, which was utterly inadequate, and composed of raw conscripts. Whereupon I declined to look at the fortifications, and requested him to order work upon them to be stopped, so that his men could get by a fire, as I then was and intended to remain. I had observed a movement of stores in passing the railway station, and now expressed the opinion that Macon was the safest place in Georgia, and advised Cobb to keep his stores. Here entered General Mackall, one of Cobb's subordinates, who was personally in charge of the defensive works, and could not credit the order he had received to stop. Cobb referred him to me, and I said : " The enemy was but twelve miles from you at noon of yesterday. Had he intended coming to Macon, you would have seen him last evening, before you had time to strengthen works or remove stores." This greatly comforted Cobb, who up to that moment held me to be a lunatic. Breakfast was suggested, to which I responded with enthusiasm, having been on short commons for many hours. While we were enjoying the meal, intelligence was brought that the enemy had disappeared from the north of Macon and marched eastward. Cobb was delighted. He pronounced me to be the wisest of generals, and said he knew nothing of military affairs, but had entered the service from a sense of duty.

Cobb had been Speaker of the United States House of Representatives, and Secretary of the Treasury in the administration of President Buchanan. Beloved and respected in his State, he had been sent to Georgia to counteract the influence of Governor Joe Brown, who, carrying out the doctrine of State rights, had placed himself in opposition to President Davis. Cobb, with his conscripts, had been near Atlanta before Sherman moved out, and gave me a laughable account of the expeditious manner in which he and " his little party " got to Macon, just as he was inditing a superb dispatch to General Lee to inform him of the impossibility of Sherman's escape.

While we were conversing Governor Brown was announced, as arrived from Milledgeville, the State capital, forty miles to the northeast. Cobb remarked that it was awkward; for Governor Brown was the only man in Georgia to whom he did not speak. But he yielded to the ancient jest, that for the time being we had best hang together, as there seemed a possibility of enjoying that amusement separately, and brought the Governor in, who told me that he had escaped from Milledgeville as the Federals entered. People said that he had brought off his cow and his cabbages, and left the State's property to take care of itself. However, Governor Brown deserves praise at my hands, for he promptly acceded to all my requests. With him were General Robert Toombs, the most original of men, and General G. W. Smith, both of whom had been in the Confederate army. Toombs had resigned to take the place of Adjutant-General of Georgia; Smith, to superintend some iron works, from which he had been driven by Sherman's movements, and was now in command of Governor Brown's "army," composed of men that he had refused to the Confederate service. This "army" had some hours before marched east toward Savannah, taking the direct route along the railway. I told the Governor that his men would be captured unless they were called back at once; and Smith, who undertook the duty in person, was just in time. "Joe Brown's army" struck the extreme right of Sherman, and suffered some loss before Smith could extricate it. To Albany, ninety miles south of Macon, there was a railway, and some forty miles farther south, across the country, Thomasville was reached. Here was the terminus of the Savannah and Gulf Railway, two hundred miles, or thereabouts, southwest of Savannah. This route I decided to take, and suggested it to the Governor as the only safe one for his troops. He acquiesced at once, and Toombs promised to have transportation ready by the time Smith returned. Taking leave of Cobb, I departed.

Several years after the close of the war General Cobb and I

happened to be in New York, accompanied by our families, but stopping at different inns. He dined with me, seemed in excellent health and spirits, and remained to a late hour, talking over former times and scenes. I walked to his lodgings with him, and promised to call with my wife on Mrs. Cobb the following day at 1 o'clock. We were there at the hour, when the servant, in answer to my request to take up our cards, stated that General Cobb had just fallen dead. I sprang up the stair, and saw his body lying on the floor of a room, his wife, dazed by the shock, looking on. A few minutes before he had written a letter and started for the office of the inn to post it, remarking to his wife that he would return immediately, as he expected our visit. A step from the threshold, and he was dead. Thus suddenly passed away one of the most genial and generous men I have known. His great fortune suffered much by the war, but to the last he shared its remains with less fortunate friends.

Traveling all night, I reached Thomasville in the early morning, and found that there was telegraphic communication with General Hardee at Savannah, whom I informed of my presence and requested to send down transportation for Governor Brown's troops. There was much delay at Thomasville, the railway people appearing to think that Sherman was swarming all over Georgia. At length I discovered an engine and a freight van, which the officials promised to get ready for me; but they were dreadfully slow, until Toombs rode into town and speedily woke them up. Smith returned to Macon after my departure, found transportation ready for his men, brought them to Albany by rail, and was now marching to Thomasville. Toombs, who had ridden on in advance, was not satisfied with Hardee's reply to my dispatch, but took possession of the telegraph and threatened dire vengeance on superintendents and road masters if they failed to have the necessary engines and carriages ready in time. He damned the dawdling creatures who had delayed me to such an extent as to make them energetic, and my engine appeared, puffing with anxiety to move. He assured me that he would not be many hours after me at

Savannah, for Smith did not intend to halt on the road, as his men could rest in the carriages. A man of extraordinary energy, this same Toombs.

Savannah was reached about midnight, and Hardee was awaiting me. A short conversation cleared the situation and enabled me to send the following report to General Lee. Augusta, Georgia, held by General Bragg with a limited force, was no longer threatened, as the enemy had passed south of it. Sherman, with sixty or seventy thousand men, was moving on the high ground between the Savannah and Ogeechee Rivers; and as this afforded a dry, sandy road direct to Savannah, where he would most readily meet the Federal fleet, it was probable that he would adhere to it. He might cross the Savannah river forty or fifty miles above and march on Charleston, but this was hardly to be expected; for, in addition to the river named, there were several others and a difficult country to pass before Charleston could be reached, and his desire to communicate with the fleet by the nearest route and in the shortest time must be considered. Hardee's force was inadequate to the defense of Savannah, and he should prepare to abandon the place before he was shut up. Uniting, Bragg and Hardee should call in the garrison from Charleston, and all scattered forces along the coast south of Wilmington, North Carolina, and be prepared to resist Sherman's march through the Carolinas, which he must be expected to undertake as soon as he had established a base on the ocean. Before this report was dispatched, Hardee read and approved it.

Meanwhile scores of absurd rumors about the enemy came in. Places I had passed within an hour were threatened by heavy columns; others, from which the enemy was distant a hundred miles, were occupied, etc. But one of importance did come. The railway from Savannah to Charleston passes near the coast. The officer commanding at Pocotaligo, midway of the two places, reported an advance of the enemy from Port Royal, and that he must abandon his post the following morning unless reënforced. To lose the Charleston line would seriously interfere with the concentration just recommended.

Hardee said that he could ill spare men, and had no means of moving them promptly. I bethought me of Toombs, Smith, and Governor Brown's "army." The energetic Toombs had frightened the railway people into moving him, and, from his telegrams, might be expected before dawn. Hardee thought but little of the suggestion, because the ground of quarrel between Governor Brown and President Davis was the refusal of the former to allow his guards to serve beyond their state. However, I had faith in Toombs and Smith. A short distance to the south of Savannah, on the Gulf road, was a switch by which carriages could be shunted on to a connection with the Charleston line. I wrote to Toombs of the emergency, and sent one of Hardee's staff to meet him at the switch. The governor's army was quietly shunted off and woke up at Pocotaligo in South Carolina, where it was just in time to repulse the enemy after a spirited little action, thereby saving the railway. Doubtless the Georgians, a plucky people, would have responded to an appeal to leave their State under the circumstances, but Toombs enjoyed the joke of making them unconscious patriots.

In the past autumn Cassius Clay of Kentucky killed a colored man who had attacked him. For more than thirty years Mr. Clay had advocated the abolition of slavery, and at the risk of his life. Dining with Toombs in New York just after the event, he said to me: "Seen the story about old Cassius Clay? Been an abolitionist all his days, and ends by shooting a nigger. I knew he would." A droll fellow is Robert Toombs. Full of talent and well instructed, he affects quaint and provincial forms of speech. His influence in Georgia is great, and he is a man to know.

Two days at Savannah served to accomplish the object of my mission, and, taking leave of Hardee, I returned to my own department. An educated soldier of large experience, Hardee was among the best of our subordinate generals, and, indeed, seemed to possess the requisite qualities for supreme command; but this he steadily refused, alleging his unfitness for responsibility. Such modesty is not a common American weakness, and deserves to be recorded. General Hardee's death occurred after the close of the war.

In this journey through Georgia, at Andersonville, I passed in sight of a large stockade inclosing prisoners of war. The train stopped for a few moments, and there entered the carriage, to speak to me, a man who said his name was *Wirtz*, and that he was in charge of the prisoners near by. He complained of the inadequacy of his guard and of the want of supplies, as the adjacent region was sterile and thinly populated. He also said that the prisoners were suffering from cold, were destitute of blankets, and that he had not wagons to supply fuel. He showed me duplicates of requisitions and appeals for relief that he had made to different authorities, and these I indorsed in the strongest terms possible, hoping to accomplish some good. I know nothing of this Wirtz, whom I then met for the first and only time, but he appeared to be earnest in his desire to mitigate the condition of his prisoners. There can be but little doubt that his execution was a "sop" to the passions of the "many-headed."

Returned to Meridian, the situation of Hood in Tennessee absorbed all my attention. He had fought at Franklin, and was now near Nashville. Franklin was a bloody affair, in which Hood lost many of his best officers and troops. The previous evening, at dusk, a Federal column, retreating north, passed within pistol-shot of Hood's forces, and an attack on it might have produced results; but it reached strong works at Franklin, and held them against determined assaults, until night enabled it to withdraw quietly to Nashville. This mistake may be ascribed to Hood's want of physical activity, occasioned by severe wounds and amputations, which might have been considered before he was assigned to command. Maurice of Saxe won Fontenoy in a litter, unable from disease to mount his horse; but in war it is hazardous to convert exceptions into rules.

Notwithstanding his frightful loss at Franklin, Hood followed the enemy to Nashville, and took position south of the place, where he remained ten days or more. It is difficult to imagine what objects he had in view. The town was open to the north, whence the Federal commander, Thomas, was hourly receiving reënforcements, while he had none to hope for. His plans perfected and his reënforcements joined, Thomas moved, and Hood was driven off; and, had the Federal general possessed dash equal to his tenacity and caution, one fails to see how Hood could have brought man or gun across the Tennessee River. It is painful to criticise Hood's conduct of this campaign. Like Ney, " the bravest of the brave," he was a splendid leader in battle, and as a brigade or division commander unsurpassed; but, arrived at higher rank, he seems to have been impatient of control, and openly disapproved of Johnston's conduct of affairs between Dalton and Atlanta. Unwillingness to obey is often interpreted by governments into capacity for command.

Reaching the southern bank of the Tennessee, Hood asked to be relieved, and a telegraphic order assigned me to the duty. At Tupelo, on the Mobile and Ohio Railway, a hundred and odd miles north of Meridian, I met him and the remains of his army. Within my experience were assaults on positions, in which heavy losses were sustained without success; but the field had been held—retreats, but preceded by repulse of the foe and followed by victory. This was my first view of a beaten army, an army that for four years had shown a constancy worthy of the " Ten Thousand "; and a painful sight it was. Many guns and small arms had been lost, and the ranks were depleted by thousands of prisoners and missing. Blankets, shoes, clothing, and accouterments were wanting. I have written of the unusual severity of the weather in the latter part of November, and it was now near January. Some men perished by frost; many had the extremities severely bitten. Fleming, the active superintendent mentioned, strained the resources of his railway to transport the troops to the vicinity of Meridian, where timber for shelter and fuel was abundant and supplies convenient; and every energy was exerted to reëquip them.

Sherman was now in possession of Savannah, but an interior line of rail by Columbus, Macon, and Augusta, Georgia, and Columbia, South Carolina, was open. Mobile was not immediately threatened, and was of inferior importance as compared with the safety of Lee's army at Petersburg. Unless a force could be interposed between Sherman and Lee's rear, the game would be over when the former moved. Accordingly, I dispatched to General Lee the suggestion of sending the " Army of Tennessee " to North Carolina, where Johnston had been restored to command. He approved, and directed me to send forward the men as 'rapidly as possible. I had long dismissed all thought of the future. The duty of a soldier in the field is simple—to fight until stopped by the civil arm of his government, or his government has ceased to exist; and military men have usually come to grief by forgetting this simple duty.

Forrest had fought and worked hard in this last Tennessee campaign, and his division of cavalry was broken down. By brigades it was distributed to different points in the prairie and cane-brake regions, where forage could be had, and I hoped for time to restore the cattle and refit the command. With our limited resources of transportation, it was a slow business to forward troops to Johnston in North Carolina; but at length it was accomplished, and the month of March came round to raise the curtain for the last act of the bloody drama. Two clouds appeared on the horizon of my department. General Canby, a steady soldier, whom I had long known, had assumed command of all the Federal forces in the southwest, and was concentrating fifty thousand men at Fort Morgan and Pensacola against Mobile. In northern Alabama General Wilson had ten thousand picked mounted men ready for an expedition. At Selma was a foundry, where the best ordnance I have seen was made of Briarsfield iron, from a furnace in the vicinity; and, as this would naturally attract the enemy's attention to Selma, I endeavored to prepare for him. The Cahawba River, from the northeast, enters the Alabama below Selma, north of which it separates the barren mineral region from the fertile lands of the river basin; and at its crossing I directed Forrest to concentrate.

Wilson, with the smallest body, would probably move first; and, once disposed of, Forrest could be sent south of the Alabama

River to delay Canby and prolong the defense of Mobile. For a hundred miles north of the gulf the country is sterile, pine forest on a soil of white sand; but the northern end of the Montgomery and Pensacola Railway was in our possession, and would enable us to transport supplies. In a conference with Maury at Mobile I communicated the above to him, as I had previously to Forrest, and hastened to Selma. Distributed for forage, and still jaded by hard work, Forrest ordered his brigades to the Cahawba crossing, leading one in person. His whole force would have been inferior to Wilson's, but he was a host in himself, and a dangerous adversary to meet at any reasonable odds.

Our information of the enemy had proved extremely accurate; but in this instance the Federal commander moved with unusual rapidity, and threw out false signals. Forrest, with one weak brigade, was in the path; but two of his brigadiers permitted themselves to be deceived by reports of the enemy's movements toward Columbus, Mississippi, and turned west, while another went into camp under some misconception of orders. Forrest fought as if the world depended on his arm, and sent to advise me of the deceit practiced on two of his brigades, but hoped to stop the enemy if he could get up the third, the absence of which he could not account for. I directed such railway plant as we had to be moved out on the roads, retaining a small yard engine to take me off at the last moment. There was nothing more to be done. Forrest appeared, horse and man covered with blood, and announced the enemy at his heels, and that I must move at once to escape capture. I felt anxious for him, but he said he was unhurt and would cut his way through, as most of his men had done, whom he had ordered to meet him west of the Cahawba. My engine started toward Meridian, and barely escaped. Before headway was attained the enemy was upon us, and capture seemed inevitable. Fortunately, the group of horsemen near prevented their comrades from firing, so we had only to risk a fusillade from a dozen, who fired wild. The driver and stoker, both negroes, were as game as possible, and as we thundered across Cahawba bridge, all safe, raised a loud "Yah! yah!" of triumph, and smiled like two sable angels.

Wilson made no delay at Selma, but, crossing the Alabama River, pushed on to Montgomery, and thence into Georgia. I have never met this General Wilson, whose soldierly qualities are entitled to respect; for of all the Federal expeditions of which I have any knowledge, his was the best conducted.

It would have been useless to pursue Wilson, had there been troops disposable, as many hundred miles intervened between him and North Carolina, where Johnston commanded the nearest Confederate forces, too remote to be affected by his movements. Canby was now before the eastern defenses of Mobile, and it was too late to send Forrest to that quarter. He was therefore directed to draw together and reorganize his division near Meridian.

CHAPTER XIII.

On the 26th of March Canby invested Spanish Fort, and began the siege by regular approaches, a part of his army investing Blakeley on the same day. General R. L. Gibson, now a member of Congress from Louisiana, held Spanish Fort with twenty-five hundred men. Fighting all day and working all night, Gibson successfully resisted the efforts of the immense force against him until the evening of April 8, when the enemy effected a lodgment threatening his only route of evacuation. Under instructions from Maury, he withdrew his garrison in the night to Mobile, excepting his pickets, necessarily left. Gibson's stubborn defense and skillful retreat make this one of the best achievements of the war. Although invested on the 26th of March, the siege of Blakeley was not pressed until April 1, when Steele's corps of Canby's army joined the original force before it. Here, with a garrison of twenty-eight hundred men, commanded General Liddell, with General Cockrell, now a Senator from Missouri, as his second. Every assault of the enemy, who made but little progress, was gallantly repulsed until the afternoon of the 9th, when, learning by the evacuation of Spanish Fort how small a force had delayed him, he concentrated on Blakeley and carried it, capturing the garrison. Maury intended to withdraw Liddell during the night of the 9th. It would have been more prudent to have done so on the night of the 8th, as the enemy would naturally make an energetic effort after the fall of Spanish Fort; but he was unwilling to yield any ground until the last moment, and felt confident of holding the place another day. After dismantling his works, Maury marched out of Mobile on the 12th of April, with forty-five hundred men, including three field batteries, and was directed to Cuba Station, near Meridian. In the interest of the thirty thousand non-combatants of the town, he properly notified the enemy that the place was open. During the movement from Mobile toward Meridian occurred the last engagement of the civil war, in a cavalry affair between the Federal advance and our rear guard under Colonel Spence. Commodore Farrand took his armed vessels and all the steamers in the harbor up the Tombigby River, above its junction with the Alabama, and planted torpedoes in the stream below. Forrest and Maury had about eight thousand men, but tried and true. Cattle were shod, wagons overhauled, and every preparation for rapid movement made.

From the North, by wire and courier, I received early intelligence of passing events. Indeed, these were of a character for the enemy to disseminate rather than suppress. Before Maury left Mobile I had learned of Lee's surrender, rumors of which spreading among the troops, a number from the neighboring camps came to see me. I confirmed the rumor, and told them the astounding news, just received, of President Lincoln's assassination. For a time they were silent with amazement, then asked if it was possible that any Southern man had committed the act. There was a sense of relief expressed when they learned that the wretched assassin had no connection with the South, but was an actor, whose brains were addled by tragedies and Plutarch's fables.

It was but right to tell these gallant, faithful men the whole truth concerning our situation. The surrender of Lee left us little hope of success; but while Johnston remained in arms we must be prepared to fight our way to him. Again, the President and civil authorities of our Government were on their way to the south, and might need our protection. Granting the cause for which we had fought to be lost, we owed it to our own manhood, to the memory of the dead, and to the honor of our arms, to remain steadfast to the last. This was received, not with noisy cheers, but solemn murmurs of approval, showing

that it was understood and adopted. Forrest and Maury shared
my opinions and objects, and impressed them on their men.
Complete order was maintained throughout, and public property
protected, though it was known later that this would be turned
over to the Federal authorities. A considerable amount of gold
was near our camps, and safely guarded ; yet it is doubtful if our
united means would have sufficed to purchase a breakfast.

Members of the Confederate Congress from the adjoining
and more western States came to us. These gentlemen had
left Richmond very hurriedly, in the first days of April, and
were sorely jaded by fatigue and anxiety, as the presence of
Wilson's troops in Georgia had driven them to by-paths to
escape capture. Arrived at a well-ordered camp, occupied by a
formidable-looking force, they felt as storm-tossed mariners in a
harbor of refuge, and, ignorant of recent events, as well as uncertain of the future, were eager for news and counsel. The
struggle was virtually over, and the next few days, perhaps
hours, would decide my course. In my judgment it would
speedily become their duty to go to their respective homes.
They had been the leaders of the people, had sought and
accepted high office at their hands, and it was for them to teach
the masses, by example and precept, how best to meet impending troubles. Possibly they might suffer annoyance and perse-
cution from Federal power, but manhood and duty required
them to incur the risk. To the credit of these gentlemen it
should be recorded that they followed this advice when the time
for action came. There was one exception which deserves
mention.

Ex-Governor Harris, now a United States Senator from
Tennessee, occupied the executive chair of his State in 1862,
and withdrew from Nashville when the army of General Sidney
Johnston retreated to the Tennessee River in the spring of that
year. By the death of President Lincoln, Andrew Johnson had
succeeded to power, and he was from Tennessee, and the personal enemy of Governor Harris. The relations of their State
with the Federal Union had been restored, and Harris's return
would be productive of discord rather than peace. I urged him

to leave the country for a time, and offered to aid him in crossing the Mississippi River; but he was very unwilling to go, and only consented after a matter was arranged, which I anticipate the current of events to relate. He had brought away from Nashville the coin of the Bank of Tennessee, which, as above mentioned, was now in our camp. An official of the bank had always been in immediate charge of this coin, but Harris felt that honor was involved in its safe return. At my request, General Canby detailed an officer and escort to take the coin to Nashville, where it arrived intact; but the unhappy official accompanying it was incarcerated for his fidelity. Had he betrayed his trust, he might have received rewards instead of stripes. 'Tis dangerous to be out of harmony with the practices of one's time.

Intelligence of the Johnston-Sherman convention reached us, and Canby and I were requested by the officers making it to conform to its terms until the civil authorities acted. A meeting was arranged to take place a few miles north of Mobile, where the appearance of the two parties contrasted the fortunes of our respective causes. Canby, who preceded me at the appointed spot, a house near the railway, was escorted by a brigade with a military band, and accompanied by many officers in "full fig." With one officer, Colonel William Levy, since a member of Congress from Louisiana, I made my appearance on a hand-car, the motive power of which was two negroes. Descendants of the ancient race of Abraham, dealers in cast-off raiment, would have scorned to bargain for our rusty suits of Confederate gray. General Canby met me with much urbanity. We retired to a room, and in a few moments agreed upon a truce, terminable after forty-eight hours' notice by either party. Then, rejoining the throng of officers, introductions and many pleasant civilities passed. I was happy to recognize Commodore (afterward Admiral) James Palmer, an old friend. He was second to Admiral Thatcher, commanding United States squadron in Mobile Bay, and had come to meet me. A bountiful luncheon was spread, of which we partook, with joyous poppings of champagne corks for accompaniment, the first agreeable explo-

sive sounds I had heard for years. The air of " Hail Columbia,"
which the band in attendance struck up, was instantly changed
by Canby's order to that of " Dixie " ; but I insisted on the first,
and expressed a hope that Columbia would be again a happy
land, a sentiment honored by many libations.

There was, as ever, a skeleton at the feast, in the person of
a general officer who had recently left Germany to become a
citizen and soldier of the United States. This person, with the
strong accent and idioms of the Fatherland, comforted me by
assurances that we of the South would speedily recognize our
ignorance and errors, especially about slavery and the rights of
States, and rejoice in the results of the war. In vain Canby
and Palmer tried to suppress him. On a celebrated occasion an
Emperor of Germany proclaimed himself above grammar, and
this earnest philosopher was not to be restrained by canons of
taste. I apologized meekly for my ignorance, on the ground
that my ancestors had come from England to Virginia in 1608,
and, in the short intervening period of two hundred and fifty-
odd years, had found no time to transmit to me correct ideas of
the duties of American citizenship. Moreover, my grandfather,
commanding the 9th Virginia regiment in our Revolutionary
army, had assisted in the defeat and capture of the Hessian
mercenaries at Trenton, and I lamented that he had not, by
association with these worthies, enlightened his understanding.
My friend smiled blandly, and assured me of his willingness to
instruct me. Happily for the world, since the days of Huss
and Luther, neither tyranny nor taste can repress the Teutonic
intellect in search of truth or exposure of error. A kindly,
worthy people, the Germans, but wearing on occasions.

The party separated, Canby for Mobile, I for Meridian,
where within two days came news of Johnston's surrender in
North Carolina, the capture of President Davis in Georgia,
and notice from Canby that the truce must terminate, as his
Government disavowed the Johnston-Sherman convention. I
informed General Canby that I desired to meet him for the
purpose of negotiating a surrender of my forces, and that Commodore Farrand would accompany me to meet Admiral Thatcher.

15

The military and civil authorities of the Confederacy had fallen, and I was called to administer on the ruins as residuary legatee. It seemed absurd for the few there present to continue the struggle against a million of men. We could only secure honorable interment for the remains of our cause—a cause that for four years had fixed the attention of the world, been baptized in the blood of thousands, and whose loss would be mourned in bitter tears by countless widows and orphans throughout their lives. At the time, no doubts as to the propriety of my course entered my mind, but such have since crept in. Many Southern warriors, from the hustings and in print, have declared that they were anxious to die in the last ditch, and by implication were restrained from so doing by the readiness of their generals to surrender. One is not permitted to question the sincerity of these declarations, which have received the approval of public opinion by the elevation of the heroes uttering them to such offices as the people of the South have to bestow; and popular opinion in our land is a court from whose decisions there is no appeal on this side of the grave.

On the 8th of May, 1865, at Citronelle, forty miles north of Mobile, I delivered the epilogue of the great drama in which I had played a humble part. The terms of surrender demanded and granted were consistent with the honor of our arms; and it is due to the memory of General Canby to add that he was ready with suggestions to soothe our military pride. Officers retained their side arms, mounted men their horses, which in our service were private property; and public stores, ordnance, commissary, and quartermaster, were to be turned over to officers of the proper departments and receipted for. Paroles of the men were to be signed by their officers on rolls made out for the purpose, and I was to retain control of railways and river steamers to transport the troops as nearly as possible to their homes and feed them on the road, in order to spare the destitute people of the country the burden of their maintenance. Railways and steamers, though used by the Confederate authorities, were private property, and had been taken by force which the owners could not resist; and it was agreed that they should not be seized by civil jackals following the army without special orders from Washington. Finally, I was to notify Canby when to send his officers to my camp to receive paroles and stores.

Near the Tombigby River, to the east of Meridian, were many thousands of bales of cotton, belonging to the Confederate Government and in charge of a treasury agent. It seemed to me a duty to protect public property and transfer it to the United States, successors by victory to the extinct Confederacy. Accordingly, a guard had been placed over this cotton, though I hated the very name of the article, as the source of much corruption to our people. Canby remarked that cotton had been a curse to his side as well, and he would send to New Orleans for a United States Treasury agent, so that we might rid ourselves of this at the earliest moment. The conditions of surrender written out and signed, we had some conversation about the state of the country, disposition of the people, etc. I told him that all were weary of strife, and he would meet no opposition in any quarter, and pointed out places in the interior where supplies could be had, recommending him to station troops at such places. I was persuaded that moderation by his officers and men would lead to intercourse, traffic, and good feeling with the people. He thanked me for the suggestions, and adopted them.

The Governors of Mississippi and Alabama, Clarke and Watts, had asked for advice in the emergency produced by surrender, which they had been informed was impending, and I thought their best course would be to summon their State Legislatures. These would certainly provide for conventions of the people to repeal ordinances of secession and abolish slavery, thus smoothing the way for the restoration of their States to the Union. Such action would be in harmony with the theory and practice of the American system, and clear the road of difficulties. The North, by its Government, press, and people, had been declaring for years that the war was for the preservation of the Union and for nothing else, and Canby and I, in the innocence of our hearts, believed it. As Canby thought well of my plan, I communicated with the Governors, who acted on it; but the

Washington authorities imprisoned them for abetting a new rebellion.

Returned to Meridian, I was soon ready for the Federal officers, who came quietly to our camp and entered on their appointed work; and I have now in my possession receipts given by them for public stores. Meanwhile, I received from Canby a letter informing me that he had directed two of his corps commanders, Generals Steele and Granger, to apply to me for instructions concerning the movement of their troops, as to time, places, and numbers. It was queer for one to be placed in *quasi* command of soldiers that he had been fighting for four years, and to whom he had surrendered; but I delicately made some suggestions to these officers, which were adopted.

With two or three staff officers, I remained at Meridian until the last man had departed, and then went to Mobile. General Canby most considerately took me, Tom, and my two horses on his boat to New Orleans; else I must have begged my way. The Confederate paper (not currency, for it was without exchangeable value) in my pocket would not have served for traveling expenses; and my battered old sword could hardly be relied on for breakfasts, dinners, and horse feed.

After an absence of four years, I saw my native place and home, New Orleans. My estate had been confiscated and sold, and I was without a penny. The man of Uz admitted that naked he came into the world, and naked must leave it; but to find himself naked in the midst of it tried even his patience. My first care was to sell my horses, and a purchaser was found who agreed to take and pay for them the following morning. I felt somewhat eager to get hold of the " greenbacks," and suffered for my avarice. The best horse, one that had carried me many a weary mile and day without failing, could not move a hoof when the purchaser came to take him. Like other veterans, long unaccustomed to abundance of prog, he had overfed and was badly foundered. Fortunately, the liveryman proposed to take this animal as a consideration for the keep of the two, and the price received for the other would suffice to bring my wife and children from the Red River to New Orleans, and was sent to them for that purpose.

Awaiting the arrival of my family, I had a few days of rest at the house of an old friend, when Generals Price, Buckner, and Brent came from Shreveport, the headquarters of the "Trans-Mississippi Department," under flag of truce, and sent for me. They reported a deplorable condition of affairs in that region. Many of the troops had taken up the idea that it was designed to inveigle them into Mexico, and were greatly incensed. Some generals of the highest rank had found it convenient to fold their tents and quietly leave for the Rio Grande; others, who remained, were obliged to keep their horses in their quarters and guard them in person; and numbers of men had disbanded and gone off. By a meeting of officers, the gentlemen present were deputed to make a surrender and ask for Federal troops to restore order. The officers in question requested me to be present at their interview with General Canby, who also invited me, and I witnessed the conclusion. So, from the Charleston Convention to this point, I shared the fortunes of the Confederacy, and can say, as Grattan did of Irish freedom, that I "sat by its cradle and followed its hearse."

For some weeks after my return to New Orleans, I had various occasions to see General Canby on matters connected with the surrender, and recall no instance in which he did not conform to my wishes. Narrow perhaps in his view, and harsh in discharge of duty, he was just, upright, and honorable, and it was with regret that I learned of his murder by a band of Modoc savages.

CHAPTER XIV.

The military collapse of the South was sudden and unexpected to the world without, but by no means so to some within. I happen to know that one or two of our ablest and most trusted generals concurred with me in opinion that the failure at Gettysburg and the fall of Vicksburg in July, 1863, should have taught the Confederate Government and people the necessity of estimating the chances for defeat; but soldiers in the field can not give utterance to such opinions unless expressly solicited by the civil head of their government, and even then are liable to misconstruction.

Of many of the important battles of the civil war I have written, and desire to dwell somewhat on Shiloh, but will first say a few words about Gettysburg, because of recent publications thereanent.

Some facts concerning this battle are established beyond dispute. In the first day's fighting a part of Lee's army defeated a part of Meade's. Intending to continue the contest on that field, a commander not smitten by idiocy would desire to concentrate and push the advantage gained by previous success and its resultant *morale*. But, instead of attacking at dawn, Lee's attack was postponed until afternoon of the following day, in consequence of the absence of Longstreet's corps. Federal official reports show that some of Meade's corps reached him on the second day, several hours after sunrise, and one or two late in the afternoon. It is positively asserted by many officers present, and of high rank and character, that Longstreet was nearer to Lee on the first day than Meade's reënforcing corps to their chief, and even nearer than a division of Ewell's corps, which reached the field in time to share in the first day's success. Now, it nowhere appears in Lee's report of Gettysburg that he ordered Longstreet to him or blamed him for tardiness; but his report admits errors, and quietly takes the responsibility for them on his own broad shoulders. A recent article in the public press, signed by General Longstreet, ascribes the failure at Gettysburg to Lee's mistakes, which he (Longstreet) in vain pointed out and remonstrated against. That any subject involving the possession and exercise of intellect should be clear to Longstreet and concealed from Lee, is a startling proposition to those having knowledge of the two men. We have Biblical authority for the story that the angel in the path was visible to the ass, though unseen by the seer his master; but suppose, instead of smiting the honest, stupid animal, Balaam had caressed him and then been kicked by him, how would the story read? And thus much concerning Gettysburg.

Shiloh was a great misfortune. At the moment of his fall Sidney Johnston, with all the energy of his nature, was pressing on the routed foe. Crouching under the bank of the Tennessee River, Grant was helpless. One short hour more of life to Johnston would have completed his destruction. The second in command, Beauregard, was on another and distant part of the field, and before he could gather the reins of direction darkness fell and stopped pursuit. During the night Buell reached the northern bank of the river and crossed his troops. Wallace, with a fresh division, got up from below. Together, they advanced in the morning, found the Confederates rioting in the plunder of captured camps, and drove them back with loss. But all this was as nothing compared to the calamity of Johnston's death.

Educated at West Point, Johnston remained for eight years in the army of the United States, and acquired a thorough knowledge of the details of military duty. Resigning to aid the cause of the infant Republic of Texas, he became her Adjutant-General, Senior Brigadier, and Secretary of War. During our contest with Mexico, he raised a regiment of Texans to join

General Zachary Taylor, and was greatly distinguished in the fighting around and capture of Monterey. General Taylor, with whom the early years of his service had been passed, declared him to be the best soldier he had ever commanded. More than once I have heard General Zachary Taylor express this opinion. Two cavalry regiments were added to the United States army in 1854, and to the colonelcy of one of these Johnston was appointed. Subsequently, a brigadier by brevet, he commanded the expedition against the Mormons in Utah.

Thus he brought to the Southern cause a civil and military experience surpassing that of any other leader. Born in Kentucky, descended from an honorable colonial race, connected by marriage with influential families in the West, where his life had been passed, he was peculiarly fitted to command western armies. With him at the helm, there would have been no Vicksburg, no Missionary Ridge, no Atlanta. His character was lofty and pure, his presence and demeanor dignified and courteous, with the simplicity of a child; and he at once inspired the respect and gained the confidence of cultivated gentlemen and rugged frontiersmen.

Besides, he had passed through the furnace of ignorant newspapers, hotter than that of the Babylonian tyrant. Commanding some raw, unequipped forces at Bowling Green, Kentucky, the habitual American exaggeration represented him as at the head of a vast army prepared and eager for conquest. Before time was given him to organize and train his men, the absurdly constructed works on his left flank were captured. At Fort Donelson on the Cumberland were certain political generals, who, with a self-abnegation worthy of Plutarch's heroes, were anxious to get away and leave the glory and renown of defense to others. Johnston was in no sense responsible for the construction of the forts, nor the assignment to their command of these self-denying warriors; but his line of communication was uncovered by their fall, and he was compelled to retire to the southern bank of the Tennessee River. From the enlighteners of public opinion a howl of wrath came forth, and Johnston, who had just been Alexander, Hannibal, Cæsar, Napoleon, was now a miserable dastard and traitor, unfit to command a corporal's guard. President Davis sought to console him, and some of the noblest lines ever penned by man were written by Johnston in reply. They even wrung tears of repentance from the pachyderms who had attacked him, and will be a text and consolation to future commanders, who serve a country tolerant of an ignorant and licentious press. Like pure gold, he came forth from the furnace above the reach of slander, the foremost man of all the South; and had it been possible for one heart, one mind, and one arm to save her cause, she lost them when Albert Sidney Johnston fell on the field of Shiloh.

As soon after the war as she was permitted, the Commonwealth of Texas removed his remains from New Orleans, to inter them in a land he had long and faithfully served. I was honored by a request to accompany the coffin from the cemetery to the steamer; and as I gazed upon it there arose the feeling of the Theban who, after the downfall of the glory and independence of his country, stood by the tomb of Epaminondas.

"Amid the clash of arms laws are silent," and so was Confederate statesmanship; or at least, of its objects, efforts, and expectations little is known, save the abortive mission of Messrs. Stevens, Hunter, and Campbell to Fortress Monroe in the last months of the struggle, and about this there has recently been an unseemly wrangle.

The followers of the Calhoun school, who controlled the Government, held the right of secession to be too clear for discussion. The adverse argument of Mr. Webster, approved by a large majority of the Northern people, was considered to be founded on lust of power, not on reason. The governments of western Europe, with judgments unclouded by selfishness, would at once acknowledge it. France, whose policy since the days of the eleventh Louis had been one of intense centralization, and Germany and Italy, whose hopes and aspirations were in the same direction, would admit it, while England would not be restrained by anti-slavery sentiment. Indeed, the statesmen of these countries had devoted much time to the study of the

Constitution of the United States, knew that it was a compact, and were in complete harmony with the opinions of Mr. Calhoun. There was to be no revolution, for this, though justified by oppression, involved the recognition of some measure of obligation to the Union, from which the right to secede was manifest. Hence the haste to manufacture a paper constitution, in which the powers of different departments were as carefully weighed as are dangerous drugs by dispensing chemists. Hence two houses of Congress, refuge for mischievous twaddlers to worry the executive and embarrass the armies. Hence the Governor Browns, who, reasoning that one State had as much right to disagree with eleven as eleven with twenty, declared each of their hamlets of more importance than the cities of others. While the sections were marching through the streets, with pikes crowned by gory heads, and clamoring for more, Sieyès had his pockets stuffed with constitutions and felt that his country was safe. It is not pretended that these ideas were entertained by the larger part of the Southern people, or were confessed by the ruling minority; but they existed, nevertheless, under different forms.

Aggrieved by the action and tendencies of the Federal Government, and apprehending worse in the future, a majority of the people of the South approved secession as the only remedy suggested by their leaders. So travelers enter railway carriages, and are dragged up grades and through tunnels with utter loss of volition, the motive power, generated by fierce heat, being far in advance and beyond their control.

We set up a monarch, too, King Cotton, and hedged him with a divinity surpassing that of earthly potentates. To doubt his royalty and power was a confession of ignorance or cowardice. This potent spirit, at the nod of our Prosperos, the cotton-planters, would arrest every loom and spindle in New England, destroy her wealth, and reduce her population to beggary. The power of Old England, the growth of eight hundred years, was to wither as the prophet's gourd unless she obeyed its behests. And a right "tricksy spirit" it proved indeed. There was a complete mental derangement on this subject. The Government undertook to own all cotton that could be exported. Four millions of bales, belonging to many thousands of individuals, could be disposed of to better advantage by the Government than by the proprietors; and this was enforced by our authorities, whose ancestors for generations had been resisting the intrusion of governments into private business. All cotton, as well as naval stores, that was in danger of falling into the enemy's possession, was, by orders based on legislative enactment, to be burned; and this policy continued to the end. It was fully believed that this destruction would appall our enemies and convince the world of our earnestness. Possibly there was a lurking idea that it was necessary to convince ourselves.

In their long struggle for independence, the Dutch trafficked freely with the Spaniards, got rich by the trade, paid enormous taxes to support the war, and achieved their liberty. But the Dutch fought to rid themselves of a tyrant, while our first care was to set up one, Cotton, and worship it. Rules of common sense were not applicable to it. The Grand Monarque could not eat his dinners or take his emetics like ordinary mortals. Our people were much debauched by it. I write advisedly, for during the last two and a half years of the war I commanded in the State of Louisiana, Mississippi, and Alabama, the great producing States. Out-post officers would violate the law, and trade. In vain were they removed; the temptation was too strong, and their successors did the same. The influence on the women was dreadful, and in many cases their appeals were heart-rending. Mothers with suffering children, whose husbands were in the war or already fallen, would beseech me for permits to take cotton through the lines. It was useless to explain that it was against law and orders, and that I was without authority to act. This did not give food and clothing to their children, and they departed, believing me to be an unfeeling brute. In fact, the instincts of humanity revolted against this folly.

It is with no pleasure that I have dwelt on the foregoing topics, but the world can not properly estimate the fortitude of the Southern people unless it understands and takes account of the difficulties under which they labored. Yet, great as were their sufferings during the war, they were as nothing compared to those inflicted upon them after its close.

Extinction of slavery was expected by all and regretted by none, although loss of slaves destroyed the value of land. Existing since the earliest colonization of the Southern States, the institution was interwoven with the thoughts, habits, and daily lives of both races, and both suffered by the sudden disruption of the accustomed tie. Bank stocks, bonds, all personal property, all accumulated wealth, had disappeared. Thousands of houses, farm-buildings, work-animals, flocks and herds, had been wantonly burned, killed, or carried off. The land was filled with widows and orphans crying for aid, which the universal destitution prevented them from receiving. Humanitarians shuddered with horror and wept with grief for the imaginary woes of Africans; but their hearts were as adamant to people of their own race and blood. These had committed the unpardonable sin, had wickedly rebelled against the Lord's anointed, the majority. Blockaded during the war, and without journals to guide opinion and correct error, we were unceasingly slandered by our enemies, who held possession of every avenue to the world's ear.

Famine and pestilence have ever followed war, as if our Mother Earth resented the defilement of her fair bosom by blood, and generated fatal diseases to punish humanity for its crimes. But there fell upon the South a calamity surpassing any recorded in the annals or traditions of man. An article in the "North American Review," from the pen of Judge Black, well describes this new curse, the carpet-baggers, as worse than Attila, scourge of God. He could only destroy existing fruits, while, by the modern invention of public credit, these caterans stole the labor of unborn generations. Divines, moralists, orators, and poets throughout the North commended their thefts and bade them God-speed in spoiling the Egyptians; and the reign of these harpies is not yet over. Driven from the outworks, they hold the citadel. The epithet of August, first applied to the mighty Julius and to his successor Octavius, was continued, by force of habit, to the slobbering Claudius; and so of the Senate of the United States, which august body contained in March last several of these freebooters. Honest men regarded them as monsters, generated in the foul ooze of a past era, that had escaped destruction to linger in a wholesomer age ; and their speedy extinction was expected, when another, the most hideous of the species, was admitted. This specimen had been kept by force of bayonets for four years upon the necks of an unwilling people, had no title to a seat in the Senate, and was notoriously despised by every inhabitant of the State which he was seated to misrepresent. The Senators composing the majority by which this was done acted under solemn oaths to do the right ; but the Jove of party laughs at vows of politicians. Twelve years of triumph have not served to abate the hate of the victors in the great war. The last presidential canvass was but a crusade of vengeance against the South. The favorite candidate of his party for the nomination, though in the prime of vigor, had not been in the field, to which his eloquent appeals sent thousands, but preferred the pleasanter occupation of making money at home. He had converted the power of his great place, that of Speaker of the House of Representatives, into lucre, and was exposed. By mingled chicanery and audacity he obtained possession of his own criminating letters, flourished them in the face of the House, and, in the Cambyses vein, called on his people to rally and save the luster of his loyalty from soil at the hands of rebels ; and they came. From all the North ready acclaims went up, and women shed tears of joy, such as in King Arthur's day rewarded some peerless deed of Galahad. In truth, it was a manly thing to hide dishonorable plunder beneath the prostrate body of the South. The Emperor Commodus, in full panoply, met in the arena disabled and unarmed gladiators. The servile Romans applauded his easy victories. Ancient Pistol covers with patches the ignoble scabs of a corrupt life. The vulgar herd believes them to be wounds received in the Gallic wars, as it once believed in the virtue and patriotism of Marat and Barrère.

In the Sermon on the Mount, the Divine Moralist instructed his hearers to forgive those who had injured them ; but He knew too well the malice of the human heart to expect them to forgive those whom they had injured. The leaders of the radical masses of the North have inflicted such countless and cruel wrongs on the Southern people as to forbid any hope of disposition or ability to forgive their victims; and the land will have no rest until the last of these persecutors has passed into oblivion.

During all these years the conduct of the Southern people has been admirable. Submitting to the inevitable, they have shown fortitude and dignity, and rarely has one been found base enough to take wages of shame from the oppressor and maligner of his brethren. Accepting the harshest conditions and faithfully observing them, they have struggled in all honorable ways, and for what? For their slaves? Regret for their loss has neither been felt nor expressed. But they have striven for that which brought our forefathers to Runnymede, the privilege of exercising some influence in their own government. Yet we fought for nothing but slavery, says the world, and the late Vice-President of the Confederacy, Mr. Alexander Stephens, reëchoes the cry, declaring that it was the corner-stone of his Government.

CHAPTER XV.

THE following considerations induced me to make a pilgrimage to Washington, where, by accident of fortune, I had a larger acquaintance with influential politicians than other Southern commanders. When the Whig party dissolved, most of its Northern members joined the Republicans, and now belonged to the reigning faction; and I had consorted with many of them while my father was President and afterward.

Mention has been made of the imprisonment of Governors Clarke and Watts for adopting my advice, and it was but right for me to make an effort to have them released. Moreover, Jefferson Davis was a prisoner in irons, and it was known that his health was feeble. Lee, Johnston, and I, with our officers and men, were at large, protected by the terms of our surrenders —terms which General Grant had honorably prevented the civil authorities from violating. If Mr. Davis had sinned, we all were guilty, and I could not rest without making an attempt for his relief.

At the time, it was understood that prisoners on parole should not change their residence without military permission, and leave to go to New York was asked and obtained of General Canby. By steamer I reached that place in a week, and found that General Dix had just been relieved by General Hooker, to whom I at once reported. He uttered a shout of welcome (we were old acquaintances), declared that he was more pleased to see me than to see a church (which was doubtless true), made hospitable suggestions of luncheon, champagne, etc., and gave me a permit to go to Washington, regretting that he could not keep me with him. A warm-hearted fellow is "fighting Joe," who carried on war like a soldier.

In Washington, at Willard's—a huge inn, filled from garret to cellar with a motley crowd—an acquaintance, whom I chanced to meet, informed me that a recent disturbance had induced the belief of the existence of a new plot for assassination, and an order had been published forbidding rebels to approach the capital without the permission of the War Secretary. Having been at sea for a week, I knew nothing of this, and Hooker had not mentioned it when he gave me the permit to come to Washington. My informant apprehended my arrest, and kindly undertook to protect me. Through his intervention I received from the President, Andrew Johnson, permission to stay or go where I chose, with an invitation to visit him at a stated time.

Presenting myself at the "White House," I was ushered in to the President—a saturnine man, who made no return to my bow, but, after looking at me, asked me to take a seat. Upon succeeding to power Mr. Johnson breathed fire and hemp against the South, proclaimed that he would make treason odious by hanging traitors, and ordered the arrest of General Lee and others, when he was estopped by the action of General Grant. He had now somewhat abated his wolfish desire for vengeance, and asked many questions about the condition of the South, temper of the people, etc. I explained the conduct of Governors Clarke and Watts, how they were imprisoned for following my advice, submitted to and approved by General Canby, who would hardly have abetted a new rebellion; and he made memoranda of their cases, as well as of those of many other prisoners, confined in different forts from Boston to Savannah, all of whom were released within a short period. Fearing to trespass on his time, I left with a request that he would permit me to call again, as I had a matter of much interest to lay before him, and was told the hours at which I would be received.

Thence to the Secretary of State, Mr. Seward, who in former Whig times, as Senator from New York, had been a warm supporter of my father's administration. He greeted me cordially, and asked me to dine. A loin of veal was the *pièce de résistance* of his dinner, and he called attention to it as evidence that he had killed the fatted calf to welcome the returned prodigal. Though not entirely recovered from the injuries received in a fall from his carriage and the wounds inflicted by the knife of Payne, he was cheerful, and appeared to sympathize with the objects of my mission—at least, so far as I could gather his meaning under the cloud of words with which he was accustomed to cover the slightest thought. One or two other members of the Cabinet, to whom Mr. Seward presented me, were also favorably inclined. One, the War Secretary, I did not meet. A spy under Buchanan, a tyrant under Lincoln, and a traitor to Johnson, this man was as cruel and crafty as Domitian. I never saw him. In the end conscience, long dormant, came as Alecto, and he was not; and the temple of Justice, on whose threshold he stood, escaped profanation.

In a second interview, President Johnson heard the wish I had so much at heart, permission to visit Jefferson Davis. He pondered for some time, then replied that I must wait and call again.

Meantime, an opportunity to look upon the amazing spectacle presented by the dwellers at the capital was afforded. The things seen by the Pilgrims in a dream were at this Vanity Fair visible in the flesh : "all such merchandise sold as houses, lands, trades, places, honors, preferments, states, lusts, pleasures ; and delights of all sorts, as bawds, wives, husbands, children, masters, servants, lives, blood, bodies, souls, greenbacks, pearls, precious stones, and what not." The eye of the inspired tinker had pierced the darkness of two hundred years, and seen what was to come. The martial tread of hundreds of volunteer generals, just disbanded, resounded in the streets. Gorged with loot, they spent it as lavishly as Morgan's buccaneers after the sack of Panama. Their women sat at meat or walked the highways, resplendent in jewels, spoil of Southern matrons. The camp-followers of the army were here in high carnival, and in character and numbers rivaled the attendants of Xerxes. Courtesans swarmed everywhere, about the inns, around the Capitol, in the antechambers of the "White House," and were brokers

16

for the transaction of all business. Of a tolerant disposition and with a wide experience of earthly wickedness, I did not feel called upon to cry aloud against these enormities, remembering the fate of Faithful; but I had some doubts concerning divine justice; for why were the "cities of the Plain" overthrown and this place suffered to exist?

The officers of the army on duty at Washington were very civil to me, especially General Grant, whom I had known prior to and during the Mexican war, as a modest, amiable, but by no means promising lieutenant in a marching regiment. He came frequently to see me, was full of kindness, and anxious to promote my wishes. His action in preventing violation of the terms of surrender, and a subsequent report that he made of the condition of the South—a report not at all pleasing to the radicals—endeared him to all Southern men. Indeed, he was in a position to play a rôle second only to that of Washington, who founded the republic; for he had the power to restore it. His bearing and conduct at this time were admirable, modest and generous; and I talked much with him of the noble and beneficent work before him. While his heart seemed to respond, he declared his ignorance of and distaste for politics and politicians, with which and whom he intended to have nothing to do, but confine himself to his duties of commander-in-chief of the army. Yet he expressed a desire for the speedy restoration of good feeling between the sections, and an intention to advance it in all proper ways. We shall see when and under what influences he adopted other views.

The President put me off from day to day, receiving me to talk about Southern affairs, but declining to give an answer to my requests. I found that he always postponed action, and was of an obstinate, suspicious temper. Like a badger, one had to dig him out of his hole; and he was ever in one except when on the hustings, addressing the crowd. Of humble birth, a tailor by trade, nature gave him a strong intellect, and he had learned to read after his marriage. He had acquired much knowledge of the principles of government, and made himself a fluent speaker, but could not rise above the level of the class in which he was born and to which he always appealed. He well understood the few subjects laboriously studied, and affected to despise other knowledge, while suspicious that those possessing such would take advantage of him. Self-educated men, as they are called, deprived of the side light thrown on a particular subject by instruction in cognate matters, are narrow and dogmatic, and, with an uneasy consciousness of ignorance, soothe their own vanity by underrating the studies of others. To the vanity of this class he added that of the demagogue (I use the term in its better sense), and called the wise policy left him by his predecessor "my policy." Compelled to fight his way up from obscurity, he had contracted a dislike of those more favored of fortune, whom he was in the habit of calling "the slave-aristocracy," and became incapable of giving his confidence to any one, even to those on whose assistance he relied in a contest, just now beginning, with the Congress.

President Johnson never made a dollar by public office, abstained from quartering a horde of connections on the Treasury, refused to uphold rogues in high places, and had too just a conception of the dignity of a chief magistrate to accept presents. It may be said that these are humble qualities for a citizen to boast the possession of by a President of the United States. As well claim respect for a woman of one's family on the ground that she has preserved her virtue. Yet all whose eyes were not blinded by partisanship, whose manhood was not emasculated by servility, would in these last years have welcomed the least of them as manna in the desert.

The President, between whom and the Congressional leaders the seeds of discord were already sown, dallied with me from day to day, and at length said that it would spare him embarrassment if I could induce Stevens, Davis, and others of the House, and Sumner of the Senate, to recommend the permission to visit Jefferson Davis; and I immediately addressed myself to this unpleasant task.

Thaddeus Stevens received me with as much civility as he was capable of. Deformed in body and temper like Caliban, this was the Lord Hategood of the fair; but he was frankness itself.

He wanted no restoration of the Union under the Constitution, which he called a worthless bit of old parchment. The white people of the South ought never again to be trusted with power, for they would inevitably unite with the Northern "Copperheads" and control the Government. The only sound policy was to confiscate the lands and divide them among the negroes, to whom, sooner or later, suffrage must be given. Touching the matter in hand, Johnson was a fool to have captured Davis, whom it would have been wiser to assist in escaping. Nothing would be done with him, as the executive had only pluck enough to hang two poor devils such as Wirtz and Mrs. Surratt. Had the leading traitors been promptly strung up, well; but the time for that had passed. (Here, I thought, he looked lovingly at my neck, as Petit André was wont to do at those of his merry-go-rounds.) He concluded by saying that it was silly to refuse me permission to visit Jefferson Davis, but he would not say so publicly, as he had no desire to relieve Johnson of responsibility.

There was no excuse for longer sporting with this radical Amaryllis either in shade or in sunshine; so I sought Henry Winter Davis. Like the fallen angel, Davis preferred to rule in hell rather than serve in heaven or on earth. With the head of Medusa and the eye of the Basilisk, he might have represented Siva in a Hindoo temple, and was even more inaccessible to sentiment than Thaddeus Stevens. Others, too numerous and too insignificant to particularize, were seen. These were the cuttle-fish of the party, whose appointed duty it was to obscure popular vision by clouds of loyal declamation. As Sicilian banditti prepare for robberies and murders by pious offerings on shrines of favorite saints, these brought out the altar of the "nation," and devoted themselves afresh, whenever "Crédits Mobiliers" and kindred enormities were afoot, and sharpened every question of administration, finance, law, taxation, on the grindstone of sectional hate. So sputtering tugs tow from her moorings the stately ship, to send her forth to winds and waves of ocean, caring naught for the cargo with which she is freighted, but, grimy in zeal to earn fees, return to seek another.

Hopeless of obtaining assistance from such statesmen, I visited Mr. Charles Sumner, Senator from Massachusetts, who received me pleasantly. A rebel, a slave-driver, and, without the culture of Boston, ignorant, I was an admirable vessel into which he could pour the inexhaustible stream of his acquired eloquence. I was delighted to listen to beautiful passages from the classic as well as modern poets, dramatists, philosophers, and orators, and recalled the anecdote of the man sitting under a fluent divine, who could not refrain from muttering, " That is Jeremy Taylor ; that, South ; that, Barrow," etc. It was difficult to suppress the thought, while Mr. Sumner was talking, " That is Burke, or Howard, Wilberforce, Brougham, Macaulay, Harriet Beecher Stowe, Exeter Hall," etc. ; but I failed to get down to the particular subject that interested me. The nearest approach to the practical was his disquisition on negro suffrage, which he thought should be accompanied by education. I ventured to suggest that negro education should precede suffrage, observing that some held the opinion that the capacity of the white race for government was limited, although accumulated and transmitted through many centuries. He replied that " the ignorance of the negro was due to the tyranny of the whites," which appeared in his view to dispose of the question of the former's incapacity. He seemed over-educated— had retained, not digested his learning ; and beautiful flowers of literature were attached to him by filaments of memory, as lovely orchids to sapless sticks. Hence he failed to understand the force of language, and became the victim of his own metaphors, mistaking them for facts. He had the irritable vanity and weak nerves of a woman, and was bold to rashness in speculation, destitute as he was of the ordinary masculine sense of responsibility. Yet I hold him to have been the purest and most sincere man of his party. A lover, nay, a devotee of liberty, he thoroughly understood that it could only be preserved by upholding the supremacy of civil law, and would not sanction the garrison methods of President Grant. Without vindictiveness, he forgave his enemies as soon as they were overthrown, and one of the last efforts of his life was to remove from the flag of a common country all records of victories that perpetuated the memory of civil strife.

Foiled in this direction, I worried the President, as old Mustard would a stot, until he wrote the permission so long solicited. By steamer from Baltimore I went down Chesapeake Bay, and arrived at Fortress Monroe in the early morning. General Burton, the commander, whose civility was marked, and who bore himself like a gentleman and soldier, received me on the dock and took me to his quarters to breakfast, and to await the time to see Mr. Davis.

It was with some emotion that I reached the casemate in which Mr. Davis was confined. There were two rooms, in the outer of which, near the entrance, stood a sentinel, and in the inner was Jefferson Davis. We met in silence, with grasp of hands. After an interval he said, " This is kind, but no more than I expected of you." Pallid, worn, gray, bent, feeble, suffering from inflammation of the eyes, he was a painful sight to a friend. He uttered no plaint, and made no allusion to the irons (which had been removed) ; said the light kept all night in his room hurt his eyes a little, and, added to the noise made every two hours by relieving the sentry, prevented much sleep; but matters had changed for the better since the arrival of General Burton, who was all kindness, and strained his orders to the utmost in his behalf. I told him of my reception at Washington by the President, Mr. Seward, and others, of the attentions of Generals Grant and Humphreys, who promoted my wish to see him, and that with such aid I was confident of obtaining permission for his wife to stay with him. I could solicit favors for him, having declined any for myself. Indeed, the very accident of position, that enabled me to get access to the governing authorities, made indecent even the supposition of my acceptance of anything personal while a single man remained under the ban for serving the Southern cause ; and therefore I had no fear of misconstruction. Hope of meeting his family cheered him much, and he asked questions about the condition and prospects of the South, which I answered as favorably as possible, passing over things that would have grieved him. In

some way he had learned of attacks on his character and conduct, made by some Southern curs, thinking to ingratiate themselves with the ruling powers. I could not deny this, but remarked that the curse of unexpected defeat and suffering was
to develop the basest passions of the human heart. Had he
escaped out of the country, it was possible he might have been
made a scapegoat by the Southern people, and, great as were
the sufferings that he had endured, they were as nothing to
coward stabs from beloved hands. The attacks mentioned were
few, and too contemptible for notice; for now his calamities had
served to endear him to all. I think that he derived consolation from this view.

The day passed with much talk of a less disturbing character, and in the evening I returned to Baltimore and Washington. After some delay Mr. Davis's family was permitted to
join him, and he speedily recovered strength. Later I made a
journey or two to Richmond, Virginia, on business connected
with his trial, then supposed to be impending.

The slight service, if simple discharge of duty can be so
called, I was enabled to render Mr. Davis, was repaid ten thousand fold. In the month of March, 1875, my devoted wife was
released from suffering, long and patiently endured, originating
in grief for the loss of her children and exposure during the
war. Smitten by this calamity, to which all that had gone
before seemed as blessings, I stood by her coffin, ere it was
closed, to look for the last time upon features that death had
respected and restored to their girlish beauty. Mr. Davis came
to my side, and stooped reverently to touch the fair brow, when
the tenderness of his heart overcame him and he burst into tears.
His example completely unnerved me for the time, but was of
service in the end. For many succeeding days he came to me,
and was as gentle as a young mother with her suffering infant.
Memory will ever recall Jefferson Davis as he stood with me by
the coffin.

Duty to imprisoned friends and associates discharged, I returned to New Orleans, and remained for some weeks, when an
untoward event occurred, productive of grave consequences.

The saints and martyrs who have attained worldly success have rarely declined to employ the temporal means of sinners. While calling on Hercules, they put their own shoulders to the wheel, and, in the midst of prayer, keep their powder dry. To prepare for the reëlection of President Lincoln in 1864, pretended State governments had been set up by the Federal military in several Southern States, where fragments of territory were occupied. In the event of a close election in the North, the electoral votes in these manufactured States would be under the control of the executive authority, and serve to determine the result. For some years the Southern States were used as thimble-riggers use peas : now they were under the cup of the Union, and now they were out. During his reign in New Orleans the Federal General Banks had prepared a Louisiana pea for the above purpose.

At this time negro suffrage, as yet an unaccomplished purpose, was in the air, and the objective point of radical effort. To aid the movement, surviving accomplices of the Banks fraud were instigated to call a " State Convention " in Louisiana, though with no more authority so to do than they had to call the British Parliament. The people of New Orleans regarded the enterprise as those of London did the proposed meeting of tailors in Tooley street; and just before this debating society was to assemble, the Federal commander, General Sheridan, selected especially to restrain the alleged turbulent population of the city, started on an excursion to Texas, proving that he attached no importance to the matter and anticipated no disturbance.

Living in close retirement, I had forgotten all about the " Convention." Happening to go to the center of the town, from my residence in the upper suburb, the day on which it met, on descending from the carriage of the tramway I heard pistol shots and saw a crowd of roughs, Arabs, and negroes running across Canal Street. I walked in the direction of the noise to inquire the cause of excitement, as there was nothing visible to justify it. The crowd seemed largely composed of boys of from twelve to fifteen, and negroes. I met no acquaintance, and could obtain no information, when a negro came flying past, pursued by a white boy, certainly not above fifteen years of age, with a pistol in hand. I stopped the boy without difficulty, and made him tell what he was up to. He said the niggers were having a meeting at Mechanics' Institute to take away his vote. When asked how long he had enjoyed that inestimable right of a freeman, the boy gave it up, pocketed his "Derringer," and walked off.

By this time the row appeared to be over, so I went on my way without seeing the building called Mechanics' Institute, as it was around the corner near which the boy was stopped. Speedily the town was filled with excitement, and Baird, the Federal commander in the absence of Sheridan, occupied the streets with troops and arrested the movements of citizens. Many poor negroes had been killed most wantonly, indignation ran high among decent people, and the perpetrators of the bloody deeds deserved and would have received swift, stern punishment had civil law been permitted to act. But this did not suit the purposes of the radicals, who rejoiced as Torquemada might have done when the discovery of a score of heretics furnished him an excuse to torment and destroy a province. Applying the theory of the detective police, that among the beneficiaries of crime must be sought the perpetrators, one would conclude that the radical leaders prompted the assassination of Lincoln and the murder of negroes; for they alone derived profit from these acts.

From this time forth the entire white race of the South devoted itself to the killing of negroes. It appeared to be an inherent tendency in a slave-driver to murder a negro. It was a law of his being, as of the monkey's to steal nuts, and could not be resisted. Thousands upon thousands were slain. Favorite generals kept lists in their pockets, proving time, place, and numbers, even to the smallest piccaninny. Nay, such was the ferocity of the slave-drivers, that unborn infants were ripped from their mothers' wombs. Probably these sable Macduffs were invented to avenge the wrongs of their race on tyrants protected by satanic devices from injury at the hands of Africans of natural birth. Individual effort could not suffice the rage for slaughter, and the ancient order of "assassins" was revived, with an "Old Man" of the swamps at its head. Thus "Ku-Klux" originated, and covered the land with a network of crime. Earnest, credulous women in New England had their feelings lacerated by these stories, in which they as fondly believed as their foremothers in Salem witches.

As crocodiles conceal their prey until it becomes savory and tender and ripe for eating, so the Radicals kept these dark corpses to serve up to the public when important elections approached, or some especial villainy was to be enacted by the Congress. People who had never been south of the Potomac and Ohio Rivers knew all about this "Ku-Klux"; but I failed, after many inquiries, to find a single man in the South who ever heard of it, saving in newspapers. Doubtless there were many acts of violence. When ignorant negroes, instigated by pestilent emissaries, went beyond endurance, the whites killed them; and this was to be expected. The breed to which these whites belong has for eight centuries been the master of the earth wherever it has planted its foot. A handful conquered and holds in subjection the crowded millions of India. Another and smaller bridles the fierce Caffre tribes of South Africa. Place but a score of them on the middle course of the Congo, and they will rule unless exterminated; and all the armies and all the humanitarians can not change this, until the appointed time arrives for Ham to dominate Japhet.

Two facts may here be stated. Just in proportion as the whites recovered control of their local governments, in that proportion negroes ceased to be killed; and when it was necessary to Radical success to multiply negro votes, though no census was taken, formal statistics were published to prove large immigration of negroes into the very districts of slaughter. Certainty of death could not restrain the colored lambs, impelled by an uncontrollable ardor to vote the radical ticket, from traveling to the wolves. Such devotion deserved the tenderest consideration of Christian men and women, and all means of protection and loving care were due to this innocent, credulous race. A great bureau, the Freedmen's, was established, and in connection with it, at the seat of government, a bank.   It was of importance to teach the freedmen, unused to responsibility, industry and economy; and the bank was to encourage these virtues by affording a safe place of deposit for their small savings.   To make assurance doubly sure, the "Christian soldier of the United States army" was especially selected to keep the money, and he did —so securely, in point of fact, that it is to be apprehended the unfortunate depositors will never see it more.   After so brilliant an experience in banking, prudence might have suggested to this officer the wisdom of retiring from public view.   Fortune is sometimes jealous of great reputations and fresh laurels.   The success of his first speech prevented "Single-speech Hamilton" from rising again in the House of Commons; Frederick failed to repeat Rossbach, and Napoleon, Austerlitz; but the "Christian soldier" rushed on his fate, and met it at the hands of the Nez Percés.   The profound strategy, the skillful tactics, the ready valor that had extinguished bank balances, all failed against this wily foe.

While the excitement growing out of the untoward event mentioned was at its height, President Johnson summoned me to Washington, where I explained all the circumstances, as far as I knew them, of the recent murders, and urged him to send General Hancock to command in New Orleans.   He was sent, and immediately restored order and confidence.   A gentleman, one of the most distinguished and dashing officers of the United States army, General Hancock recognizes both the great duties of a soldier of the Republic—to defend its flag and obey its laws, discharging the last with a fidelity equal to his devotion to the first in front of battle.

The contest between the Congress and the President now waxed fierce, and Thaddeus Stevens, from his place in the House, denounced "the man at the other end of the avenue." The President had gone back to wise, lawful methods, and desired to restore the Union under the Constitution; and in this he was but following the policy declared in his last public utterance by President Lincoln.   Mr. Johnson could establish this fact by members of his predecessor's Cabinet whom he had retained, and thus strengthen his position; but his vanity forbade him, so he called it "my policy," as if it were something new.

At his instance, I had many interviews with him, and consulted influential men from different parts of the country. His Secretary of War was in close alliance with his enemies in the Congress, and constantly betraying him. This was susceptible of proof, and I so informed the President, and pointed out that, so far from assisting the people of the South, he was injuring them by inaction; for the Congress persecuted them to worry him. He was President and powerful; they were weak and helpless. In truth, President Johnson, slave to his own temper and appetites, was unfit to control others.

General Grant yet appeared to agree with me about "reconstruction," as it was called; and I was anxious to preserve good feeling on his part toward the President. In the light of subsequent events, it is curious to recall the fact that he complained of Stanton's retention in the Cabinet, because the latter's greed of power prevented the Commander-in-Chief of the army from controlling the most minute details without interference. I urged this on the President as an additional motive for dismissing his War Secretary and replacing him by some one agreeable to General Grant; but all in vain. This official "old man of the sea" kept his seat on the Presidential neck, never closing crafty eye nor traitorous mouth, and holding on with the tenacity of an octopus.

Many moderate and whilom influential Republicans determined to assemble in convention at Philadelphia, and invited delegates from all parts, North and South, to meet them. The object was to promote good feeling and an early restoration of the Union, and give aid to the President in his struggle with extremists. Averse to appearing before the public, I was reluctant to go to this Convention; but the President, who felt a deep interest in its success, insisted, and I went. It was largely attended, and by men who had founded and long led the Freesoil party. Ex-members of Lincoln's first Cabinet, Senators and members of the Congress, editors of Republican newspapers (among whom was Henry J. Raymond, the ablest political editor of the day and an eminent member of Congress as well), Southern men who had fought for the Confederacy, were there. Northern Republicans and Democrats, long estranged, buried the political hatchet and met for a common purpose, to restore the Union. Negro-worshipers from Massachusetts and slave-drivers from South Carolina entered the vast hall arm in arm. The great meeting rose to its feet, and walls and roof shook with applause. General John A. Dix of New York called the Convention to order, and, in an eloquent and felicitous speech, stated the objects of the assembly—to renew fraternal feeling between the sections, heal the wounds of war, obliterate bitter memories, and restore the Union of the fathers. Senator Doolittle of Wisconsin was chosen permanent president, and patriotic resolutions were adopted by acclamation. All this was of as little avail as the waving of a lady's fan against a typhoon. Radical wrath uprose and swept these Northern men out of political existence, and they were again taught the lesson that is ever forgotten, namely, that it is an easy task to inflame the passions of the multitude, an impossible one to arrest them. From selfish ambition, from thoughtless zeal, from reckless partisanship, from the low motives governing demagogues in a country of universal suffrage, men are ever sowing the wind, thinking they can control the whirlwind; and the story of the Gironde and the Mountain has been related in vain.

The President was charmed with the Convention. Believing the people—his god—to be with him, his crest rose, and he felt every inch a President. Again I urged him to dismiss his War Secretary and replace Mr. Seward, Secretary of State, now in disfavor with his own creation, the Radical party, by General Dix, who was rewarded for his services at Philadelphia by the appointment of Naval Officer at New York. He was an exception to the rule above mentioned. A more cautious pilot than Palinurus, this respectable person is the "Vicar of Bray" of American politics; and like that eminent divine, his creeds sit so lightly as to permit him to take office under all circumstances. Secretary of the Treasury in the closing weeks of President Buchanan, he aroused the North by sending his immortal dispatch to the commander of a revenue cutter : " If any man attempts to haul down the American flag, shoot him on the spot." This bespoke the heart of the patriot, loving his country's banner, and the arm of the hero, ready to defend it ; and, clad in this armor of proof, he has since been invulnerable. The President took kindly to the proposition concerning General Dix, and I flattered myself that it would come off, when suddenly the General was appointed Minister Plenipotentiary to France. I imagine that Mr. Seward had got wind of the project and hurried Dix out of the way. Thus, in a few days General Dix had the offer of the Netherlands, Naval Office, and France. " Glamis, and thane of Cawdor " ; and his old age is yet so green, mayhap " the greatest is behind."

To air his eloquence and enlighten the minds of his dear people, the President made a tour through the North and West, in which his conduct and declarations were so extraordinary as to defeat any hopes of success for " my policy."

A circumstance connected with the Philadelphia Convention made an impression on me at the time. Mr. Raymond was editor of the " New York Times," the most powerful Republican journal in the North. Among many who had gained large wealth by speculations during the war was Mr. Leonard Jerome, a Republican in politics. This gentleman spent his fortune so lavishly that his acquaintances and the public shared its enjoyment. With other property, Mr. Jerome owned the controlling interest in the " Times," then very valuable. Dining in New York with him and Mr. Raymond, the latter told me it was useless to support the President, who was daily becoming more unpopular, and that the circulation and influence of his paper were rapidly diminishing in consequence of his adherence to " my policy." Whereupon Mr. Jerome replied : " I know but little about politics ; but if you think it right to stand by the President, I will pay all losses that the ' Times ' may suffer to the other proprietors." This was unselfish and patriotic ; and I record it with the more pleasure, because Mr. Jerome has lost much of his wealth, and I fear, like many another Timon, some friends with it.

After this period I saw little of President Johnson, who fought his fight in his own way, had his hands completely tied, and barely escaped impeachment; the Congress, meanwhile, making a whipping-post of the South, and inflicting upon it every humiliation that malignity could devise.

CHAPTER XVI.

BEFORE the conventions to nominate candidates for the Presidency met in 1868, I had much intercourse with General Grant, and found him ever modest and determined to steer clear of politics, or at least not permit himself to be used by partisans; and I have no doubt that he was sincere. But the Radical Satan took him up to the high places and promised him dominion over all in view. Perhaps none but a divine being can resist such temptation. He accepted the nomination from the Radicals, and was elected; and though I received friendly messages from him, I did not see him until near the close of his first administration. As ignorant of civil government as of the characters on the Moabitish stone, President Grant begun badly, and went from bad to worse. The appointments to office that he made, the associates whom he gathered around him, were astounding. All his own relatives, all his wife's relatives, all the relatives of these relatives, to the remotest cousinhood, were quartered on the public treasury. Never, since King Jamie crossed the Tweed with the hungry Scotch nation at his heels, has the like been seen; and the soul of old Newcastle, greatest of English nepotists, must have turned green with envy. The influence of this on the public was most disastrous. Already shortened by the war, the standard of morality, honesty, and right was buried out of sight.

For two or three years I was much in the North, and especially in New York, where I had dear friends. The war had afforded opportunity and stimulated appetite for reckless speculation. Vast fortunes had been acquired by new men, destitute of manners, taste, or principles. The vulgar insolence of wealth held complete possession of public places and carried by storm the citadels of society. Indeed, society disappeared. As in the middle ages, to escape pollution, honorable men and refined women (and there are many such in the North) fled to sanctuary and desert, or, like early Christians in the catacombs, met secretly and in fear. The masses sank into a condition that would disgrace Australian natives, and lost all power of discrimination.

The Vice-President of the United States accepted bribes, and perjured himself in vain to escape exposure. President Grant wrote him a letter to assure him of his continued esteem and confidence, and this Vice-President has since lectured before "Young Men's Christian Associations." Plunderings by members of the Congress excited no attention so long as they were confined to individuals or corporations. It was only when they voted themselves money out of taxes paid by the people, that these last growled and frightened some of the statesmen into returning it. A banker, the pet of the Government, holding the same especial relation to it that the Bank of England held to William of Orange, discovered that "a great national debt was a blessing," and was commended and rewarded therefor. With a palace on the shores of the Delaware, this banker owned a summer retreat on a lovely isle amid the waters of Lake Erie. A pious man, he filled this with many divines, who blessed all his enterprises. He contributed largely, too, to the support of an influential Christian journal to aid in disseminating truth to Jew, Gentile, and heathen. The divines and the Christian journal were employed to persuade widows and weak men to purchase his rotten securities, as things too righteous to occasion loss.

The most eloquent preacher in the land, of a race devoted to adoration of negroes, as Hannibal to hatred of Rome, compromised the wife of a member of his congregation. Discovered by the husband, he groveled before him in humiliation as before "his God" (his own expression). Brought before the public, he swore that he was innocent, and denied the meaning of his own written words. The scandal endured for months and gave an opportunity to the metropolitan journals to display

17

their enterprise by furnishing daily and minute reports of all details to their readers. The influence of the preacher was increased by this. His congregation flocked to him as the Anabaptists to John of Leyden, and shopkeepers profitably advertised their wares by doubling their subscriptions to augment his salary. Far from concealing this wound inflicted on his domestic honor, the injured husband proclaimed it from the housetops, clothed himself in it as in a robe of price, and has successfully used it to become a popular lecturer.

To represent the country at the capital of an ancient monarchy, a man was selected whom, it is no abuse of language to declare, Titus Oates after his release from the pillory would have blushed to recognize. On the eve of his departure, as one may learn from the newspapers of the day, all that was richest and best in New York gathered around a banquet in his honor, congratulated the country to which he was accredited, and lamented the misfortune of their own that it would be deprived, even temporarily, of such virtue. Another was sent to an empire which is assured by our oft-succeeding envoys that it is the object of our particular affection. To the aristocracy of the realm this genial person taught the favorite game of the mighty West. A man of broad views, feeling that diplomatic attentions were due to commons as well as to crown and nobles, he occasionally withdrew himself from the social pleasures of the "West End" to inform the stags of Capel Court of the value of American mines. Benefactors are ever misjudged. Aristocracy and the many-antlered have since united to defame him; but Galileo in the dungeon, Pascal by his solitary lamp, More, Sidney, and Russell on the scaffold, will console him; and in the broad bosom of his native Ohio he has found the exception to the rule that prophets are not without honor but in their own country.

The years of Methuselah and the pen of Juvenal would not suffice to exhaust the list, or depict the benighted state into which we had fallen; but it can be asserted of the popular idols of the day that unveiled, they resemble Mokanna, and can each exclaim:

" Here, judge if hell, with all its power to damn,
  Can add one curse to the foul thing I am! "

The examples of thousands of pure and upright people in the North were as powerless to mitigate the general corruption as song of seraphim to purify the orgies of harlots and burglars; for they were not in harmony with the brutal passions of the masses.

In Boston, July, 1872, as co-trustees of the fund left by the late Mr. Peabody for the education of the poor in the Southern States, President Grant and I met for the first time since he had accepted the nomination from the Radical party. He was a candidate for reëlection, and much worshiped; and, though cordial with me, his general manner had something of "I am the State." Stopping at the same inn, he passed an evening in my room, to which he came alone; and there, avoiding public affairs, we smoked and chatted about the Nueces, Rio Grande, Palo Alto, etc.—things twenty-five years agone, when we were youngsters beginning life. He was reëlected in November by a large majority of electoral votes; but the people of Louisiana elected a Democratic Governor and Assembly. When, in January following, the time of meeting of the Assembly arrived, the country, habituated as it was to violent methods, was startled by the succeeding occurrences.

The night before the Assembly was to meet, the Federal Judge in the city of New Orleans, a drunken reprobate, obtained from the commander of the United States troops a portion of his force, and stationed it in the State House. In the morning the members elect were refused admittance, and others not elected, many not even candidates during the election, were allowed to enter. One Packard, Marshal of the Federal Court, a bitter partisan and worthy adjunct of such a judge, had provided for an Assembly to suit himself by giving tickets to his friends, whom the soldiers passed in, excluding the elected members. The ring-streaked, spotted, and speckled among the cattle and goats, and the brown among the sheep, were turned into the supplanters' folds, which were filled with lowing herds and bleating flocks, while Laban had neither horn nor hoof. There was not a solitary return produced in favor of this Packard body, nor of the Governor subsequently installed; but the Radicals asserted that their friends would have been elected had the people voted as they wished, for every negro and some whites in the State upheld their party. By this time the charming credulity of the negroes had abated, and they answered the statement that slave-drivers were murdering their race in adjacent regions by saying that slave-drivers, at least, did not tell them lies nor steal their money.

All the whites and many of the blacks in Louisiana felt themselves cruelly wronged by the action of the Federal authorities. Two Assemblies were in session and two Governors claiming power in New Orleans. Excitement was intense, business arrested, and collision between the parties imminent. As the Packard faction was supported by Federal troops, the situation looked grave, and a number of worthy people urged me to go to Washington, where my personal relations with the President might secure me access to him. It was by no means a desirable mission, but duty seemed to require me to undertake it.

Accompanied by Thomas F. Bayard, Senator from Delaware, my first step in Washington was to call on the leader of the Radicals in the Senate, Morton of Indiana, when a long conversation ensued, from which I derived no encouragement. Senator Morton was the Couthon of his party, and this single interview prepared me for one of his dying utterances to warn the country against the insidious efforts of slave-driving rebels to regain influence in the Government. The author of the natural history of Ireland would doubtless have welcomed one specimen, by describing which he could have filled out a chapter on snakes; and there is temptation to dwell on the character of Senator Morton as one of the few Radical leaders who kept his hands clean of plunder. But it may be observed that one absorbing passion excludes all others from the human heart; and the small portion of his being in which disease had left vitality was set on vengeance. Death has recently clutched him, and would not be denied; and he is bewailed throughout the land as though he had possessed the knightly tenderness of Sir Philip Sidney and the lofty patriotism of Chatham.

The President received me pleasantly, gave much time to the Louisiana difficulty, and, in order to afford himself opportunity for full information, asked me frequently to dine with his immediate family, composed of kindly, worthy people. I also received attention and hospitality from some members of his Cabinet, who with him seemed desirous to find a remedy for the wrong. More especially was this true of the Secretary of State, Hamilton Fish, with whom and whose refined family I had an acquaintance. Of a distinguished Revolutionary race, possessor of a good estate, and with charming, cultivated surroundings, this gentleman seemed the Noah of the political world. Perhaps his retention in the Cabinet was due to a belief that, under the new and milder dispensation, the presence of one righteous man might avert the doom of Gomorrah. An exception existed in the person of the Attorney-General, a man, as eminent barristers declare, ignorant of law and self-willed and vulgar. For some reason he had much influence with the President, who later appointed him Chief Justice of the United States; but the Senatorial gorge, indelicate as it had proved, rose at this, as the easy-shaving barber's did at the coal-heaver, and rejected him.

Weeks elapsed, during which I felt hopeful from the earnestness manifested in my mission by the President and several of his Cabinet. Parties were in hostile array in New Orleans, but my friends were restrained by daily reports of the situation at Washington. Only my opinion that there was some ground for hope could be forwarded. Conversations at dinner tables or in private interviews with the Executive and his advisers could not, then or since, be repeated; and this of necessity gave room for misconstruction, as will appear. At length, on the day before the Congress was by law to adjourn, the President sent a message to the Senate, informing that body that, in the event the Congress failed to take action on the Louisiana matter, he should esteem it his duty to uphold the Government created by the Federal Judge. I left Washington at once, and did not revisit it for nearly four years.

I believe that President Grant was sincere with me, and went as far as he felt it safe. No doubt the Senatorial hyenas brought him to understand these unspoken words: "We have supported your acts, confirmed your appointments, protected and whitewashed your friends; but there are bones which we can not give up without showing our teeth, and Louisiana is one of them."

The failure to obtain relief for the State of my birth, and whose soil covered the remains of all most dear, was sad enough, and the attempt had involved much unpleasant work; but I had my reward. Downfall of hope, long sustained, was bitter to the people, especially to the leaders expectant of office; and I became an object of distrust. "Nothing succeeds like success," and nothing fails like failure, and the world is quite right to denounce it. The British Ministry shot an admiral for failing to relieve Minorca — to encourage others, as Voltaire remarked. Byng died silent, without plaint, which was best. The drunken Federal Judge, author of the outrages, was universally condemned, with one exception, of which more anon. Both branches of the Congress, controlled by Radicals, pronounced his conduct to have been illegal and unjust, and he was driven from the bench with articles of impeachment hanging over him. Nevertheless, the Government evolved from his unjudicial consciousness was upheld by President Grant with Federal bayonets.

Two years later the people of Louisiana elected an Assembly, a majority of whose members were opposed to the fraudulent Governor, Kellogg. The President sent United States soldiers into the halls of the Assembly to expel members at the point of the bayonet. Lieutenant-General Sheridan, the military maid of all (such) work, came especially to superintend this business, and it was now that he expressed the desire to exterminate "banditti." The destruction of buildings and food in the Valley of Virginia, to the confusion of the crows, was his Salamanca; but this was his Waterloo, and great was the fame of the Lieutenant-General of the Radicals.

This *Governor* Kellogg is the Senator recently seated, of whom mention has been made, and, if a lesser quantity than zero be conceivable, with a worse title to the office than he had to that of Governor of Louisiana. So far as known, he is a commonplace rogue; but his party has always rallied to his support, as the "Tenth Legion" to its eagles. Indeed, it is difficult to understand the qualities or objects that enlist the devotion and compel the worship of humanity. Travelers in the Orient tell of majestic fanes, whose mighty walls and countless columns are rich with elaborate carvings. Hall succeeds hall, each more beautifully wrought than the other, until the innermost, the holy of holies, is reached, and there is found enshrined—a shriveled ape.

The sole exception referred to in the case of the drunken Federal Judge was a lawyer of small repute, who had been Democratic in his political tendencies. Languishing in obscurity, he saw and seized his opportunity, and rushed into print in defense of the Judge and in commendation of the President for upholding such judicial action. It is of record that this lawyer, in the society of some men of letters, declared Dante to be the author of the Decameron; but one may be ignorant of the Italian poets and thoroughly read in French memoirs. During the war of the Spanish succession, the Duke of Vendôme, filthiest of generals, not excepting Suvaroff, commanded the French army in Italy. To negotiate protection for their States, the Italian princes sent agents to Vendôme; but the agents sent by the Duke of Parma were so insulted by the bestialities of the French commander as to go back to their master without negotiating, and no decent man would consent to return. A starving little abbé volunteered for the service, and, possessing a special aptitude for baseness, succeeded in his mission. Thus Alberoni, afterward Cardinal and Prime Minister of Spain, got his foot on the first rung of the ladder of fame. The details of the story are too gross to repeat, and the Memoirs of the Duke of St. Simon must be consulted for them; but our lawyer assuredly had read them. Many may imitate Homer, however feebly; one genius originated his epics.

Having entered on this lofty career, our Alberoni stuck to it with the tenacity of a ferret in pursuit of rabbits, and was rewarded, though not at the time nor to the extent he had reason to expect. The mission to England was promised him by the reigning powers, when, on the very eve of securing his prize, a stick was put in the wheels of his progress, and by a brother's hand. Another legal personage, practicing at the same bar, that of New York, and a friend, did the deed. "Chloe was false, Chloe was common, but constant while possessed"; but here Chloe was without the last quality. In 1868, General Grant's election pending, Chloe was affiliated with the Democratic party, and had been chosen one of the captains of its citadel, a sachem of Tammany. Scenting success for Grant, with the keenness of the vulture for his prey, he attended a Radical meeting and announced his intention to give twenty thousand dollars to the Radical election fund. This sum appears to have been the market value of a seat in the Cabinet, to which ultimately he was called. When the English mission became vacant by the resignation of the incumbent, disgusted by British ingratitude, Chloe quitted the Cabinet to take it, and Alberoni was left wearing weeds. Yet much allowance is due to family affection, the foundation of social organization. Descended from a noble stock, though under a somewhat different name, Chloe from mystic sources learned that his English relatives pined for his society, and devotion to family ties tempted him to betray his friend. Subsequently Alberoni was appointed to a more northern country, where he may find congenial society; for, in a despotism tempered only by assassination, the knees of all become pliant before power.

It is pleasant to mark the early steps of nascent ambition. In the time of the great Napoleon every conscript carried the baton of a marshal in his knapsack; and in our happy land every rogue may be said to have an appointment to office in his pocket. This is also pleasant.

Since the spring of 1873, when he gave himself up to the

worst elements of his party, I have not seen President Grant; but his career suggests some curious reflections to one who has known him for thirty-odd years. What the waiting-woman promised in jest, Dame Fortune has seriously bestowed on this Malvolio, and his political cross-garterings not only find favor with the Radical Olivia, but are admired by the Sir Tobys of the European world. Indeed, Fortune has conceits as quaint as those of Haroun al-Raschid. The beggar, from profound sleep, awoke in the Caliph's bed. Amazed and frightened by his surroundings, he slowly gained composure as courtier after courtier entered, bowing low, to proclaim him King of kings, Light of the World, Commander of the Faithful; and he speedily came to believe that the present had always existed, while the real past was an idle dream. Of a nature kindly and modest, President Grant was assured by all about him that he was the delight of the Radicals, greatest captain of the age, and saviour of the nation's life. It was inevitable that he should begin by believing some of this, and end by believing it all. Though he had wasted but little time on books since leaving West Point, where in his day the curriculum was limited, he had found out to the last shilling the various sums voted by Parliament to the Duke of Wellington, and spoke of them in a manner indicating his opinion that he was another example of the ingratitude of republics. The gentle temper and sense of justice of Othello resisted the insidious wiles of Iago; but ignorance and inexperience yielded in the end to malignity and craft. President Grant was brought not only to smother the Desdemona of his early preferences and intentions, but to feel no remorse for the deed, and take to his bosom the harridan of radicalism. As Phalaris did those of Agrigentum opposed to his rule, he finished by hating Southerners and Democrats.

During the struggle for the Presidency in the autumn of 1876, he permitted a member of his Cabinet, the Secretary of the Interior, to become the manager of the Radicals and use all the power of his office, established for the public service, to promote the success of his party's candidate.

Monsieur Fourtou, Minister of the Interior, removed prefects and mayors to strengthen the power of De Broglie; where-upon all the newspapers in our land published long essays to show and lament the ignorance of the French and their want of experience in republican methods. One might suppose these articles to have been written by the "seven sleepers," so forgetful were they of yesterday's occurrences at home; but beams near at hand are ever blinked in our search of distant motes. The election over, but the result in dispute, President Grant, in Philadelphia, alarmed thoughtful people by declaring that "no man could take the great office of President upon whose title thereto the faintest shadow of doubt rested," and then, with all the power of the Government, successfully led the search for this non-existing person. To insure fairness in the count, so that none could carp, he requested eminent statesmen to visit South Carolina, Florida, and Louisiana, the electoral votes of which were claimed by both parties; but the statesmen were, without exception, the bitterest and most unscrupulous partisans, personally interested in securing victory for their candidate, and have since received their hire. Soldiers were quartered in the capitals of the three States to aid the equitable statesmen in reaching a correct result by applying the bayonet if the figures proved refractory. With equity and force at work, the country might confidently expect justice; and justice was done —that justice ever accorded by unscrupulous power to weakness.

But one House of the Congress was controlled by the Democrats, and these, Herod-like, were seeking to slay the child, the Nation. To guard against this, President Grant ordered other troops to Washington and a ship of war to be anchored in the Potomac, and the child was preserved. Again, the 4th of March, appointed by law for the installation of Presidents, fell on Sunday. President Grant is of Scotch descent, and doubtless learned in the traditions of the land o' cakes. The example of Kirkpatrick at Dumfries taught him that it was wise to "mak sicker"; so the incoming man and the Chief Justice were smuggled into the White House on the sabbath day, and the oath of office was administered. If the chair of George Washington was to be filched, it were best done under cover. The value of the loot inspired caution.

In Paris, at a banquet, Maître Gambetta recently toasted our ex-President " as the great commander who had sacredly obeyed and preserved his country's laws." Whether this was said in irony or ignorance, had General Grant taken with him to Paris his late Secretary of the Interior, the accomplished Z. Chandler, the pair might have furnished suggestions to Marshal MacMahon and Fourtou that would have changed the dulcet strains of Maître Gambetta into dismal howls.

CHAPTER XVII.

Dismissing hope of making my small voice heard in mitigation of the woes of my State, in May, 1873, I went to Europe and remained many months. Returned to New York, I found that the characters on the wall, so long invisible, had blazed forth, and the vast factitious wealth, like the gold of the dervish, withered and faded in a night. The scenes depicted of Paris and London, after the collapse of Mississippi schemes and South Sea bubbles, were here repeated on a greater scale and in more aggravated form. To most, the loss of wealth was loss of ancestry, repute, respectability, decency, recognition of their fellows—all. Small wonder that their withers were fearfully wrung, and their wails piteous. Enterprise and prosperity were frozen as in a sea of everlasting ice, and guardians of trusts, like Ugolino, plunged their robber fangs into the scalps and entrails of the property confided to them.

A public journal has recently published a detailed list, showing that there has been plundered by fiduciaries since 1873 the amazing amount of thirty millions of money; and the work goes on. Scarce a newspaper is printed in whose columns may not be found some fresh instance of breach of trust. As poisoning in the time of Brinvilliers, stealing is epidemic, and the watch-dogs of the flocks are transformed into wolves.

Since the tocsin sounded we have gone from bad to worse. During the past summer (1877) laborers, striking for increased wages or to resist diminution thereof, seized and held for many days the railway lines between East and West, stopping all traffic. Aided by mobs, they took possession of great towns and destroyed vast property. At Pittsburgh, in Pennsylvania, State troops attempting to restore order were attacked and driven off. Police and State authorities in most cases proved impotent, and the arm of Federal power was invoked to stay the evil.

Thousands of the people are without employment, which they seek in vain; and from our cities issue heart-rending appeals in behalf of the suffering poor. From the Atlantic as far to the west as the young State of Nebraska, there has fallen upon the land a calamity like that afflicting Germany after the Thirty Years' War. Hordes of idle, vicious tramps penetrate rural districts in all directions, rendering property and even life unsafe; and no remedy for this new disease has been discovered. Let us remember that these things are occurring in a country of millions upon millions of acres of vacant lands, to be had almost for the asking, and where, even in the parts first colonized, density of population bears but a small relation to that of western Europe. Yet we daily assure ourselves and the world that we have the best government under the canopy of heaven, and the happiest land, hope and refuge of humanity.

Purified by fire and sword, the South has escaped many of these evils; but her enemies have sown the seeds of a pestilence more deadly than that rising from Pontine marshes. Now that Federal bayonets have been turned from her bosom, this poison, the influence of three fourths of a million of negro voters, will speedily ascend and sap her vigor and intelligence. Greed of office, curse of democracies, will impel demagogues to grovel deeper and deeper in the mire in pursuit of ignorant votes. Her old breed of statesmen has largely passed away during and since the civil war, and the few survivors are naturally distrusted, as responsible for past errors. Numbers of her gentry fell in battle, and the men now on the stage were youths at the outbreak of strife, which arrested their education. This last is also measurably true of the North. Throughout the land the experience of the active portion of the present generation only comprises conditions of discord and violence. The story of the six centuries of sturdy effort by which our English forefathers wrought out their liberties is unknown, certainly unappreciated.

Even the struggles of our grandfathers are forgotten, and the names of Washington, Adams, Hamilton, Jay, Marshall, Madison, and Story awaken no fresher memories in our minds, no deeper emotions in our hearts, than do those of Solon, Leonidas, and Pericles. But respect for the memories and deeds of our ancestors is security for the present, seed-corn for the future; and, in the language of Burke, "Those will not look forward to their posterity who never look backward to their ancestors."

Traditions are mighty influences in restraining peoples. The light that reaches us from above takes countless ages to traverse the awful chasm separating us from its parent star; yet it comes straight and true to our eyes, because each tender wavelet is linked to the other, receiving and transmitting the luminous ray. Once break the continuity of the stream, and men will deny its heavenly origin, and seek its source in the feeble glimmer of earthly corruption.

INDEX.

18

THE END.

RECENT
American History and Biography.

I.

Four Years with General Lee :

Being a Summary of the more Important Events touching the Career of General Robert E. Lee, in the War between the States; together with an Authoritative Statement of the Strength of the Army which he commanded in the Field. By WILLIAM H. TAYLOR, of his Staff, and late Adjutant-General of the Army of Northern Virginia. 8vo. Cloth, $2.00.

II.

The Life of General Albert Sidney Johnston.

By his Son, Colonel WILLIAM PRESTON JOHNSTON. One large octavo volume, 774 pages. With Maps, a fine Portrait on Steel, and 8 full-page Illustrations. Cloth, $5.00; sheep, $6.00; half turkey, $7.00.

III.

The Autobiography of William H. Seward (1801–1834).

With a later Memoir by his Son, FREDERICK W. SEWARD, late Assistant Secretary of State. Per volume, over 800 pages, cloth, $4.25; sheep, $5.25; half turkey, $6.25; full turkey, $8.25.

IV.

Military History of General U. S. Grant,

from April, 1861, to April, 1865. By ADAM BADEAU, Colonel and Aide-de-Camp to the General-in-Chief, Brevet Brigadier-General U. S. A. With Portrait, and numerous Maps. Vol. I. 8vo. Cloth, $4.00; half calf, extra, $6.50.

V.

Memoirs of W. T. Sherman.

By Himself. (With a Military Map showing the Marches of the United States Forces under General Sherman's command.) Two handsome vols., 8vo. Blue cloth, $5.50; sheep, $7.00; half morocco, $8.50; full morocco, $12.00.
Cheap edition. 1 vol. Cloth, $3.50.

D. APPLETON & CO., PUBLISHERS, 549 & 551 BROADWAY, NEW YORK.

AMERICAN PAINTERS:

Biographical Sketches of Fifty American Artists.

WITH EIGHTY-THREE EXAMPLES OF THEIR WORKS,

ENGRAVED ON WOOD IN A PERFECT MANNER.

Quarto; cloth, extra gilt.................Price, $7.00; full morocco, $13.00.

The painters represented in this work are as follows:

CHURCH,	HUNT,	J. H. BEARD,
INNES,	WHITTREDGE,	W. H. BEARD,
HUNTINGTON,	W. HART,	PORTER,
PAGE,	J. M. HART,	G. L. BROWN,
SANFORD GIFFORD,	McENTEE,	APPLETON BROWN,
SWAIN GIFFORD,	COLMAN,	CROPSEY,
DURAND,	HICKS,	CASILEAR,
R. W. WEIR,	WINSLOW HOMER,	E. JOHNSON,
W. T. RICHARDS,	DE HAAS,	SHIRLAW,
T. MORAN,	J. G. BROWN,	CHASE,
P. MORAN,	WYANT,	BRICHER,
PERRY,	WOOD,	ROBBINS,
BELLOWS,	BRISTOL,	WILMARTH,
SHATTUCK,	REINHART,	EATON,
MILLER,	BRIDGMAN,	GUY,
J. F. WEIR,	BIERSTADT,	QUARTLEY,
	HOPKINSON SMITH,	MEEKER.

The publishers feel justified in saying that the contemporaneous art of no country has ever been so adequately represented in a single volume as our American Painters are in this work, while the engravings are equal in execution to the finest examples of wood-engraving produced here or abroad.

OPINIONS OF THE PRESS.

"The richest and in many ways the most notable of fine art books is 'American Painters,' just published, with unstinted liberality in the making. Eighty-three examples of the work of American artists, reproduced in the very best style of wood-engraving, and printed with rare skill, constitute the chief purpose of the book; while the text which accompanies them, the work of Mr. George W. Sheldon, is a series of bright and entertaining biographical sketches of the artists, with a running commentary—critical, but not too critical—upon the peculiarities of their several methods, purposes, and conceptions."—*New York Evening Post.*

"The volume gives good evidence of the progress of American art. It shows that we have deft hands and imaginative brains among painters of the country, and it shows, moreover, that we have publishers who are liberal and cultured enough to present their works in a handsome and luxurious form that will make them acceptable. 'American Painters' will adorn the table of many a drawing-room where art is loved, and where it is made still dearer from the fact that it is native."—*New York Express.*

"It is at once a biographical dictionary of artists, a gallery of pen portraits and of beautiful scenes, sketched by the painters and multiplied by the engraver. It is in all respects a work of art, and will meet the wants of a large class whose tastes are in that direction."—*New York Observer.*

"One of the most delightful volumes issued from the press of this country."
—*New York Daily Graphic.*

"Outside and inside it is a thing of beauty. The text is in large, clear type, the paper is of the finest, the margins broad, and the illustrations printed with artistic care. The volume contains brief sketches of fifty prominent American artists, with examples from their works. Some idea of the time and labor expended in bringing out the work may be gathered from the fact that to bring it before the public in its present form cost the publishers over $12,000."—*Boston Evening Transcript.*

"This book is a notable one, and among the many fine art books it will rank as one of the choicest, and one of the most elegant, considered as an ornament or parlor decoration. The engravings are in the highest style known to art. Mr. Sheldon has accompanied the illustrations with a series of very entertaining biographical sketches. As far as possible, he has made the artists their own interpreters, giving their own commentaries upon art and upon their purposes in its practice instead of his own."—*Boston Post.*

"'American Painters' consists of biographical sketches of fifty leading American artists, with eighty-three examples of their works, engraved on wood with consummate skill, delicacy of touch, and appreciation of distinctive manner. It is a gallery of contemporary American art."—*Philadelphia Press.*

"This work is one of surpassing interest, and of marvelous typographical and illustrative beauty."—*Philadelphia Item.*

"The whole undertaking is a noble one, illustrative of the best period of American art, and as such deserves the attention and support of the public."—*Chicago Tribune.*

D. APPLETON & CO., Publishers, 549 & 551 Broadway, New York.

THE

FRENCH REVOLUTIONARY EPOCH.

Being a History of France from the Beginning of the First French
Revolution to the End of the Second Empire.

BY

HENRI VAN LAUN,

Author of "History of French Literature," etc.

In 2 vols., 12mo. . . . . Cloth, $3.50.

"As a history for readers who are not disposed to make an exhaustive study of the subject treated, the book impresses us as eminently good."—*N. Y. Evening Post.*

"This work throws a flood of light on the problems which are now perplexing the politicians and statesmen of Europe."—*N. Y. Daily Graphic.*

"This is a work for which there is no substitute at present in the English language. For American readers it may be said to have secured a temporary monopoly of a most interesting topic. Educated persons can scarcely afford to neglect it."—*N. Y. Sun.*

"The opinion is here advanced and tolerably well fortified that Napoleon would have been beaten at Waterloo if Blücher had not come up. The book is a compendium of the events between 1789 and 1871: it is a popular treatment of the subject for students and family reading."—*Chicago Tribune.*

"Nothing can surpass the clearness of the narrative, and it may be truly said that this history is as interesting as a romance."—*Philadelphia Press.*

"The general reader will get, as he goes along with it, a more distinct idea of the salient features which marked the course of events than he might from some of the thousand and one more picturesque and more dramatic, but less truthful, histories of the same epoch."—*N. Y. Express.*

"We heartily commend it to our readers as one of the most compact, attractive, trustworthy, and instructive historical works in existence."—*Utica Daily Observer.*

"The author shows judgment and skill in culling from the large materials at command that which is of value, and also a masterly ability in presenting them tersely, and at the same time throwing in enough of incident and the lighter thought to make the volumes wholly enjoyable."—*Chicago Inter-Ocean.*

"If you desire to read facts and not theories, events and not imaginings, in chaste though vigorous language, peruse these volumes."—*Providence Press.*

"The author has accomplished a difficult and much-needed undertaking in a very satisfactory way."—*Boston Journal.*

"No student of American history can afford to be without this book."—*St. Louis Times-Journal.*

D. APPLETON & CO., PUBLISHERS, 549 & 551 BROADWAY, NEW YORK.

WILLIAM CULLEN BRYANT'S

POETICAL WORKS.

Illustrated 8vo Edition of Bryant's Poetical Works. 100 Engravings by Birket Foster, Harry Fenn, Alfred Fredericks, and other Artists. 1 vol., 8vo. Cloth, gilt side and edge, $4.00; half calf, marble edge, $6.00; full morocco, antique, $8.00; tree calf, $10.00.

Household Edition. 1 vol., 12mo. Cloth, $2.00; half calf, $4.00; morocco, $5.00; tree calf, $5.00.

Red-Line Edition. With 24 Illustrations, and Portrait of Bryant on Steel. Printed on tinted paper, with red line. Square 12mo. Cloth, extra, $3.00; half calf, $5.00; morocco, $7.00; tree calf, $8.00.

Blue-and-Gold Edition. 18mo. Cloth, gilt edge, $1.50; half calf, marble edge, $3.00; morocco, gilt edge, $4.00.

The Song of the Sower. Illustrated with 42 Engravings on Wood, from Original Designs by Hennessy, Fenn, Winslow Homer, Hows, Griswold, Nehlig, and Perkins; engraved in the most perfect manner by our best Artists. Elegantly printed and bound. Cloth, extra gilt $5.00; morocco, antique, $9.00.

The Story of the Fountain. With 42 Illustrations by Harry Fenn, Alfred Fredericks, John A. Hows, Winslow Homer, and others. In one handsome quarto volume. Printed in the most perfect manner, on heavy calendered paper. Uniform with "The Song of the Sower." 8vo. Square cloth, extra gilt, $5.00; morocco, antique, $9.00.

The Little People of the Snow. Illustrated with exquisite Engravings, printed in Tints, from Designs by Alfred Fredericks. Cloth, $5.00; morocco, $9.00.

D. APPLETON & CO., Publishers, 549 & 551 Broadway, New York.

The Poet and Painter;

OR, GEMS OF ART AND SONG.

An imperial 8vo volume, containing Choice Selections from the English Poets. Superbly illustrated with Ninety-nine Steel Engravings. Printed in the best manner on the page with the text. New edition : cloth, extra, $12.00 ; morocco, antique, or extra, $20.00.

The Household Book of Poetry.

BY CHARLES A. DANA.

New edition, enlarged, with Additions from recent Authors. Illustrated with Steel Engravings by celebrated Artists. 1 vol., royal 8vo. Cloth, extra, gilt edges, $5.00 ; morocco, antique, $10.00 ; crushed levant, $15.00.
The Household Book of Poetry. New cheap edition. Cloth, extra, red edges, $3.50 ; morocco, gilt edges, $7.00.

Fitz-Greene Halleck's Poetical Works.

EDITED BY JAMES GRANT WILSON.

Complete Poetical Works. 1 vol., 12mo. Cloth, $2.50 ; half calf, extra, $4.50 ; morocco, antique, $6.00.
Large-paper copy of the same. 8vo. Cloth, $10.00 ; morocco, antique, $15.00.
Complete Poetical Works. 1 vol., 18mo. In blue-and-gold, $1.00 ; morocco, antique, $3.00.

Appletons' Library of the British Poets

FROM CHAUCER TO TENNYSON AND THE LATER POETS.

EDITED BY ROSSITER JOHNSON.

Complete in three large 8vo volumes. Illustrated with Portraits and Views on Steel. Price, per volume, cloth, $5.00 ; sheep, $6.00 ; half turkey, $7.00 ; half russia, $8.00 ; full russia or full turkey, $10.00.

D. APPLETON & CO., PUBLISHERS, 549 & 551 BROADWAY, NEW YORK.

Library of Congress Cataloguing in Publication Data

Taylor, Richard, 1826-1879.
Destruction and reconstruction.
(Collector's library of the Civil War)
Reprint. Originally published: New York:
D. Appleton, 1879.
Includes index.
1. United States—History—Civil War, 1861-1865—
Campaigns. 2. Reconstruction. 3. Taylor, Richard, 1826-
1879. 4. United States—History—Civil War, 1861-
1865—Personal narratives, Confederate. 5. Soldiers—
Southern States—Biography. I. Title. II. Series.
E470.T24   1983   973.7'82   82-16991
ISBN 0-8094-4281-7
ISBN 0-8094-4280-9 (library)
ISBN 0-8094-4279-5 (retail)

Printed in the United States of America

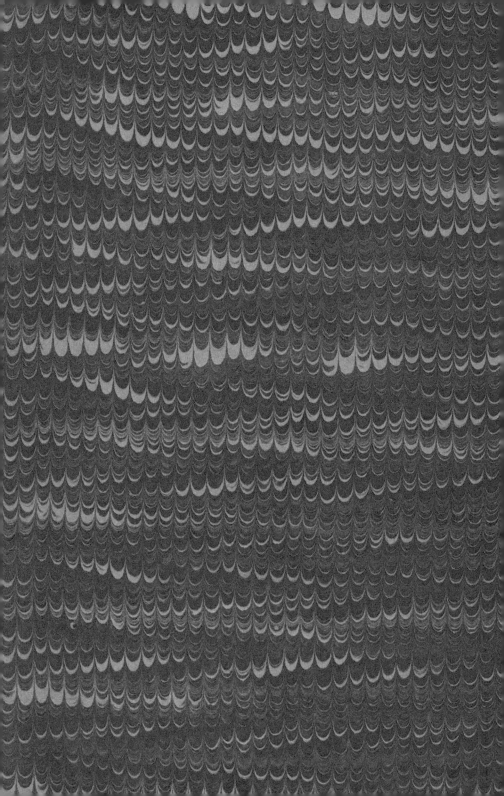